TREES OF
FIRE

NICK TOGNIETTI

ISBN: 9798325938931

Praise For...

"This book is captivating, thought provoking, and life changing! Pastor Nick has captured the heart and mind of Father Adonai. I honestly recommend this book for new converts and seasoned saints alike. This manuscript will not only enhance your walk with God, but it will challenge you to go deeper into the realm of the Holy Spirit, to seek out what's needed for our lives. This book will cause you to self-examine your life to make sure that you are studying properly, praying effectively, loving your fellow brothers and sisters correctly, etc... Pastor Nick Nick masterfully takes us on a journey that he himself has taken and continues to take as he discovers more and more what the Father has in store for him and the believers. I encourage each of you to not only invest, but to investigate what Pastor Nick has conveyed in this book so that when you're done reading this book, you will say, 'I must do more for God!'"

-Dr. Paul Speights
President and Founding Teacher Of Theos Spiritual Institute

"Nick Tognietti is one of the most anointed, gifted, and dedicated scholars of scripture in our generation. His newest revelation "Trees For Fire" is filled with divine knowledge given to him by the Holy Spirit. Nick's deep understanding of the Torah and how it translates to the New Testament is revealed in this amazing publication. Chapter by chapter I felt my faith and knowledge grow. Page by Page I could feel the fire burning in me. Line by line I found myself being fill with a fresh zeal. I too, now, am a Tree of Fire for our Messiah Yeshua."

-Kelley Knox
Youth Pastor, CHH Artist

"The ultimate job of the Holy Spirit is to transform you and I into the image of the Messiah (Romans 8:29, 1 John 2:6). That is God's number one concern and top priority for our lives. (Pg 200 - Trees of Fire)

I can't walk in His power if I won't walk in His image or with His heart. (Pg 128- Trees of Fire)

These 2 statements jumped off the page to me. What you are holding in your hands is an ignition switch to a deeper, more relevant study and understanding of the Word of God. Pastor Nick Tognetti has harnessed his powerful testimony of the reality of what God will do through one that authentically seeks Him as the Spirit leads. The beauty of the book is that Pastor Nick reminds us our all powerful God has not left His children without power or an inheritance, in fact, it is quite the opposite. Make no mistake, Trees of Fire is a call to come up higher and is not to be read for more head knowledge. Pastor Nick provides scriptural evidence of why and how God's people becoming consumed by the Holy Spirit and Fire is forever life changing. I am proud to call Pastor Nick a friend, a mentor and more importantly, an on fire, on mission brother in Christ and I gladly commend Trees of Fire to your reading and application.

We can become encouraged by another man's revelation, but we can't live off it. We need our own revelation and roots of understanding in God, that gives us the boldness to declare as Pastor Nick does:

I don't walk on the waters of wishful thinking when it comes to my relationship with my Father. I know my Father and I walk very closely with Him. (Pg 128)"

-Pastor Moses Francis
Pastor of God's House of Praise (GHOP):

*"As someone deeply entrenched in the field of preaching and exploring the Word of God, I have encountered numerous works attempting to distill complex ideas into accessible narratives. Nevertheless, '***Trees of Fire***' stands out*

as a beacon of clarity and insight on the Holy Spirit from the Old Testament. **Nick Tognetti** has masterfully woven together the Revelations of the Holy Spirit with Jewish Perspective and Hebrew understanding, presenting a comprehensive yet easily digestible exploration of the WORD of GOD.

What sets 'Trees of Fire' apart is its ability to not only inform but also inspire. Through poignant anecdotes and meticulously researched evidence, **Pastor Nick** not only illuminates the intricacies of The Baptism Of The Holy Spirit And Fire, but also compels readers to reflect deeply on their own perspectives. As I delved into its pages, I found myself challenged, enlightened, and ultimately enriched by the profound wisdom contained within.

Whether you're a seasoned professional seeking new spiritual insights or a curious novice eager to explore uncharted territory, 'Trees of Fire' offers something invaluable to every [believer] reader. It is with great enthusiasm that I endorse this remarkable work, confident that its impact will resonate far beyond the confines of its pages."

-Pastor Shashi Kiran Pulukuri
Shalowm Covenant Church
Hyderabad, TS, India.

"'Trees of Fire' is a very powerful revelation Maria and I were personally able to witness being birthed by Our Heavenly Father through Nick Tognietti. From the time we met him in Jerusalem to the time he moved to Shiloh Farm with us, it has been a blessing to be a witness of God's powerful presence, with healing, revelation, prophecy, dreams, and visions, and now to read about it through Nick's anointed perspective allows us to see the full picture. As you read this book, it will ignite a hunger for more of Our Heavenly Father's presence in your life. We pray that you, too, will become a 'TREE of Fire' in the Army of YHWH taking ground for the Kingdom of Heaven."

Be Blessed and be a Blessing to others,
-Apostolic Ministers Todd & Maria Cleppe

Nick, Todd, and Maria in Jerusalem

Table of Contents

Foreword

For two and a half years, beginning in October of 2021 through the first half of 2024, I was in the hardest season of my life, which is saying a lot, considering everything I went through as a child and young adult. During that period of time, the evil one nearly took me out of ministry completely. Things were rising up against me left and right from my health, ministry, and much, much more. In 2022, I took a sabbatical lasting almost half of the year. The amount of witchcraft that came against me and the revelations I received will be explained in depth in another volume, God willing. It would have killed me had it not been for the grace of God, as it is written in 2 Corinthians 1:8-10:

> "But, my brothers, we wish you to know, concerning the affliction that was upon us in Asia, that we were afflicted exceedingly, beyond our strength, to the extent that our life was ready to terminate. And we passed a death sentence upon ourselves, that our confidence might not be in ourselves, but in God Who raises up the dead, Who rescued us from imminent death, and we hope that He will again rescue us."

I cannot tell you how many days I would have to go lay back in bed by noon or 2-3pm because I could hardly stand or think. I cannot tell you how many times I was in tears before God during this time, alone, with no one that could successfully comfort me. There was nothing flesh and blood could give me that would relieve me of what I was facing. But the anointing oil only comes through great crushing, and the gold and silver only come out of the oppressions of Egypt (Exodus 3:21-22). The more the enemy trampled me like a winepress, the more new wine (Matthew 9:16-17) that began to overflow, and the more revelation that poured out upon me daily (Exodus 1:7-12). I would say the evil one overdid himself, and what the enemy meant for harm, God used for good (Genesis 50:20).

People were trampling me, but God was allowing it to produce a Psalms 37 meekness within me. It was the season of meekness He told me, and I continually was on my face before Him. But it was during this time that the Holy Spirit began to take me into the deepest places of intimacy and revelation, while training my hands for war in the Holy Spirit like I had never encountered, even with all the mighty things I had already encountered in the Holy Spirit before this. As I began receiving the abundance of downloads from the Holy Spirit, started preaching about it, and being revealed to a new power and anointing, all hell broke out against me beginning February of 2022. The revelation was so deep, and the power that manifested, and the chains that were breaking off of people as I preached became so evident, I knew we were stepping into a precious time, and so did everyone who was listening to my messages, hearing me privately in homes, or guest speaking.

In fact, a man and woman reached out to me from Arizona whom I had never met, who had been watching my broadcasts. We jumped on a Zoom call, and they said, "Starting in October of 2021 your messages changed. They became so full of the Spirit of God, and the Holy Spirit showed us that you were at war against a spirit of witchcraft that was coming against you." They began reaching out regularly to tell me how every week the Holy Spirit was setting them free through my teachings. I had another reach out who said, "Today I decided to close myself inside a room with the Holy Spirit and listen to all of your videos. It was the best day ever."

When I came to the LORD in September of 2017, I immediately began having encounters with the Holy Spirit and experiencing things of the Spirit. Due to me not growing up in the faith, I had no preconceived thoughts, ideologies, or traditional chains of theology weighing me down, but rather I was like blank tablets of stone for the Holy Spirit to write on whatever He pleases. All I knew was that I love Jesus, what I was reading in the Bible, and the tangible encounters that allowed me to taste the goodness of God (Psalms 34:9) in a way that the world became bland to me, and I to the world (Galatians 6:14). I say this to say, I never had to go through the questions of, "Is the Holy Spirit real today? Are the gifts of the Holy Spirit still operating? Can we still cast out devils? Are there still apostles, prophets, evangelists, pastors, and teachers (Ephesians 4:11-12)?" I had been experiencing all of this, so to even contemplate that all of these were not still here for today was outrageous to me, especially due to the encounters I had in the supernatural from day one of my faith, and I didn't know how so many Christians, pastors, elders, etc., could even come to such an erroneous conclusion, or live a Christian life without encountering these things.

I was fresh in the faith, and these things immediately flowed like a river to one degree or another. I began getting dreams every night, prophecy, demonic attacks, and much more immediately took place in my life from the start of my walk with the LORD. As time went on, I began experiencing things so heavily in the Holy Spirit with the prophetic anointing, words of knowledge, speaking in tongues, interpretation of tongues, preaching, gold dust manifesting while I preached, seeing healings, devils cast out, dreams and visions, and even being transfigured before others as Moses and Jesus were, etc. This was my walk not only as a believer, but also as I entered into full time ministry in October of 2018 as well.

However, in late 2021, the revelation and power I began encountering in the Holy Spirit went to such a level that it almost made me forget any of the former (Jeremiah 23:7-8, Isaiah 43:18-19). With these encounters came not only a new hunger and a new desperation, but a ridiculous dissatisfaction for anything that was less than what we see in the book of Acts, or stepping into Jesus' words in John 14:12, "Amen, amen, I say to you, whoever believes in Me, he will also do the works that I do, and he will do greater than these, because I go to the Father." As I studied the Scripture now to a new depth, the Holy Spirit began brewing in me a desperation that could not be quenched by anything less than the fullness of the identity, righteousness, and power that Yeshua proclaimed we would walk in as believers.

As the Father sent Him, so is Jesus sending us (John 20:21), which means every ounce of Jesus' walk on earth is what we are expected to walk in-repentance, obedience, power, miracles, persecutions, and all. But as I said, the more I pressed into this, and the deeper the revelations I began preaching, the more hell put my name on its "to kill" list each and every day. I was hard pressed on every side, persecuted, black balled, slandered, mocked, hit with unexplained sickness after sickness, and so much more, while due to the labor of the grace of God within me (1 Corinthians 15:10), others were being set free, empowered, lit on fire, healed, learning how to war against witchcraft, and baptized in the Holy Spirit and fire (2 Corinthians 4:8-12). The thing was, the more the evil one came against me, the more the revelation poured out upon me (Exodus 1:12).

In April of 2022, I was visiting some mentors and dear friends of mine, Pastor Todd and his wife, Pastor Maria, on their 180 acres of Shiloh Farm in Chelsea, Iowa. One morning I was walking back and forth in prayer, looking at all the naked trees since the leaves had fallen from winter. It was after a few minutes of pressing into prayer that the Holy Spirit gripped me and gave me an open eyed vision of Mark 8:24, which says, "and he gazed, and he said, 'I see people like trees walking.'" As I looked at all the naked trees, the Holy Spirit spoke through me and said:

> "Father, I don't want to see people like trees walking, I
> want to see people like trees on fire! I want to see this tree
> on fire, and for its branch to touch that tree's branch, so
> that it will be lit on fire, and start a forest fire."

Immediately He showed me one tree lit on fire, and as its branch touched the other, it caught fire, and the next, until the entire place was in a forest fire on Shiloh Farm.

That day I shared with Todd and Maria what He showed me, and from that point on, the LORD showed me there was going to be such a move of the Holy Spirit and fire setting His people ablaze, and I began crying out for this movement of Trees Of Fire. I went back to Dallas-Fort Worth, where I was living at that time, and every day I was so unsatisfied, longing for this vision to manifest in the earth. I became obsessed with it, and I could no longer sit still until I saw God do this in the earth. Just months after this vision, Todd was preaching to a congregation in Pakistan, and without knowing anything about my vision, the pastor of the Pakistani congregation said that as Todd preached, he saw fire coming out of his mouth and his exact words was that he saw "trees catching on fire." Todd immediately called me to share this with me, as we knew it was confirmation of the open eyed vision I had received from the Holy Spirit.

The next month after this vision, in May of 2022, Maria had a dream that my preaching had gotten taken to a new level of power, vulnerability, and revelation, as I stood preaching on the hilltop at Shiloh Farm. The LORD had shown very clearly that I was to move out to Iowa from Dallas-Fort Worth where I was currently living. I moved out there for about seven months and finished the year of 2022 in Iowa, secluded on their 180 acre farm in the small town of Chelsea, Iowa, which has a population of just over 200 people. During those seven months, it was me and the Spirit of God only, with no distractions from the time I wake up until I go to bed, and even in bed I was getting revelations, dreams, and angelic visitations. It was during this time that I took off a third of the year from ministry. Todd, Maria, and I entered into a season of prayer, study, and desperation for more of Him. During those seven months of 2022 in Iowa, I cannot tell you how many nights we were up late in prayer, and getting things from the Holy Spirit, and how many times we were up at 4am sharing revelations, dreams, and visions in the Holy Spirit, which we still continue to do today.

Due to everything that came against me and all the hardships I was enduring at this time, the LORD led me in July of 2022 to go into what I thought was a four week sabbatical but ended up being over four months until mid-late November. Nobody knew at the time, neither people close in my ministry, nor even my family, but due to everything I was going through, during my sabbatical I quit ministry to the LORD. I wouldn't even preach at Todd and Maria's ministry when they would ask. I told the LORD:

> "Father, I will not go on another broadcast, write another blog, preach another sermon, or do anything else unless You show me very clearly. I will not go if You aren't with me (Exodus 33:15). I will not do a thing in the flesh. I know that ministry was a promise from You, but I am crucifying it as Abraham was willing to crucify the

promise of his son, Isaac (Genesis 22), because if it is truly from You, You will resurrect it incorruptible (Hebrews 11:17-19, 1 Corinthians 15:42). I am done."

Every time I reminisce on this it brings me to tears, because just as Isaac meant so much to Abraham, so does ministry to me. But even a promise from God that we are not willing to crucify to Him has become an idol. The LORD showed me to do this with everything, and whatever is from Him He will make evident in its proper time, so I have carried this method into just about everything I do.

I had never told anyone that, meanwhile, I had family, friends, students, and people from all over the world emailing into the ministry asking when I would be back in public ministry. I didn't have an answer, and I had to continually lift everyone to be under the LORD's Shepherding. The LORD sent me an angel one night that November (2022) in Iowa, and the angel began sealing my instruction for moving forward. Then, the following night, the LORD came to me in a dream and anointed my head with oil and was sending me back into ministry. Also, in the dream a dear friend, Jennifer Rowan, said to me, "These have been the best seventeen weeks of our life." When I woke up, little did I know, seventeen weeks prior was the very week I had begun my sabbatical. Those seventeen weeks were truly the best weeks I ever had in the Holy Spirit up until that point. Revelation flowed like rivers of living water, which is incredible considering Shiloh Farm where I was living and still spend much of my time, Todd and Maria's ministry there is called "Rivers Of Living Water Ministries." It was such a tough season day to day, but as I said, the greater the hardships, persecutions, and attacks, the heavier the Presence of God rested upon me. The LORD told me that I was now coming out of sabbatical, and that He wanted me to focus on one thing very specifically, preaching and teaching on the anointing and the power of the Holy Spirit. Like I said, I didn't tell anyone about my crucifying ministry.

In order to bring even more confirmation to everything, I received a text message late one night from a woman I had baptized a couple years before in Houston, but really hadn't spoken to since, nor did I even have her number anymore. I had taken her through freedom ministry years before, and she was baptized in the Holy Spirit and fire and began speaking in tongues. The breakthrough that day was incredible. She ended up getting plugged into another ministry, and she has a beautiful prophetic anointing. She texted me and said:

> "Hey Nick, how are you? I am reaching out because I had a dream with you two weeks ago. It is really weird for me to dream about certain people, especially when I have not had contact in a long time. I knew my dream was from God because today I was reminded of it again, and it left me with discomfort. So, in my dream you were sad and doubtful about your calling with the LORD, and it looked like you even wanted to leave your calling behind. I saw you speaking with your elders about how you couldn't keep going, and in the dream, I came in to encourage you and remind you that this is what the LORD called you to since the beginning."

I called her the next day and was brought to tears, because like I said, neither she nor anyone else knew what I was doing behind the scenes when I quit ministry to the LORD, and she confirmed everything for me that I not only did, but also as I was literally entering back into ministry after the angel and the LORD visited me. I was empowered so heavily knowing that this was the resurrection from the LORD I had been seeking the entire time. Nothing going forward was in the flesh, but with the power and revelation of the Holy Spirit. The week she shared this, I had actually began raising up leaders, elders, pastors, and teachers behind the scenes, telling them about my crucifying of not only my ministry, but myself in ministry period, and it all went perfectly with her dream.

As I came back into ministry, with everything I began speaking about from the baptism of the Holy Spirit and fire, an entire series on witchcraft, prophecy, the anointing, gifts of the spirit, etc., I literally had people and congregational leaders reaching out to me and viewing from all over the world such as Finland, Spain, Malaysia, Belgium, Fiji, Germany, Mexico, Indonesia, Sri Lanka, Australia, South Africa, Kenya, Tanzania, UK, France, India, Amsterdam, Austria, and all over the US telling me how they were getting baptized in the Holy Spirit during the teachings, set free from witchcraft, and a deep hunger was taking place for more of the Holy Spirit. God was opening doors to not only reach people worldwide, but leaders of congregations, in order to pour into them and raise them up, so they can pour into their flocks. I knew God's movement of my vision of the Trees Of Fire was beginning. This was all the Father, I have simply been a vessel, and I won't touch His glory. Very quickly, about two months after I had entered back into ministry, I wanted to bring it all to God again, and I asked Him one Saturday night, January 21, 2023, at about 8pm, "Father, do You still want me to push out these teachings? Are they bearing fruit?" The Father answered me very quickly. Four hours later at 12:57am, a woman who was living in Sri Lanka reaches out to the ministry by email and says:

> "Shalom Pastor Nick. I am in awe of the messages. I cannot explain or even begin to describe how these messages are opening up revelation and understanding to me. I started sending your messages to someone that is going through a difficult time, and she has been so blessed. She

is actually listening to them two and three times over. She has been struggling with understanding the Bible and some of the translations. Listening to your Hebrew explanations of Scripture has started her journey into understanding the Bible better."

There was literally a continual river of God's voice and favor because the ministry was now operating in the resurrection power of the Holy Spirit after I crucified it all to Him. God showed me a new revelation and movement in the Holy Spirit, but this time, the pour out wasn't coming from above. It was coming from below, from within us. It was not so much a pour out, but a removal of the bushel (Matthew 5:15-16) that covers up the flame, which would take place through repentance, prayer, and ceasing from dead works (Hebrews 6:1), as it is written in Psalms 85:12, "Truth will sprout from the earth, and righteousness will look down from heaven." People were commenting on the anointing that was not only taking place through the teachings, but that was being imparted to them. A woman commented on my broadcast on "Overcoming Witchcraft Part 2," saying:

> "Thank God for setting me free from prison by the word of discernment through Pastor Nick! I see the LORD has renewed and empowered him again with the power of the Word of Truth and a stronger prophetic spirit than ever before, in order to rescue other victims and to help us be restored for His calling to a prophetic ministry."

I couldn't help but praise God through all that I was starting to see. It reminded me of a prophetic word that a mighty woman of God had spoken over me at a ministry I was visiting in Houston on February 18,

2019. It was my first time there. She approached me with her husband and said God gave her a prophetic word for me, saying:

> "I see you and I hear you. The more you seek Me, the more I will continue to reveal to you. You are going to know My voice, you will know. I am going to speak, and you will know it's Me. I have given you an authority and you are about to walk into that authority, but I need you to stay humble. I need you to stay humble. There are coming times you will need to speak. Don't worry about what you will speak, at that moment I will give you every word to speak. I am pouring out My anointing onto you, even now you will have the anointing. People will see you from every side, from everywhere all around you and say, 'I want what you have, I want that.' I see you and I hear you. The more you keep seeking, the more I will give you."

This began happening in every place I would go to. Pastors, doctors, teachers, believers, and even unbelievers kept saying they wanted what I had, and that there was a Godly jealousy being aroused in them to want more of God, more revelation, more intimacy, more of Him. Within about six months of coming out of the 2022 sabbatical, I had produced over 120 teachings, and within four of those months, I wrote this book. The overflow in the Holy Spirit was absolutely unparalleled to anything that I had experienced before this. I had a pastor walk into my office after he realized how many teachings the LORD had produced through me in that short amount of time, and he said, "Nick, I have preached three Sundays in a row, and I am exhausted, I don't know how you have done that." It wasn't me, but the Holy Spirit within me (Galatians 2:20). I never expected to see the fruit that I did as I came out of that sabbatical, but honestly, I was also caught off guard with how much persecution and resistance I got as well. With apostolic anointing, also comes apostolic persecution, and I might even say more so with a prophetic anointing.

On May 9, 2022, the LORD gave me a dream that I was invited to preach before 3,000 people. The man that invited me was commending me on my boldness to preach the way I do. It was known in the dream that the 3,000 people were readied by the Holy Spirit for my preaching. In this dream, I had a sermon written in my notebook that I used to prepare all of my sermons in, but when I opened it up, it was written with black sharpie and water was spilled all over it, smearing it, so I couldn't read a thing. I panicked in the dream as I was about to step before 3,000 people with no prepared sermon. The Holy Spirit told me in the dream what I was to teach on in regards to entering into His Presence from a revelation I had received from Leviticus 16, which I didn't have written down, but the message was burning inside of me by the Holy Spirit, just as the prophetic word above that the woman spoke over me, that the Holy Spirit would give me words in its time of need (Matthew 10:19-20). When I woke up the LORD told me the interpretation of the dream. The 3,000 people were the same 3,000 who got saved on the day of Pentecost in Acts 2:41 as Peter stood up and preached boldly. He told me that if I will never again prepare notes beforehand, the Holy Spirit will always give me words to speak, Pentecost will come, and Trees Of Fire will be realized, as it is written in Acts 2:40-41:

> "And with many other words he (Peter) would witness to them, and he would beseech them, while saying, 'be saved from this perverse generation.' And in that day about 3,000 souls were added to them."

Ever since I came back into ministry in November of 2022, I have never used a single note. I became so filled with the Word of God and clothed in the Spirit that I wouldn't even hardly open my Bible when preaching because the Holy Spirit brought me to memorize the Scriptures by heart. People became amazed as they saw I never used a single note. As Jesus is the walking Word of God, and He lives in me, we can become a co-heir with Him (Romans 8:17), and we too, can become the walking Word of God as it is no longer we who live, but Messiah within us (Leviticus 26:11-12, Galatians 2:20). As the Father sent Him, so Jesus is sending us (John 20:21).

I wouldn't trade the hardship of those times for anything. It was hands down the darkest and most oppressive season of my life, but I would walk it all again in order to receive what He imparted to me, as well as the intimacy I experienced and gained with the Holy Spirit, so that I may impart it to His people. This book, and the revelations contained within it were birthed out of much pain, as a woman in birth pangs. It was birthed out of tears and bruised knees as I begged God on all fours to sustain me through His cloud by day and fire by night (Exodus 13:21, Numbers 9:15-23). It was birthed out of an unparalleled devotion to intimacy with God in the secret place, which is now being proclaimed upon the roof tops in the marketplace (Matthew 10:27).

It was through my painful oppressions in Egypt that I came out with a new vision and understanding of what God was wanting to do in the earth. It was to create Trees Of Fire. He found a man during a time of desperation, broke him, and baptized him in a season of prayer and desperation that began to shake the heavens and the earth, as it is written in 2 Chronicles 16:9, "For the eyes of the LORD run to and fro throughout the entire earth to grant strength with those whose heart is whole towards Him." My goal in this volume is that people see the Holy Spirit, and if people see me, may it only be what the Holy Spirit has done through me, as it is written in Romans 15:18, "For I presume not to speak of anything, which the Messiah has not done by me in word or in deed for the obedience of the Gentiles."

Acknowledgements:

There were a small handful of people that walked step by step with me through that great season of trial, never leaving my side, and bearing every ounce of my burden (Galatians 6:2). I want to publicly honor these individuals, because they are the only ones who can truly read between the lines of the foreword.

Terry and Deedee Tognietti (my parents):

The only thing I can think of is the Scriptures in Luke, as Simon speaks to the mother of Jesus when Jesus was born, as it is written in Luke 2:34-35:

> "Behold, this One is appointed for the fall and for the rise of many in Israel, and for a sign of dispute, and in your own soul a spear will pass through, so that the thoughts of many hearts may be revealed."

Jesus' mother was told, due to the mission of Jesus in the earth, it would be as a spear piercing through her soul because of the pain of the calling on His life. Regardless of persecutions, being misunderstood, and many divisions due to the things of the Holy Spirit, you two have stood near and seen the power of God manifest, confirming that we are walking with Him (Mark 16:15-18). Although rare for many to see and realize, the life of a true apostle is one of great hardship, as it is written in 1 Corinthians 4:9-13:

> "But I suppose that God has placed us apostles last, as if condemned for death, since we have become a spectacle to the world, to angels, and to men. We are fools on

account of Messiah, but you are wise in Messiah. We are weak, but you are strong. You are praised, we are hated. Up until this hour, we hunger, and thirst, and are naked, and are buffeted, and have no permanent home. And we toil, working with our own hands. They defame us, and we bless, they persecute us, and we endure it, they revile us, and we beg to them. We are as the filth of the world, and the expiation for all men up to this time."

However, with all the hardships, I have always come with not only the Word of God by revelation of the Holy Spirit, but also with the power of the Holy Spirit (1 Corinthians 2:4/4:20), not I, but the grace of God in me (1 Corinthians 15:10). Mom, as you have said, "Nick, everywhere you go, something gets stirred up." As we always say, when you walk in the Holy Spirit, this will either fill up a room, or clear it out (Genesis 3:8), but this comes with the calling, as it is written in 1 Corinthians 12:12, "I performed the signs of the apostles among you with all patience, and with signs, and with wonders, and with mighty deeds." There is not much you two have been able to do in order to bring comfort or save me from the hardships this walk has brought, however, you have given me the greatest thing any parent can give their child, which is full love and support. Pondering upon this, I am reminded of a story Kobe Bryant said about his dad:

"When I was young, I went an entire summer where I didn't score a single point in a game. I was devastated. My father came up to me and told me, 'whether you score zero points or sixty points, I will always love you.' What my father gave me was the most important thing a parent could give their child, which is the confidence to fail."

I have always walked in great boldness and conviction, and ever since I was a child, which never wavered through the days of my entering into the faith in 2017, you two have stood by me against all odds. I will continue to run the race and fight the good fight (2 Timothy 4:7). As has been required of me, I have been willing to lose all for the sake of pressing on, in order to fulfill the call of God upon my life (Philippians 3:14), as the Holy Spirit continually leads, as Jesus said in Luke 14:25-27:

> "And as the great multitudes went with Him, He turned and said to them, 'Whoever comes to Me and he does not hate his father, and his mother, and his brothers, and his sisters, and his wife, and his sons, and also himself, he is not able to be My disciple. And whoever does not take his cross and come after me, he is not able to be My disciple.'"

Although I love you two, our family, friends, etc., as I always preach, He must come first before any and all things. Loyalty to the King of kings and LORD of lords comes before us, our comfort zones, and our desires. Regardless of how tough it gets, He is faithful through it all, as He also said in Luke 18:29-30:

> "Yeshua said to them, 'Amen, I say to you, there is no man who has forsaken houses, or parents, or brothers, or wife, or children for the sake of the Kingdom of God, and he will not receive many times over in this time, and eternal life in the world to come.'"

Just as the reason Joseph named his firstborn son, Manashe (Genesis 41:51), for Manashe's name means "He has made me to forget," in regards to God's causing such a good life for Joseph in the end, that Joseph forgot all the pain of his father's house, so too, God is redeeming every ounce of hardship we have ever faced, and the goodness in Him to come will cause us to forget all of our toil and pains (Romans 8:18). The enemy will be forced to vomit up everything he has swallowed (Job 20:15).

Todd and Maria Cleppe:

There is no Pastor Nick or Trees Of Fire as it is today without Shiloh Farm, and what God did through you two and your family during that tough season, and still continues to do through you both. You have opened up the entire land for me, have given me my own place to live, and continually allowed me to get the rest and recovery I have needed in the Holy Spirit. During those seven months in 2022, every day you allowed me to walk into your offices, and you would stop any and all work in order to pray with me and minister to me. The continual late nights of prayer, and early mornings of revelation will always be treasured, which continues even until today. Your entire family has taken me in fully as family, there is no distinction. Although we have been family since we met in Jerusalem, Israel in 2017, those seven months in 2022 brought new depths of relationship, calling, and foundational roots that God is bearing and will continue to bear so much fruit through.

We have gone to war against so much together, and I thank God I get to go to battle side by side with you two. If I am Joseph, you two are Pharaoh. If I am Betzalel or Joshua, you two are Moses. If I am Solomon, you two are David. If I am Elisha, you two are Elijah. If I am Paul, you two are Gamliel. You two have gone before me in so many ways, poured into me, invested in me, believed in me, and as Todd has said about me continually since 2019, "The Father has shown us clearly that we are to do whatever we are able in order to get you to where He has called you." I have seen how important it is to have someone over them to walk with, look to, be encouraged by, and to be corrected by as well. That is you two.

Muhammad Ali said that he is the greatest, but he never won a championship without Angelo Dundee, and Michael Jordan never won

a championship without Phil Jackson. All of those who have done anything great have always had someone see something in them that others,
or even themselves can't see about themselves at one point or another.
You saw me in Jerusalem, but you didn't see an ignorant, tatted up bodybuilder in a Lakers jersey, rather, you saw a zealous, young, on fire believer who was on a mission to convert all of Jerusalem to the faith in Jesus.
You never judged me according to the flesh, but by revelation of the Holy
Spirit, not for who I was, but who I was called to be, and from the first
night I met you two in the lobby of the Eldan Hotel in Jerusalem during
happy hour on Shabbat, you spoke into that calling on my life that was
not yet realized by others, or even myself. There is no such thing as
"self-made." There is only iron sharpening iron (Proverbs 27:17), while
both irons bow down to the One Who holds and fashions them, which
is Messiah Himself (John 15:4-5). There is no Muhammad Ali without
Angelo Dundee, and there is no Michael Jordan without Phil Jackson,
and as I said, there is no Trees Of Fire and who I am today without what
God has done, and is continually doing through you two, just as there is
no Joseph, Betzalel, Joshua, Solomon, Elisha, or Paul without Pharaoh,
Moses, David, Elijah, and Gamliel.

Mike Lockwood:

You started out as my student, grew to be my friend, and without
a doubt, have become my brother. Your continual words of encourage-
ment, and our weekly talks continually fueled me during those tough
times. I will never forget in May of 2022 when we sat on the curb in
front of my parents' house, and talked about everything I was facing.
While many left me, you stayed by my side without hesitation. When
others left in the fear of man, you truly proved yourself to be a man that
fears God, and one of the few that I can genuinely look anyone else in the
eyes and say, "I trust him." I am so proud to be your pastor and teacher,
but I am most thankful to be your friend and brother. Our stories are so

similar since 2017, it only makes sense that we walk so close, as it is said "birds of a feather flock together." Your loyalty towards me and having my back is nothing short of the love and loyalty Jonathan showed David.

You are a foundational piece of what God is doing and will do through Trees Of Fire in its apostolic calling. You continually fulfill Galatians 6:2, "Each man bears the burden of his friend, for in this, you fulfill the Torah of the Messiah." Due to your continually bearing my burdens, you remind me of when Simon of Cyrene helped bear the cross of Jesus. You are without a doubt Simon in my life, Mike, and I simply don't have the words to thank you enough, or praise Him for all that you have done, and continually do for me. Just know one thing, Mike, as you pass through the waters, I will be with you (Isaiah 43:2).

John and Jennifer Rowan:

Since the first time we met, I remember telling you both, "There is only one other couple (Todd and Maria Cleppe) whom when I met them, I knew it was the LORD, and although I don't know what it is, I know that there is more for us together." I immediately knew the cloth you two were cut from. You are loyal, bold, unwavering, and uncompromising soldiers for the King. During the summer of 2022, as we were going to meet in person for the second time to have breakfast at First Watch, and while I was in the middle of such hardship, I won't forget the dream where God visited me just a couple of nights before and said, "These two will help bring you relief from your troubles." That statement and dream couldn't have been more true.

Every day you two stood by my side, had my back, and saw something within me that many have not. John, you started out as a friend, grew to be my brother, and quickly became one of my top students, however, I am most thankful that you are my brother and best friend (Proverbs 18:24). You two and your entire family have truly embraced me as nothing short of family and "Uncle Nick." You two have not only continually opened up your house to me, but have even gone as far as urging me to stay the night every week I am in town as if I were an angel, as it is written in Genesis 19:1-3:

> "And the two angels came to Sodom in the evening, and Lot was sitting in the gate of Sodom, and Lot saw and arose toward them, and he prostrated himself on his face toward the ground. And he said, 'behold now, my lords, please turn to your servant's house and stay overnight and wash your feet, and you shall arise early and go on your way.' And they said, 'no, but we will stay overnight in the street.' And he urged them strongly, and they turned into him, and came into his house, and he made them a feast, and he baked unleavened bread, and they ate."

Without a doubt, you two are Aquilla and Priscilla to me, as well as the Shunemite woman and her husband, as you two have not only continually asked me to stay with you, but have even discussed building a place for me on your property, as it is written in 2 Kings 4:8-11:

> "And it was that day that Elisha went as far as Shunem, and there was a prominent woman who prevailed upon him to eat a meal, and it was, whenever he would pass, he would stop there to eat a meal. And she said to her husband, 'Behold, now I know that he is a holy man of God that passes by us continually. Now let us make a small walled upper chamber, and place a bed there for him, a table, a chair, and a lamp, and when he comes to us, he will turn there.' And it was one day that he went there, he turned into the upper chamber and laid there."

You two have continually given me a place to stay, to eat, to study, and to work.

For years to come I think we will continue to laugh at when your daughter, Emma, walked in the house and walks up to you two, and myself, saying, "I realized something...my father has a slumber party with his best friend every weekend." Spirit filled "slumber parties" consisting of late nights, which end up overflowing into the morning, while talking about the Holy Spirit (Acts 20:7-12) and encountering the power of God.

You two very quickly became a part of what God is doing with Trees Of Fire, and I am honored that God has allowed me to find such favor with you two, your family, and those whom you have introduced me too. The things we have experienced in the Holy Spirit together in such a short time, very few of which will be mentioned in this book, are too many to put here in such a short acknowledgement. Thank you for being who you are in Him. You two are repairers of the breach.

CHAPTER 1

The Baptism Of
The Holy Spirit And Fire

There are only about five things that we find in all four gospels of Matthew, Mark, Luke, and John. Each gospel has its own perspectives with different details, which gives us a fuller picture of the life of Jesus, however, there are only about five topics that are discussed in all four gospel accounts, one of which is the baptism of the Holy Spirit and fire (Matthew 3:11, Mark 1:8, Luke 3:16, and John 1:33). It is mentioned in every gospel due to its significance. John the Baptist says very clearly that he comes baptizing with water, which is a baptism of repentance, but the Messiah would come after him baptizing with the Holy Spirit and fire. What is the baptism of the Holy Spirit and fire? I will go as far as even saying, most Christians today do not know what it is, as they are only familiar with the baptism of John, which is a baptism in water (Acts 19:1-4).

I used to always wonder why some people would get baptized in the Holy Spirit and fire and others wouldn't. Many people that I would lay hands on would get hit with the Holy Spirit, the glory would take them to the ground, some would speak in tongues, some would have a literal fire come upon them and they would be drenched in sweat, some may start prophesying, etc. Similarly, in John 18:1-6 when the men would come to arrest Jesus, Scripture says that when they approached Him, they fell down backwards because of the glory that He carried. One thing worth mentioning is the word glory (כבוד) comes from the word "caveid (כבד)," which means "to be heavy." The glory of God is a thick, heavy, tangible presence. These things happen many times when people get baptized with the Holy Spirit and fire, which also happened to me as I will share.

It was these things, why some had this happen, and some didn't, that intrigued me, and during my sabbatical in 2022 the Holy Spirit unraveled these things to me in great detail-the secrets of the baptism of the Holy Spirit and its prerequisites. Apart from the baptism of the Holy Spirit, you will not walk in the power that God desires for you and your life or ministry (Acts 1:4-8). You don't need to be a pastor or teacher to receive these things, and if you are not a pastor or teacher, it doesn't mean you don't need the baptism of the Holy Spirit. Your life, job, family, etc., is your ministry. Power is not something for a preacher, it is for believers in Jesus (Mark 16:15-18).

In fact, to prove to you that this power is not just for apostles, prophets, evangelists, pastors, and teachers, the Scripture specifically says in Acts 6 that the disciples were looking for seven faithful men to go and work because Peter says it is not good for the ministers to work, but rather to focus on full time ministry, because he who preaches from the gospel is to live from the gospel (1 Corinthians 9:14), which was a theme that we find starting all the way back in the book of Genesis, which is why the Levites, the ministers, lived from the tithes and offerings of the people (Numbers 18). So too, Peter said that they needed to find seven men with a good name, and filled with the Holy Spirit and wisdom, and they will do these things. These seven men are not apostles. They are believers filled with the Holy Spirit, one of which was Stephen, who was martyred. It is written in Acts 6:8 "and Stephen was full of grace and power, and he did signs and wonders in the midst of the people." This was a disciple of Jesus doing mighty deeds with great power, not an apostle, prophet, evangelist, pastor, or teacher. These signs will follow them that believe (Mark 16:17), after you become baptized in the Holy Spirit and fire as Jesus said in Acts 1:4-8.

This is not to say that God cannot use you or do mighty things through you before you get baptized in the Holy Spirit, however, when you become baptized in the Holy Spirit and fire there is a new power, a new cleansing, a new unctioning, a new wisdom, a new revelation, and a new intimacy with the LORD that I can guarantee will not happen without it. In Luke 24:49 Jesus says to His disciples "I will send you the promise of the Father but wait in the city of Jerusalem until you are clothed with power from on high." Jesus is telling us that He has many things for us to do, but until we receive this power, we can't fulfill all that we need to do, because many times the Scripture says about Jesus and His disciples that it is because of the signs and wonders that people believed (John 2:23, Acts 8:6). In Acts 1:5 Jesus says, "For John baptized in water, but you will be baptized in the Holy Spirit not many days from now." Then Jesus continues in verse 8, saying, "But when the Holy Spirit comes upon you, you will receive power, and you will be My witnesses in Jerusalem, in all of Judah, among the Samaritans, and unto the ends of the earth."

We have to understand, John 20:19 says the disciples were walking in absolute fear of the Jews before they were baptized in the Holy Spirit. They were in hiding after Yeshua died and resurrected. But then in Acts 2:14-39 Peter and the others become baptized in the Holy Spirit, speaking boldly before the crowd with deep revelation, which resulted in converting 3,000 souls. This theme continued in Acts 4:8-32 as they spoke before the rulers with all boldness. The Holy Spirit is needed for so many things, as we will see throughout this book.

I want to first make something clear. When we truly come to faith in Jesus and truly repent, one is given a new heart, where the old heart of stone and sin is removed, and a new heart of flesh is given, and the Holy Spirit begins a new work inside of you, as it is expressed very clearly in Jeremiah 31:31-33, and Ezekiel 36:26-27, which is later quoted by Paul in Hebrews 10:15-16, "And the Holy Spirit also testifies to us by saying, 'This is the covenant which I will give them after those days, says the LORD: I will put My Torah into their minds and inscribe it on their hearts.'" The Holy Spirit immediately begins a work of sanctification when you truly repent, and this evidence will be the fruits of repentance (Matthew 3:8), leading you to be a completely new creation (Galatians 6:15), and a new person born from the beginning (John 3:7, Galatians 6:15), as Paul also says in 2 Corinthians 5:17-18:

> "Therefore, whoever is in the Messiah is a new creation. The old things have passed away, and all things have become new from God who reconciled us to Himself by the Messiah and has given to us the ministry of reconciliation."

With that said, there are some passages in the Scripture that also must be weighed in the balance to recognize the baptism of the Holy Spirit being a separate work of God. There is no doubt that the Holy Spirit will do a work in our life, but it doesn't mean one has been baptized in the Holy Spirit and fire and clothed with power from on high.

I will give a little bit of my experience. I came to the LORD in September of 2017 at 23 years old, and I immediately was transformed, and so much sin was removed from my life. I had a new heart, new desires, new attributes. Drugs, alcohol, violence, anger, and sexual immorality seemed to be completely removed. There were other things that were a process, such as cussing, and my music preferences, but so much was changed. There was a girl I was dating at the time, and we had been together for about a year and a half, and I was about to propose to her. However, within weeks of me coming to the LORD she said, "Nick, I don't even know who you are anymore, you are a different person." This was not a compliment from her, although to me, it was. She didn't join me on my walk with the LORD, and we broke up within a couple of weeks.

I didn't want to party anymore, do drugs, get drunk, gossip, or have sex before marriage. People began messaging me all over because I immediately started preaching on Facebook. I became obsessed with the Word of God, immediately reading it for 6-12 hours a day, cover to cover, and it became a fire in my bones I couldn't contain (Jeremiah 20:9), so I preached constantly on social media, as Paul did when he came to Jesus in Acts 9:18-21:

> "And at once something that resembled scales fell from his eyes, and his eyes were opened. And he arose and he was baptized. And he received nourishment and was strengthened and was with the disciples, those who were in Damascus. And immediately he was in the assembly of the Jews preaching about Yeshua that He is the Son of God. And all those who were hearing him were amazed, and they were saying, 'Was not this he who was persecuting all those who were calling on this name in Jerusalem? He was even sent here for this same reason to bind and take them away to the chief priests!'"

I remember I was living with my parents at the time, and I didn't tell them I came to the LORD. They just began noticing things. I remember very clearly one day eating at the table and my dad was in the living room, and not meaning to be rude by any means, he said, "Nick, do you feel the need to share Scripture on Facebook? You know people will call you a hypocrite with your lifestyle." He said this because I never told him I came to the LORD and that I was no longer doing drugs or anything else. He had no idea. I figured, people will know me by my fruits, as Jesus said in Matthew 7:20, "Therefore, you will recognize them by their fruits." I remember I kept quiet as I ate at the table that day.

It wasn't hardly a couple weeks after this that I was reading the Bible in the office I had at my parents, and my dad walked in and said, "Nick, what is going on with you? I have never seen you so calm and peaceful before like I have been lately?"

I simply said, "I gave my life to Jesus." He didn't give much reaction at that moment, walked out of the office, and carried on with his day, and I with my reading the Bible. The following week he came back in and said the same thing, and I responded, "Dad, I gave my life to Jesus." He responded the same way.

The following week, now being the third time, my dad came in, saying, "Nick, what is this? You are so calm. I've never seen you like this in your entire life. You aren't angry or anything. What happened to you?"

I turned my whole body around and said, "Dad, I recently gave my life to Jesus. He has completely changed me into a new person." I am now my dad's pastor and teacher, and as I will share later on in this chapter, during worship one day in my parents living room he walked up to me, I laid hands on him, and he got baptized in the Holy Spirit and fire.

I say this to say, the Holy Spirit began doing a sanctification work in my life immediately, which is continual today. I immediately started receiving dreams and even seeing demons and angels in the spirit realm. Hearing the voice of God was as clear to me as the music in peoples' headphones. Immediately I had different giftings working through me, such as prophecy and words of knowledge, but there was still a holy power that I was missing as I measured my life with what was promised in the Scriptures. I didn't get baptized in the Holy Spirit until April 14, 2018, roughly 8 months after I came to the LORD, however, I got water baptized in the Jordan River in Israel in December of 2017, just three months after I became a believer.

So initially, how did I start to learn more about the baptism of the Holy Spirit, tongues, etc.? Pastor Todd and Pastor Maria, whom I mentioned in the introduction of this book, I met during that trip in Israel in December of 2017. My first day there I was upstairs in my hotel room at the Eldan Hotel in Jerusalem during my first evening there, and I will never forget I was reading in 1 Kings as Solomon was building the Temple. It was 7pm on the dot and the Holy Spirit told me, "Go downstairs now." I kid you not, I remember very clearly telling the LORD out loud in my hotel room, "No, I am studying LORD, I will go eat dinner at 7:30." The LORD told me again, "Go downstairs now." He took my focus away to where I had to read one verse over and over and over and would still forget what I just read. The LORD won that battle. I had no idea what I was going to do downstairs, but I got dressed and went, figuring I would go get dinner early.

As I get down there, the hotel was hosting a happy hour, and as I walked to the dessert table, a man with his wife and another family on my right called out to me as I passed by, and this man said, "Your arms look small. You may need to work out." This was Pastor Todd. I used to be a heavyweight bodybuilder and had just placed top five at the Mr. Texas competition the year prior, hence, his joke. He asked me about my business in Israel, and I told him I was told by God to come to Israel alone. He asked me to sit down, and I shared my testimony with he and those with him. Little did I know that he came to Israel almost a dozen times a year for ministry and business. They took me under their wing that trip, introducing me to people, and he began to mentor me. He is now a dear brother of mine, his family is like my family, and he and

Maria are my greatest mentors. I had no idea what the LORD had in store for me when He changed my plans up in my hotel room that night. We ended up going to dinner and became family ever since.

Immediately Todd began speaking to me about the Holy Spirit, and the signs and wonders that God has done in his life, things you only hear about from the Scriptures. His whole emphasis was on the baptism of the Holy Spirit, and I remember he prayed over me in the lobby of the hotel, and when he prayed, he began speaking in tongues, which I had never heard before. His tongues sounded like the language of Arabic, so I thought he was speaking Arabic, then he interpreted the tongues with a powerful prophetic word that ended up being spot on years later. During that trip, he prayed that I would be baptized in the Holy Spirit, but the Father told Todd that I wouldn't be baptized in the Holy Spirit and fire as of yet, but it would come, and that I would speak in tongues as well.

This planted such a seed of hunger in my life that I remember as soon as I got back to Houston, I was crying to God, yelling, night and day for the baptism of the Holy Spirit, to speak in tongues, and for a great prophetic anointing. I kid you not, as a I lived in the newest high-rise in downtown Houston, it is a good thing that when I lived there it wasn't over ten percent capacity yet, because all of the fourteenth floor would have heard me yelling all day, every day, desperate for the Holy Spirit, crying out, "Father, fill me with the Holy Spirit! I want to speak in tongues, prophecy, heal the sick, raise the dead. Baptize me in the Holy Spirit and fire!" I knew there was more. This wasn't going to be an empty hunger, but it was the LORD emptying me of myself so that I could be filled with Him. The LORD was preparing His soil and ripening the wheat within me for Pentecost.

In April I heard that there was a conference in Dallas-Fort Worth, where a mighty evangelist would have many people get baptized in the Holy Spirit and fire. People would walk through what is commonly referred to as a fire tunnel (not to be confused with the passing of children into the fire to the god of Moloch, as Scripture states), and people on your left and right would lay hands on you as you walked through it, and as they would lay hands, the Holy Spirit would move powerfully. I determined in my mind to go, expectant for the power of God to fall on me. I was actually headed to Peru the next month as an evangelist, traveling alone to do God's work, but I knew, as Jesus said in Luke 24:49 and Acts 1:8, "Tarry in Jerusalem until you have become clothed with power from on high." I needed to be baptized in the Holy Spirit and fire.

At the conference, it was almost midnight, and the man who is running the conference sees me in the first two or three rows and calls me out in front of thousands. I was wearing a white shirt that complimented my bodybuilding physique at the time, and seeing the hunger in my eyes as Paul saw with a man in Acts 14:9, he said, "Do you all see this young man? He will fall like a tree tonight," and everyone starts laughing. He said "No, I am serious. This guy is huge. Wait until the Holy Spirit comes upon him because he will get nailed tonight." So, as they setup the fire tunnel of people, I am one of the first to walk through it. I kid you not, I didn't even make it to the second or third person. The moment hands were laid on me, I was paralyzed from the neck down in the weighty glory of God. My body collapsed, and a man came behind me, picked me up under my arms, and the moment he removed his arms I collapsed again under the glory. Remember, the word glory means "weighty." The Presence of God consumed me. I was on fire. It was truly a moment of 2 Chronicles 5:13-14:

> "There was unison among the trumpeters and the singers, sounding out in one voice to praise and give thanksgiving to the LORD, and when the sound of the trumpets and cymbals and other musical instruments sounded

out with praise of the LORD 'for He is good, for His mercy endures forever,' and the priests could not stand and minister because of the cloud, for the glory of the LORD filled the temple of God."

The glory came upon me so heavily, I was paralyzed from the neck down and on fire. At this moment, I realized why it is so important to encounter the LORD. Nobody will ever be able to tell me this isn't real. It's not hearsay, I encountered it. Theology has no place in the conversation anymore, but rather a real experience with the King of kings and LORD of lords. At this moment, in order to get me out of the way, two men grabbed each of my arms and dragged me about twenty yards because I couldn't move, and people were falling like dominos. A little later I was finally able to move again, and I just sat there with the LORD. I had gotten everything I cried for. It was almost midnight as I was leaving, and I remember I was staying at a friend's house in downtown Dallas, but as I was filling up my car with gas that night, I was literally still on fire like a flame while at the gas pump. I was baptized in water in Israel four months prior, but now, I was baptized in the Holy Spirit and fire by King Jesus Himself. When I got back to my friend's place, I said, "There's no way I can sleep tonight." I packed my stuff and headed home at midnight, praising God for four hours the entire way back home. Rather than driving to my place in downtown Houston, I drove to my parents and got there after 4am. My parents can tell you, the next morning I was completely different again. God had ruined me for the world that night. The world was crucified to me, and I to the world (Galatians 6:14). There was no turning back (Genesis 19:17). God had marked me in His jealousy (Exodus 34:14) and sanctified me by His glory (Exodus 29:43).

What was interesting was at this point I had been walking with the LORD for about eight months but had never brought someone to the

LORD. People would become inspired by my walk, and even jealous with a Godly jealousy, but I never saw actual conversions, a non-believer into a believer, or the radical manifestations of the Holy Spirit that I really wanted to see. All of the sudden, within just a couple of weeks, people I came across began giving their lives to the LORD left and right. I lost count. It was just as when Peter stood up on Pentecost and the 3,000 were saved. This continued for me the next month in Peru, and really with anyone I came in contact with. God was having His way, for His glory.

One morning there was a Hispanic man sitting at the bus stop right outside of my high-rise as I was walking my dog, Kaia. As I walked past him, the Holy Spirit moved me, and I said, "Sir, are you a believer in Jesus?" He said, "No, my sister got raped by a priest at seven years old. Ever since, I stay away from all of that." I sat down with him, and I didn't speak to him with the persuasions of men, but with demonstration and the power of the Spirit (1 Corinthians 2:4). By the end of that conversation, this man gave his life to Jesus. I saw this over, and over, and over, and over again within just weeks of being baptized in the Holy Spirit and fire.

I saw that after being baptized in the Holy Spirit, the word of God on my tongue was like a sword cutting to the hearts of the people (Leviticus 26:7-8). It was like Stephen in Acts 6:15 as he spoke by the Holy Spirit, Scripture says the leaders saw his face as the face of an angel. Another time, I was in my office in the Woodlands, and walked out in order to step next door into HeBrews Coffee shop. As I walk past the coffee bar to go to the restroom, on my way out of the restroom, I walk back past that coffee bar and two men stopped me. One of them said, "As you walked by on your way to the restroom, the glory of your presence fell upon me and I was healed, and I feel incredible." I told him I had just read Acts 5:15 that morning, which says, "They brought out the sick (while lying on pallets) into the markets so that when Simon should come, at least his shadow might rest on them." We began praising God right there. This happened similarly to me as I was preaching in Iowa in 2019, and two pastors walked up to me after I preached and said, "As you preached, gold dust was manifesting on your forehead." I say what I have said so far in order to say, we need the baptism of the Holy Spirit so that we can do the work of the ministry and build the Kingdom of God with power.

I want to point out a couple instances in the book of Acts where there is a clear distinction between believing in Jesus, being water baptized, and then being baptized in the Holy Spirit. The first place I want to jump to is Acts 8:5-18:

> "Now Phillip went down to a city of the Samaritans, and he preached to them concerning Messiah. And men, who when they heard his word there, heeded him and were persuaded by all that he said because they saw the signs that he did. For many that were seized by unclean spirits cried out in a loud voice, and they went out from them. And others, paralytics and lame were healed. And a great joy was there in that city. Now there was a certain man there whose name was Simon who lived in that city a long time and deceived the people of Samaria by his sorcery while magnifying himself and saying, 'I am great!' And they followed after him, all of them great and small. And they said, 'this is the great power of God.' And they listened to him because for a long time he had persuaded them with his sorceries. But when they believed Phillip who had preached the kingdom of God in the name of our Master Yeshua the Messiah, men and women were baptized. And even Simon believed, and he was baptized

and adhered to Phillip. And when he saw the great signs and miracles that occurred by his hand he was amazed, and he marveled. And when the apostles who were in Jerusalem heard that the people of Samaria had received the word of God, they sent Simon Peter and John to them. And they went down and prayed over them that they would receive the Holy Spirit, for it was not upon one of them yet. They were only baptized now in the name of our Master Yeshua. Then they placed a hand upon them, and they received the Holy Spirit. And when Simon saw that by the placing of a hand of the apostles the Holy Spirit was given, he offered silver to them."

In this passage we see Phillip goes to Samaria and is doing signs and wonders among them, and notice it was the signs that converted them. Just as Jesus Himself said in John 14:10-11 that if they don't believe in Him (Jesus), at least believe in Him for the signs which He does. If we do not carry the power of the Holy Spirit, our word is nothing more than a theological debate. In 1 Kings 18 it was Elijah's word against the prophets of Baal, that is, until Elijah brought fire from heaven. Now, notice in the passage above, the Samaritans were converted. They became believers in Jesus and were even water baptized, yet the Scripture goes on to say that John and Peter went down to pray over them and lay hands, so that they would receive the Holy Spirit, because it was not upon any of them, for they had only been baptized in the name of our Master Yeshua!

Before we go any further, which we will, right here in the book of Acts we have believers who have not been baptized in the Holy Spirit. Their belief with Phillip, and the Holy Spirit coming upon them when Peter and John arrive and lay hands on them are two completely different events. I want to say, God can baptize people in the Holy Spirit without the laying of hands, such as in Acts 10:44 when Peter is preaching to the house of Cornelius and the Holy Spirit falls upon them. I have seen people get baptized in the Holy Spirit in this way while I was preaching.

There was a time I was preaching, and that day I had picked up a homeless man on the side of the road and asked him to come to service and told him that my family would feed him before service. He was not a believer. During my preaching, he gave his life to the LORD and was baptized in the Holy Spirit and fire. After service he said, "Pastor Nick, as you preached, a great fire fell upon me and consumed me, and I knew I was to give my life to Jesus." Weeks later I saw him on the street, and he was now having a seer anointing from 2 Kings 6:17-20, seeing demons and angels in the Spirit, and a smile from one ear to the other.

My original point with acts 8 is there was a clear difference between believers and the baptism of the Holy Spirit. There is one more passage I want to bring up on this very topic from Acts 18:24-19:6:

> "And a certain Jewish man from Alexandria named Apollos, who was trained to eloquence and well taught in the Scriptures came to Ephesus. He had been instructed in the ways of the LORD, and was fervent in spirit, and he discoursed and taught fully respecting Yeshua, while yet he knew nothing except the baptism of John. And he began to speak boldly in the synagogue. And when Aquilla and Priscilla heard him, they took him to their house, and fully showed him the way of the LORD. And when he was disposed to go to Achaia, the brothers anticipated him, and wrote to the disciples to receive him. And by going, through grace, he greatly assisted all of them that believed. For he reasoned powerfully against the Jews before the congregation, and showed from the

Scriptures respecting Yeshua, that He is the Messiah. And while Apollos was at Corinth, Paul traveled over the upper countries to Ephesus, and he inquired of the disciples whom he found there, 'have you received the Holy Spirit since you believed?' They answered and said to him, 'if there be a Holy Spirit, it has not come to our hearing.' He said to them, 'into what then were you baptized?' They said, 'into the baptism of John.' Paul said to them, 'John baptized the people with the baptism of repentance, while he told them to believe in Him who was to come after him, that is, Yeshua the Messiah.' And when they heard these things, they were baptized in the name of our Master Yeshua Messiah, and Paul laid a land upon them, and the Holy Spirit came upon them, and they spoke in various tongues and prophesied."

This learned man, Apollos, whom Paul also speaks about in 1 Corinthians 3, only knew about the water baptism of John Scripture says, until Aquilla and Priscilla took him in to show him also the baptism of the Holy Spirit. Now, notice Paul asks the disciples if they have received the Holy Spirit since they believed. Paul is a theological genius, so why would he find it necessary to ask this question to believers, unless they are, or at least can be, separate events?

I remember towards the end of 2022 I was at a Bible study with a man who was leading that has been teaching the Word of God and been in ministry since maybe as long as I have been alive. My dad had invited me one week and has attended this study every week, and up to this point had been with them for a while, as they are men that he is friends with and within the same age group. That week when I was invited, they happened to be reading from the Acts 8 passage we discussed with

Phillip, and during the study, I had purposed to keep my mouth shut because it is not my study, I am new, and I didn't want to barge in. As they are going back and forth about Acts 8, they all give insight and completely miss the part of the baptism of the Holy Spirit, and that the disciples in Samaria had not received the Holy Spirit after they had believed. The Holy Spirit was building up inside of me and was about to spill out of me as I kept trying to remain quiet. In my mind I am thinking, "We are missing the entire point." The Holy Spirit finally took my tongue, and I brought up that very topic within the passage, and said, "I think this is what we need to focus on."

My dad had already been baptized in the Holy Spirit, and knew this passage very well, as I taught it to him a couple years before in great depth, but as I said this, everyone is silenced and kind of scratching their heads, and the leader goes, "Nick, you are right, and theologically, this creates a big problem, because common thought is you get filled with the Holy Spirit as you receive Jesus." Right then I began to share my testimony of how I got baptized in the Holy Spirit and fire eight months after I gave my life to Jesus, and four months after my water baptism in the Jordan River in Israel. The entire atmosphere shifted, and now He made room for me to pour out to these men of God, who, like Apollos, were trained in Scripture, but knew nothing except the baptism of John. I began sharing stories about what God has done in my life with signs and wonders, and how I hear His voice with precision.

I shared with them a story that had just happened a couple months before in Iowa. I was sitting at my desk, and I heard the Holy Spirit say, "Write Todd and Maria a $5,000 check from Revelation Church, but DO NOT fill out the name. Leave it blank." So, I write the check, and head to their house on the property, and as I give it to them, I told them, "I don't know why, but the Holy Spirit wouldn't let me fill out the name. I was just to hand it to you both." So, Todd and Maria take a few

days to pray about what to do with it, whether it was to them personally, ministry, the farm, or something else. About 2-3 days later, Todd's
mentor, whom I met months earlier, called Todd very discouraged, and
shared with Todd about how they had taken a man in to stay with them,
and they just found out that this man stole 5,000 dollars from them.
Immediately the Holy Spirit told Todd that this is why I was told not to
fill out the name, because Todd would send it to his mentor. God already
had on His mind how to reimburse this man who was being stolen from,
who was living in another state. We serve such an amazing, gracious,
all knowing God. Todd's mentor, Pastor Gene, lived in Illinois. Months
earlier when I met Gene, I began sharing with him my revelations of the
baptism of the Holy Spirit, and it was he who initially told me to write
this book. Gene tells Todd, "Tell Nick to keep hearing from the LORD."

I always teach about how we have to hear the Spirit of God with
precision. The men at this Bible study were absolutely amazed, asking,
"How do you hear God so precisely?" And another in the group said,
"Nick, I am so glad you are here. This blessed me, and now I have to go
study the Scriptures about this (the baptism of the Holy Spirit). I have
never seen this." Neither did Apollos or the disciples at Ephesus. This was
no coincidence that my dad had been going to this study for a very long
time, but on this week, he just randomly invited me.

Now that we have clearly established that there is an event known
as the baptism of the Holy Spirit and fire, we have to take it deeper. My
question for a long time was, "Father, why do some get baptized in the
Holy Spirit, and others don't?" God is not a respecter of persons, so what
is it? Well, we need to begin with the first time believers in Jesus got baptized in the Holy Spirit and fire, which is at Pentecost in Acts 2, however,
this will just be our springboard, because the answer itself is not there.

As we step into Acts 2, one thing people know that I preach and
quote almost every single week is Ecclesiastes 1:9-10:

"That which has been is what will be, and that which has been done is what will be done. There is nothing new under the sun. There is a matter which one will say, 'see, this is new.' It has already been from ancient times before us."

As well as Job 8:8-10:

"For ask now of the former generation, and be prepared to search out their fathers, for we are of yesterday and we do not know, because our days are a shadow upon the earth. Will they not teach you? They will tell you, and they will bring out words from their heart."

Anytime we want to understand something in the New Testament, we must understand that everything is a paradigm, and NOTHING is new under the sun, meaning, in order to know what will be, and in order to know the future, or even current events, we have to go backwards, because whatever has been done is what will be done, because nothing is new under the sun. The forefathers before us encountered the same, and if we will study the first generations and dive into the Torah of Moses, they will continue to teach us today. Nothing is new in the New Testament, and the same goes for the baptism of the Holy Spirit and fire. I tell people continually, everything you want to know about the New Testament is found in the Torah of Moses. I have numerous teachings on this, proving this fact.

We must go backwards in order to understand the context of Acts 2. Acts 2 is about the day of Pentecost, when Scripture says that the Holy Spirit would be given, and the Holy Spirit will write the Torah on the tablet of our hearts (Jeremiah 31:31-34, Ezekiel 36:26-27, Hebrews 10:16-17). We must go back to Exodus 19-20, the day of Pentecost when the Torah was given on tablets of stone. In order to learn about the New Testament Pentecost, we must understand it through the lenses of the Old Testament Pentecost. Through this, we will find out not only how one becomes prepared to receive the baptism of the Holy Spirit and fire, but why some people don't receive it at certain times, such as myself when Todd prayed for me in Israel. There are prerequisites for the preparing of oneself to be ready and ripe for wheat harvest, as Pentecost is the wheat harvest.

We must now go back to Exodus 19, as God tells Moses how to prepare the people for the third day, which is the day of Pentecost. Exodus 19:11, "And they shall be ready on the third day, because on the third day the LORD will descend before all the people upon Mount Sinai." On the third day, the day of Pentecost, the LORD would descend and meet the people, just as He did on Pentecost in Acts 2 with the Holy Spirit, but God says they must be "ready," meaning, in order for you to receive what He wants to give on Pentecost-the Holy Spirit-you have to be "ready." God goes on to tell them what they need to do in order to help with this preparation, however, we have to understand, there is yet, another paradigm found within this verse, which will cause us to go back even further than Exodus! Exodus 19:11 says, "On the third day (בַּיּוֹם הַשְּׁלִשִׁי)," and then again in Exodus 19:16 "on the third day (בַיֹּם הַשְּׁלִישִׁי)," however, verse 16 is spelled differently by one letter that verse 13 is missing.

There is something in Rabbinic literature in regard to Jewish hermeneutics, or methods of interpretation, called "gizra shava," which means, equal weight or an equivalence of expressions. What this means is, if we find a phrase spelled exactly the same in Hebrew in one place, and then also in another, they carry the same weight and understanding, and they are pointing to each other to have a fuller perspective. This is important because in Hebrew, many times we have "missing" or "added" letters even by just one letter, which is done purposely by God so that it brings a separation, but if they are the same, Scripture is begging us, saying, "Look here also!" There is a time earlier where we see this same phrase, letter for letter, in Hebrew, "On the third day." In Genesis 22 Abraham is told by God to offer his promised son, Isaac, as an offering, specifically as a burnt offering, which we will get too in a moment. It says in Genesis 22:4, "On the third day (בַּיּוֹם הַשְּׁלִישִׁי) Abraham lifted his eyes and saw the place from afar." There is a paradigm and pattern that we must be able to see with the day of Pentecost, because through this, we will see the roots of the baptism of the Holy Spirit and fire.

Once again, just as Pentecost was said to be on the third day in Exodus 19:11/16, Abraham is offering Isaac as a burnt offering on the third day (Genesis 22:4), which is a day of repentance. Why do I say a day of repentance? The third day has to do with the resurrection (Luke 24:46-47), as it is written in Hosea 6:2, "He will revive us after two days. In the third day He will raise us up, and we will live before Him." The resurrection and living in the Spirit rather than the flesh has to do with a fullness of repentance in order to walk in the Spirit (Galatians 5:16). But not only this, there is something known as gematria, which is a numerical system I have taught on extensively on my Youtube channel (Nick Tognietti). Gematria is a numerical system used all throughout rabbinic literature and Jewish thought, as well as by the writers of the New Testament. In Hebrew, we have 22 letters, each of which has a specific numerical value. When you get a word, phrase, or even a verse, and add up its numerical value, if there is another word, phrase, or verse that is equivalent in its gematria or numerical value, it means there is a direct connection.

This is the secret behind the 153 fish in John 21, or the man whose name is equivalent to 666 in Revelation 13, who is the anti-messiah. John says a man with wisdom will be able to interpret this, and that the man's name will be equivalent to 666, and if you don't get the number of his mark, you can't buy or sell. This is actually telling us about Shechem, the son of Chamor in Genesis 34. "Shechem, the son of Chamor (שכם בן חמור)" in gematria is 666, and Genesis 34 tells us if the sons of Jacob didn't do what he wanted, they can't trade in the land, but if they do, they can trade, aka, they can buy, sell, and do business. Shechem is a picture of the anti-messiah and the context of that entire Revelation 13 passage, which is another example to prove my point, everything is found in the Torah of Moses, which is the greatest book of prophecy (Deuteronomy 34:10). Nothing is new under the sun, but to know what will be, we must know what has been (Ecclesiastes 1:9-10, Job 8:8-10).

I explain this to give clarity on why I say the third day has to do with repentance. The phrase in Exodus 19:16 and Genesis 22:4, "On the third day (בַּיּוֹם הַשְּׁלִישִׁי)" has a gematria of 713, which is equivalent to "repentance (תשובה)." This baptism of the Holy Spirit with the third day and being prepared for Pentecost is going to have to do with us having a fully repentant posture towards God, and holding nothing back from Him, as it is written in Acts 5:32, "The Holy Spirit, which God gives to those who obey Him." As I mentioned though, we must understand, Isaac was being offered specifically on this third day as a burnt offering, as Israel was commanded to be "ready" on third day, which was Pentecost. Meaning, in order to be "ready" as God commanded Israel on Pentecost in Exodus 19, we must come before the LORD as a burnt offering as Isaac was. Here is the thing, there are six different offerings in the Torah of Moses in Leviticus 1-5. Leviticus 1-burnt offering, Leviticus 2-meal offering, Leviticus 3-peace offering, Leviticus 4-sin offering, Leviticus 5-guilt offering and a trespass offering, and each of these have their own implications, practicalities, and prophetic insights in the Holy Spirit.

The question remains, if we have to come to the LORD as a burnt offering in order to be ready for the baptism of the Holy Spirit, what does it mean to be a burnt offering? Because without this understanding, one won't be "prepared" to receive the baptism of the Holy Spirit and fire as the children of Israel had to be "prepared" on the third day, the day of Pentecost in Exodus 19-20. This will also show why someone may have encountered the LORD deeply previously, but years have gone by without encountering Him the way you used to. This is the secret that the Holy Spirit showed me, because for so long I wondered why some people get baptized with the Holy Spirit, and some don't.

I remember when I first started Revelation Church in my parents living room in 2018 at 24 years old, and I spoke on the baptism of the Holy Spirit constantly, and after weeks of preaching on this topic, I stood up and asked, "Who wants the baptism?" My dad walks up, and right as I lay hands on his head, he hits the ground under the weighty glory, then another woman, same thing. I had a man walk in my parents' house who was about 6'5", and he came in with his box of drugs, placing it on their table before everyone, saying, "I don't want this, I want the baptism." I laid hands on him, and this massive man falls face flat in the glory. Not everyone gets hit under the glory the same way, some people may start speaking in tongues, or prophesying, or some may get consumed in fire, which is how my mom encountered it on Pentecost at a meeting I held in the Upper Room at Hebrews Woodlands coffee shop, as I mentioned earlier with the homeless man. I had a man up in Iowa after service come up to me and asked me to pray because he wanted the baptism. I laid my hand on his forehead, and my palm turned into a flame of fire, and I kid you not, he starts dripping in sweat as I prayed. As the fire came upon him, he verbally starts repenting of all these different sins. The fire cleanses, consumes, and purifies. My point is, the Holy Spirit will manifest however He sees fit. Not all will speak in tongues right then. In Acts 8 they didn't, but in Acts 19 some of them did.

It's not my job to tell you what will happen, but it is my job to tell you how we become "ready," which is by being a burnt offering. Leviticus

1 tells us about the burnt offering, and it is different than every other offering, because unlike other offerings, none of the burnt offering is given to the priest, and none is given to the one who offers it, such as the peace offering in Leviticus 3. The burnt offering is given completely to God. There is one prerequisite, apart from it being a male, without blemish (Leviticus 1:3), the burnt offering has to be flayed, or skinned (Leviticus 1:6). Skin it or flay it and lay the rest of the entire offering on the altar, and the fire of God will fall and consume it as we see in Leviticus 9:24, "And fire went out from before the LORD and consumed the burnt offering upon the altar, and the fat, and all the people saw, and they shouted and fell on their faces."

This is a picture of the baptism of the Holy Spirit and fire found in the Torah in Leviticus 9:24. The burnt offering is called a "burnt offering, a fire offering, a sweet smelling aroma to the LORD" in Leviticus 1:9. The word for "fire offering (אִשֶּׁה)" pronounced "isheh," is the same exact word in Hebrew in the Scriptures for the word "wife (אִשָּׁה)," pronounced "ishah." All of the offerings tell us not only about the Messiah, but also about us as the bride, and the more we study them, the more we become them. The burnt offering is a picture of the bride of Messiah, and their needed posture to be ready to be consumed by the LORD in the Holy Spirit and fire.

What this is telling us is we have to be skinned or flayed of the things of this world, the things of the flesh, removed and crucified with Messiah, and your life, like the burnt offering, has to be fully given to the LORD in repentance. Remember, I said the third day is about repentance that says, "LORD I am yours. I want to be flayed and skinned of the things of this world, holding nothing back from You," just as the man who walked in my parents' house and lays down his box of drugs, and says he is done with all of it, because he would rather be filled with the fullness of the Spirit of God. For the ones who give lip service and

45

claim this, if you haven't experienced it, I am telling you right now, the
LORD weighs the hearts and minds, and words don't fool him, nor is
God a liar, as it is written in Galatians 6:7, "Do not deceive yourselves, as
God is not deceived, for what the sons of men sow, they will also reap."
God looks at the heart (1 Samuel 16:7) and doesn't see as man sees. Fire
falls on very specific circumstances, and all the rest is just show.

This concept is shown first in the Torah quite clearly in Genesis 4. We
can always see whom God chooses when there are two opposing parties
in Scripture, and each time, God answers by fire, such as with Elijah and
the false prophets (1 Kings 18:20-40), and with Moses and the Korah
rebellion (Numbers 16). In fact, with Elijah and the false prophets, when
God answers Elijah by fire, it is written in 1 Kings 18:36, "And when the
offering was being offered, Elijah the prophet drew near, and he said, 'O
LORD God of Abraham, Isaac, and Israel, today, let it be known that
you are God in Israel, and I am Your servant, and by Your word I have
done all these things.'" Out of the six different kinds of offerings we have
given to us in Leviticus 1-5, the word here for "the offering (הַמִּנְחָה)"
is "mincha," which is the same word "offering" in regard to Cain and
Abel's offerings in Genesis 4:3-4, as well as the offering of Korah against
Moses (Numbers 16:15). These passages, especially revealed through the
"incense" in Numbers 16, is referring to whom God is going to answer
in prayer. Incense always has to do with prayer, as it was also the prayer
of Elijah or the prayer of the false prophets that would be answered. As I
said, God always answers by fire in these circumstances with two people/
parties. So too, with Cain and Abel and their offerings (mincha) to God.
It is written in Genesis 4:2-5:

> "And she gave birth again to Abel, his brother, and Abel
> was a shepherd of sheep, and Cain was a worker of the
> ground. And at the end of days Cain brought some of the

fruit of the ground as an offering to the LORD, and Abel also brought from the firstborns of his flock, and from their fat, and God looked to Abel and to his offering, and to Cain and his offering God did not look, and Cain became very angry, and his countenance fell."

Have you ever stopped and asked yourself, "How did they know whose offering God looked too? What did that look like practically?" Well, due to Ecclesiastes 1:9-10, and knowing that nothing is new under the sun, we can go to the latter stories of Torah and the Scriptures, such as Moses and Korah, or Elijah and the false prophets (and other stories) and realize that God would have answered by fire between these two individuals in order to make distinction. Rather than looking at earlier stories and using prophecy going forward, as nothing is new under the sun, and whatever will be has already been, and what has been done, will be done (Ecclesiastes 1:9-10), we can take latter stories and use "reverse prophecy" for proper Scriptural analysis, and we see that they knew whose offering God looked to through His answering by fire, for this is the nature of God, as it is written in Hebrews 12:29, "For our God is a consuming fire."

Being someone who is heavily involved in mathematics, and the quantitative dimension of Scripture, reverse prophecy would be similar to using reverse division/multiplication to get back to the beginning of an equation. God's fire fell on Abel's offering. Why? Because Cain only brought an offering that was convenient for him to bring, meanwhile, Torah says that Abel brought not only the firstborns, which is what is always commanded of us, but also their fat, which is always the choicest portion of the offerings, and the most flavorful, as we see throughout the rest of Scripture (Leviticus 3:16-17). Scripture doesn't say that Cain brought the first fruits, but says, "Some of the fruit of the ground (מִפְּרִי

47

הָאֲדָמָה)," just as someone may just give "some of themselves to God," rather than the best of them, or the first parts of them, in which case the rest follows suit, and the first fruits of who they are, for "if the first fruits are holy, then the rest is holy, and if the root is holy, so too, are the branches (Romans 11:16)."

This same scenario is with the baptism of the Holy Spirit and fire. Those who do things out of convenience, but it isn't their whole heart, their whole life, and sold out devotion, they have not and will not receive the fire, and I have personally seen these individuals not only not get the fire of God, but they become bitter and angry towards God and towards those getting encounters in the Holy Spirit and fire, just as Cain became very angry towards God and attacked his brother, Abel, because he didn't get the encounter he was looking for. What a man sows, surely he will reap (2 Corinthians 9:6, Galatians 6:7). But God is no respecter of persons, and He tells Cain that if we will all come to Him as Abel, we will receive the fire of God, as it is written in Genesis 4:6-7:

> "And the LORD said to Cain, 'Why are you angry, and why has your countenance fallen? If you do well, will you not be lifted up? And if you do not do well, sin lies at the door, and its desire is for you, but you shall rule over it.'"

One cannot fool God, regardless of how convincing they may seem in the eyes of man. In fact, in Jerusalem when I met Pastor Todd and he prayed for me, remember, I said I didn't get the baptism at that time. There were still things I was holding back from the LORD. I loved Him, but there were things of the world I was dabbling with. After Israel, for the next two months I got attacked spiritually with great temptations, and because my roots weren't fully established, I was back and forth for the next two months between God and the world. I was wrestling with God (Genesis 32:25-33). I remember very clearly; I had gone through another breakup, and I didn't handle it well when I got back from Israel. A couple months later, I went to New York with an old friend for the weekend for my 24th birthday and spent ten grand on that weekend alone, falling back into the old life with women, alcohol, weed, cocaine, bottle service, etc. We ended up missing our flights back to Houston because the party was going even until the morning at the end of the weekend.

I was living in the newest high-rise in Houston at the time, and my friend lived in one of the penthouses on the top floor. Literally, as we got back from the trip, the Uber drops us off at our high-rise from the airport and he already has women in his penthouse with lines of cocaine ready for us as we walked in to continue the New York party we just got home from. It was after this weekend that I felt so convicted, so empty, and the fear of God fell upon me so heavily that this was my official turning point. As I walked in his penthouse, rather than continuing to party, I went down to my place for a moment and my heart was rent before God. I was asking the LORD what was happening to me. I couldn't continue with this void in my heart, and the conviction and fear of Him caused me not to go back up and party with them that night.

From this moment I said, "LORD I am yours." I never looked back. At this moment God had gripped me in the fear of the LORD, and for the next several weeks, He was preparing me for the third day, the day of Pentecost when I would have a face to face encounter with the glory of God in Dallas, Texas. The LORD knew, "Nick is now a burnt offering. He has been flayed from the world. He is an offering to Me without blemish." "Without blemish (תָּמִים)" in Hebrew, pronounced "tamim," actually means completely "devoted." It is the same word for describing Noah as "perfect" in Genesis 6:9 "these are the generations of Noah. Noah, a righteous man, perfect (tamim) in his generations. Noah continually walked with God (אֵלֶּה תּוֹלְדֹת נֹחַ נֹחַ אִישׁ צַדִּיק תָּמִים הָיָה בְּדֹרֹתָיו אֶת־הָאֱלֹהִים הִתְהַלֶּךְ־נֹחַ).‎"

Noah was "perfect/without blemish (tamim)" in his generation's, meaning, the sins you see in the world, you didn't see on Noah. Full devotion. An offering worthy of receiving that fire to fall as it was in Torah. Sometimes, this takes time. I make mistakes and have to repent daily, just as Noah did, but there is always this posture of full devotion to Him, even when I fall short. There is a shift of devotion and belief. Unbelief will ruin the atmosphere for the Holy Spirit (Matthew 13:58). There comes a point where the devotion shifts, and you become unsatisfied with everything else. No matter how much you drink, no matter what you eat, no matter whom you have sex with, no matter how much money you make-none of it fills you, and you are not satisfied. The burnt offering is the key to the baptism of the Holy Spirit and fire. Through this, you will be filled, and you will move with power. God is no respecter of persons (Deuteronomy 16:19, Romans 2:11, Galatians 2:6, Ephesians 6:9, Colossians 3:25).

Only after I received the baptism did the LORD start sending me out as an evangelist, and that is when I began to see the power manifest in many different ways. It is also worth noting, I didn't receive the gift of tongues when I got the baptism. About three months later, there was a woman I water baptized, and I wanted her to get the baptism of the Holy Spirit and fire. We were at a church service and after service as people were crying for the baptism, God gripped me, and I laid hands on her while praying for fire. As I was praying in English, she got completely consumed in the fire of God, weeping, and burning on the altar, and minutes into me praying, without even realizing, I was speaking another language, a heavenly language as fluent, or even more so, than I speak in English. I received the gift of tongues. Afterwards another woman who was next to me heard me say that was my first time speaking in tongues, and she said, "Nick it sounded like you have been doing that for years." It's a faulty theology that a large movement today says that if you don't speak in tongues, you never got the baptism. I rebuke this theology with the authority of heaven and the Scriptures. In Acts 19 they did speak in tongues, but in Acts 8 they didn't, and neither did I right when I got the baptism.

The baptism of the Holy Spirit and fire is not just about the "nine gifts" that we commonly quote from 1 Corinthians 9, including tongues, interpreting tongues, prophecy, healing, etc. Moving in power doesn't just mean you walk with signs and wonders, or someone came out of a wheelchair. This is walking in power, but it is not the only manifestation of the power of the Holy Spirit. If this hasn't happened, it's okay, because the Holy Spirit was given for much more than that, as we will see throughout this book. It says in Acts 2 that when they got baptized in the Holy Spirit and fire, Peter now stands up boldly. The one who was hiding in the upper room, and denied Jesus, is now filled with all boldness and eloquence in the Scriptures, and 3,000 people get saved that day. Also, Stephen, preaching in Acts 6-7 before the Sanhedrin, recounting the entire Gospel from the book of Genesis and going forward. That kind of boldness, eloquence, understanding, and revelation takes POWER in the Holy Spirit, however, Stephen and Peter both had signs and wonders as well.

In 1 Corinthians 12 after Paul lists the "nine gifts" of the Holy Spirit, Paul says in 1 Corinthians 12:28-30:

> "For God has placed in His assembly, first, apostles, after them, prophets, after them, teachers, after them, workers of miracles, after them, gifts of healing, and helpers, and leaders, and various tongues. Are they all apostles? Are they all prophets? Are they all teachers? Are they all

workers of miracles? Have all of them gifts of healing? Do they all speak with tongues?"

Notice, Paul references a few of the commonly referred nine gifts of the Holy Spirit, but now, in the same context, interwoven with those, he discusses being teachers, helpers, and leaders. What Paul is saying is, it's not just about the nine gifts of the Holy Spirit with miracles and tongues. He is saying, you can't even be the proper teacher or leader that you are called to be. Without the baptism, neither Peter nor Stephen could have preached those powerful sermons, quoting the Scriptures by heart with absolute revelation and eloquence, and no prepared notes. You can't even lead with boldness and authority without it. Jesus said in John 14-16 that when the Holy Spirit comes, He will remind us of all things Jesus said, and teach us all things, as well as telling us of future events. Read the book of Acts. It wasn't until the baptism of the Holy Spirit and fire that Scripture would say "and the disciples now understood or remembered what Jesus had told them." They needed the Interpreter, the Holy Spirit. For 3.5 years they hardly understood Jesus, but then after Acts 2, revelation opens and flows like rivers of living water out of their belly (John 7:38).

You can't be a leader in your home, with your family, in your marriage ministry, in your Bible studies, in your prophetic ministry, at your workplace, or anything else without the Holy Spirit. There is an authority and boldness with the Holy Spirit. What I found interesting is if you study the gospels, look at what happens at every home Jesus enters, even a Pharisee's home. Jesus ends up taking the scene with authority, even at only thirty years old. Everywhere He goes, people listen, and He doesn't shy away. Jesus is always about business, Kingdom business. Every Bible study I go too, every house I enter, every ministry I walk into, at some point, I end up being the one teaching, and everyone in the room recognizes the authority, just as the prophetic word the woman spoke over me in 2019 that I discussed in the foreword of this book. I don't say this arrogantly, but it seems to happen everywhere. I have leaders in ministry saying this same thing about me.

Because I press into the Holy Spirit, He has given such eloquence and revelation, and the people listen. I remember a man who runs a marriage ministry said to me right when he met me, "Nick, I don't know how to explain it, but there is such a confidence and authority about you. It isn't arrogance, but such a confidence." I know who I am, and I know Whose I am. I also know that I am called to walk just as He walked (1 John 2:6), and as the Father sent Him, so He sends me (John 20:21). I let no one despise my words or my age (writing this book at 29 years old), and I am always prepared (1 Timothy 4:12-16). This comes with the baptism, and daily intimacy with the Holy Spirit in the secret place.

Right before I came back into ministry from my long sabbatical in 2022, He gave me a dream and baptized me afresh in the fire, but this time with a new anointing as well. In the dream, there was a mighty prophet that asked me to come preach at his ministry. He sat to my right, and as I opened up in prayer, he placed his right hand on my forehead and suddenly I stopped praying. I leaned back and the Spirit caught me in the air, filling me and enveloping me. I immediately was on fire in the dream dripping sweat, and I started praying in tongues while he prayed over me. I was simply consumed by the Holy Spirit. It was the best thing I could ever explain, and the dream was more real than being awake. As I was in the Spirit, I was made aware that the fifty people in the crowd knew I was in the Spirit as they sat before me. Suddenly, a man named John came over and told the prophet who was laying his hand on me, "the Jordan river is about to stop up." When I awoke, I was drenched in my bed with sweat, burning on fire. The LORD immediately took me to 2 Kings 2, where Elijah the prophet (who was later called John the

Baptist who baptized in the Jordan River-Matthew 11:7-14,17:11-13) and Elisha the prophet are going to cross the Jordan, and a double portion anointing would be transferred from Elijah to Elisha. As the Jordan river was split, the two of them passed over, and a chariot of fire took Elijah, and there were fifty prophets that recognized the spirit of Elijah fell on Elisha.

This was all my dream to the T, as I was consumed in fire, passing over the Jordan with a mighty prophet (Elijah), and there were fifty disciples before me who knew I was in the Spirit, and I was receiving a greater prophetic anointing from the prophet laying his hand upon me. I knew the LORD baptized me again, but this time, with a heavier prophetic anointing to walk in. This is exactly what the other woman said about me that I typed out in the foreword of this book. Once again, I was truly marked by God that night. I couldn't get over the fire and experience. I called Todd and Maria around 4am that morning to share this encounter.

I have always wanted another baptism, with a deeper calling in Him. He gave it to me as I went through the fires faithfully for those few years. Be "ready" for Pentecost as God commanded for Israel to be ready in Exodus 19:11. Be a burnt offering, flayed from the world and the lusts of the flesh. He wants to bring Pentecost every day. In Mark 16:15-18, Jesus says these signs will follow "them that believe." I hold Jesus to His Word, but first, I have to bring my body under subjection, lest I become disqualified (1 Corinthians 9:27), and hold myself to His Word as well. If I hold Him to this standard, I must hold myself to the same. The movement is here and now. He is fanning the flame to create Trees Of Fire.

Chapter 2

The Purpose Of The Blood

The point of this chapter is to bring us to the first chapter with the baptism of the Holy Spirit and fire, as I believe this chapter is the prerequisite to come to that point of being ripe for the harvest of the Holy Spirit and fire on Pentecost. When we talk about Pentecost and the baptism of the Holy Spirit and fire, one can't help but discuss Passover and the blood of the Lamb. Not only can you not discuss Pentecost without Passover, because Pentecost doesn't take place without Passover, but you also can't discuss Passover without Pentecost, because Passover, as we will see, was literally for the sake of Pentecost.

As crazy as it may sound, I do believe we have not only watered down Jesus' Passover sacrifice, but we have also limited its power due to a contextual misunderstanding, and missing the lenses we should be viewing His Passover sacrifice through. The context of Jesus' first coming and His death on the cross has everything to do with fulfilling the Passover, meaning, if we don't fully understand what the Passover is from the Torah, we will miss a lot of what Jesus said in the New Testament. John the Baptist says in John 1:29, "and on the next day, John saw Yeshua coming to him, and he said, 'behold, the Lamb of God who takes away the sin of the world.'" Again, John says in John 1:36 "and he stared at Yeshua, and He was walking, and he said, 'behold, the Lamb of God.'"

We as believers fully recognize that Jesus came and took away our sins, but we can't stop there, because His sacrifice, as understood through the Passover, carries so much more significance to not only heal our past, but also to empower our present and our future. We must grasp the purpose of the Passover. What is the purpose of the blood of Jesus (Passover)? Throughout the New Testament we are shown that through the shedding of His blood, if one repents of sin and believes in Him, they receive the forgiveness of sins, as Jesus also declared in Luke 24:46-47:

> "And He said to them, 'thus it is written, and thus it is fitting that the Messiah will suffer and rise from the dead on the third day. And that repentance should be preached in His name for the forgiveness of sins in all the nations, beginning from Jerusalem.'"

Jesus' words as we see from the original Aramaic Peshitta text of the New Testament specifically state "repentance FOR the forgiveness of sins," meaning, without repentance, you are still in your sins and unforgiven, as Jesus also said in Luke 13:3 "no, but I tell you, that also all of you, if you do not repent, you will perish," which Jesus repeats in Luke 13:5 as well. This same thought is said by John in 1 John 1:7 "but if we walk in the light, as He is in the light, we have fellowship with each other, and the blood of Yeshua His Son purifies us from all of our sins."

But was this the only reason for the blood of Jesus? Was it just to have forgiveness of sins? I ask again, what is the purpose of the blood of Jesus as the Passover Lamb of God? We have to start seeking for this understanding from what is commonly referred to as the "Last Supper," specifically from Luke 22, but it is really a Passover seder. Jesus sits with His twelve disciples, and He says in Luke 22:15-20:

"I have greatly longed to eat this Passover with you before I suffer. I say to you that from now on, I will not eat it until it will be perfected in the Kingdom of God. And He took the cup, and He gave thanks, and He said, 'take this, and divide it amongst yourselves. For I say to you, that I will not drink of the fruit of the vine until the Kingdom of God will come.' And He took the bread, and He gave thanks and broke it, and He gave it to them, saying, 'this is my body that is given for your sakes. Do this in remembrance of Me.' And thus He also did with the cup after they ate, and He said, 'this cup is the New Covenant in My blood that is poured out for your sakes.'"

Notice Jesus is doing something with the bread and the wine, which is nothing new. He is doing a Passover seder meal with His disciples. But what He is saying is, what Israel has done for thousands of years at the Passover seder with unleavened bread and wine, Jesus now interprets this as His body and His blood. A very old tradition, with a new interpretation, also known as a "chidush." Like I said, we cannot understand the blood of Jesus apart from the context of Passover, because He specifically says in the passage above, "I have greatly longed to eat this Passover with you." So, when we talk about the Passover, the blood of Jesus, we are actually talking about what took place in Exodus 12, and everything preceding it from Exodus 1-12, because the first twelve chapters are actually one thought, and Chapter 12 being the Passover, was actually the culmination of the first eleven chapters, and it was done because of the first eleven chapters. All twelve chapters must be read together, or we will miss the reason that the Passover was given in Chapter 12 in the first place. It is the culmination of the ten plagues God displayed against Egypt. These plagues, and Israel's freedom finalizes with Passover when

God "passes over," or leaps over the houses of Israel and smites all of the firstborn in Egypt from the least to the greatest (Exodus 12::23/27), from the son of Pharaoh who sits on his throne, down to the animals (Exodus 12:29) that did not have the blood on their lentil and doorposts (Exodus 12:7/13). There was not a single house where there was not one who was dead (Exodus 12:30).

The question now becomes, what were the plagues for? The Passover itself was a plague, so what was the purpose of the plagues, including the Passover? The Torah continually tells us throughout the first twelve chapters of Exodus. More than six times the LORD tells Pharaoh "let My people go so that they may serve Me (Exodus 7:16, 7:26, 8:16, 9:1, 9:13, 10:3)!" God continually sends Moses and Aaron to Pharaoh before these plagues, telling Pharaoh to let the people of Israel go, specifically for one purpose, so that they may serve the LORD. That is the purpose of all of these plagues, including the final plague-Passover. God is wanting to free the people from Egypt in order to come serve Him at Mount Sinai, so that they may come and celebrate Pentecost! The tenth plague, the Passover, was no different than the first nine in the context of its purpose, the only difference is, within it, is the power to set them free. Within the blood of Jesus, the Passover Lamb of God, is that power, nevertheless, its purpose is to come to Pentecost as we will see.

The blood is not there for you to stay in Egypt. The purpose of the blood was in order to have you leave Egypt and to forsake sin (Proverbs 28:13), not to remain in it and make the blood of Jesus, the Passover, of no effect. Notice in all the verses I listed above, where God says, "let my people go so they may serve Me," those Scriptures don't tell us what that looks like exactly, however, before these, God already told us. The answer, and purpose of the blood is found in Exodus 5:1 "and afterwards Moses and Aaron came, and they said to Pharaoh, 'thus says the LORD God of Israel, send out My people, so that they may celebrate a feast to

Me in the wilderness.'" What is this feast? This feast in Hebrew is called a "chag (חג)." There are three feasts listed for us in the Torah of Moses (Exodus 23:14-17, Deuteronomy 16:16) that Israel was to appear before the LORD for, which is the feast of Passover/Unleavened Bread, the feast of Pentecost (also called the feast of the Harvest), and the feast of Tabernacles (also called the feast of Ingathering).

Passover, Pentecost, and Tabernacles are the three feasts, but which is the one God is specifying here that they are being set free in order to do? He is talking about Pentecost in Exodus 19-20! God is saying, the entire reason He wants the children of Israel to leave Egypt and come to Him at Mount Sinai is so that they may come to Pentecost, so they can come and receive His Torah, in order that they will know how to serve Him. Ultimately, so they may come and get all that Pentecost has to offer, which means to get baptized in the Holy Spirit and fire as the disciples on Pentecost in Acts 2. You are being set free from being a slave to the master of sin (Pharaoh/Satan), to now being a slave to the Master of the universe (Messiah Yeshua). You are being set free from the orphanage and spirit to the bondage of sin, to now receiving the Spirit of adoption by whom we cry out Abba, Father (Romans 8:15).

We always hear the phrase, "let my people go, let my people go," but why? What was the purpose? The institution of Passover was solely to come to Pentecost. As I mentioned at the beginning of this chapter, without Passover, there is no Pentecost, but without Pentecost, the blood of the Passover isn't needed. The blood is for the sake of coming to Pentecost and being baptized in the Holy Spirit and fire. The blood of Jesus is not meant to just be used in confession so that we can continue to abide in Egypt in our sin and live a powerless life, so that we can continue to be trampled by the Evil One, but rather, the blood of the Passover Lamb of God is to set us free from the bondage of the sins of the flesh, to leave Egypt, and to come to the LORD and walk in the Holy Spirit, as Paul said in Galatians 5:16 "I am saying, walk in the Spirit, and you shall not fulfill the desire of the flesh." God wants us to come celebrate a festival with Him daily-Pentecost. At Pentecost in Exodus 19-20, the Torah was given on Tablets of Stone, but it says in Jeremiah 31:31-34 and Ezekiel 36:26-27, that under the New Covenant, the Torah will now be written upon the tablet of our heart by the Holy Spirit, which is also repeated in Hebrews 10:16-17. So, both times, the Passover in Exodus and the Passover with Jesus, the Passover was so that we may leave Egypt, turning from sin, coming to Pentecost, so that His ways may penetrate our deepest parts in order to serve Him well. Pentecost is where the believers got baptized in the Holy Spirit, so that they may walk free from sin, set others free from sin, and trample serpents, scorpions, and over all of the power of the Evil One (Luke 10:19).

Many have taken the blood of Jesus, without recognizing its power, trampling the Son of God underfoot, by using His name in a way that doesn't match His character, or the purpose of His blood. People have perverted the grace of God to use the blood and then stay in Egypt, as it is written in Titus 1:16 "and they profess that they know God, but in their works they deny Him, and they are odious, and disobedient, and reprobates to every good work." Again, in Jude 1:4:

> "For some have obtained entrance who from the begin-
> ning were registered beforehand under this condemna-
> tion: wicked men who pervert the grace of God to im-
> purity and deny Him who is the only Lord God and our
> Master Yeshua the Messiah."

But God's desires for us are explained clearly in Titus 2:11-15:

> "For the all resurrecting grace of God is revealed to all
> men, and it teaches us to deny that which is without God

and worldly lusts, and to live in this world in sobriety, and in uprightness, and in the fear of God, looking for the blessed hope and the manifestation of the glory of the great God and our Life-giver, Yeshua the Messiah, Who gave Himself for us that He might recover us from all iniquity and purify for Himself a new people who are zealous in good works. Speak and encourage these things and point out with all authority and let no one despise you."

Again, in 1 Thessalonians 4:3-7:

"For this is the will of God, your sanctification, and that you be separated from all sexual sin, and that each one of you might know how to possess his vessel in sanctity and in honor, and not in the passion of lust, like the rest of the Gentiles who do not know God, and that no-one transgress and overreach his brother in this matter, because our Master is the Avenger of all these, as also we have said and testified to you in time past. For God did not call you to impurity, but to sanctification."

1 John 2:6 says that if we say we are His, we also ought to walk as He walked, and we are continually told to be "imitators of God (1 Corinthians 11:1, Ephesians 5:1)." The purpose of the blood of Jesus is so that we can come out of our old ways and come to Pentecost. Pentecost is where we get baptized in the Holy Spirit and receive instruction in order to learn how to serve the LORD, so that we can enter into the Promise Land. Ecclesiastes 7:11 says "wisdom is good with the inheritance," meaning, wisdom and knowing God's ways is good with the Promise Land, because if you don't know how to honor God within the Promise

Land, you will get vomited out quicker than you came in (see 2 Kings 17, but notice specifically verses 24-28, also see Leviticus 18:28, 20:22, and Revelation 3:16).

Coming to the cross and leaving Egypt is critical, and without it, nothing else matters, however, it is not where we stop, it is only the beginning. The cross wasn't the end of our walk, it was the end of our old life. The cross was actually a starting point in a resurrected life by the power of the Holy Spirit, and "it is finished (John 19:30)" is referring to the power that sin has over us as Satan accuses us in the eyes of the Father (Zechariah 3:1-10). It is through the revelation of the cross, our confession and repentance, that we come to Pentecost in order to get baptized in the Holy Spirit and fire, in order to walk in power, righteousness, and in the fear of the LORD, and to enter into and remain in the promise lands that God has for each of our lives. Many today have either come to the blood of Jesus and remained in the Egyptian lifestyle, or they have skipped Mount Sinai and Pentecost in order go straight to the promise land, both of which will end in death and a returning to Egypt one way or another (Acts 7:39). A walk without Pentecost is a powerless life, one that won't stand before the wars that the wilderness and promise lands contain, nor will you truly be changed and continually transformed into the image of the Son of God (Romans 8:29).

On this topic of Passover, and the purpose of the blood, it is important for us to now go back even further to Genesis 19 with Lot, Abraham's nephew. In Genesis 18, three angels, one of which was the Messiah Himself, come to visit Abraham. Then in Genesis 19, two of these angels come to Sodom and visit Lot, in order to see if the sins of Sodom are as bad as what has been heard (Genesis 18:20-21). I bring this chapter up because of a principal I explained in Chapter 1, which is the principle of "nothing is new under the sun (Ecclesiastes 1:9-10, Job 8:8-10)," and that everything is found in the Torah of Moses. Ecclesiastes 1:9-10" that which has been is what will be, and that which has been done is what will be done. There is nothing new under the sun. There is a matter which one will say, 'see, this is new. 'It has already been from ancient times before us." It is important to understand something about the book of Genesis, because it is quite different than the rest of the Torah of Moses. It isn't a book that is filled with a bunch of commandments, and descriptions of the feasts, but rather it is more narrative based. However, those commandments and feasts are actually taking place without being directly referenced. We have to pick up on the clues and view them through Ecclesiastes 1:9-10. Certain instances where we can go, "oh, this was Passover," or, "this commandment in Deuteronomy is a direct reference to this passage in Genesis."

The Passover is first officially instituted in detail in Exodus 12, and then again in Leviticus 23, but Passover actually took place in Genesis 19 in Sodom and Gomorrah, and I will show it here, as well as Genesis 12-13 (which I won't get into in this book). Genesis 19:3 "and he (Lot) urged them (the two angels) greatly, and they turned to him, and they came to his house, and he made a feast for them and baked unleavened bread and they ate." Notice they ate unleavened bread. Unleavened bread is only eaten one time in Scripture-Passover/feast of Unleavened Bread. Lot could have just made bread, and who in their right mind would choose unleavened bread over regular bread? The Scripture is hinting that they are having a Passover seder. Go further in Genesis 19, and what happens? That night and the following day, God destroys the sinners along with Sodom and Gomorrah, and redeems Lot and his family. The same thing happened with the Passover in Egypt, as God has Israel eat Unleavened Bread for Passover, and then that night and the next day destroys Egypt while redeeming Israel. The same thing with us in Messiah, as God destroys our bondage to sin, and redeems us by the Passover blood of Jesus. There is nothing new under the sun.

Why am I bringing this up with Genesis 19? Because we will get to see the continued emphasis on what the Passover is for, and the purpose of the blood, through what the angels tell Lot and his family in Genesis 19:17 "and as he brought them outside of the city, he said, 'escape for your life. Do not gaze behind you and do not stand in all of the plot of land. Flee to the mountain lest you be destroyed.'" Notice the emphasis is, when leaving Sodom, we must get you out of the city (Genesis 19:22), and do not turn back to gaze at the city. Don't look back at the old lifestyle you are being saved from, lest it be like you are returning to Egypt in your hearts, as it is written in Acts 7:39 "and our fathers did not desire to obey Him, but they forsook Him and turned to Egypt in their hearts," and again in Numbers 14:4 "and they said to each other, 'let us appoint a leader, and we will return to Egypt.'" As Jesus said in Luke 9:62 "there is no one who puts his hand to the plough and gazes behind him that is fit for the kingdom of God."

Then later in Genesis 19, as Lot and his family flee from the city, verse 26 says about Lot's wife, "and his wife gazed behind him, and she became a pillar of salt." Jesus, when speaking about the time before His second coming, also references this very thing in Luke 17:32-33 "remember Lot's wife. Whoever desires to save his soul will lose it, but whoever will lose his soul will save it."

In regard to Lot's wife, Scripture doesn't say she "looks" behind her in the Hebrew, although, many English Bibles translate it this way. The Hebrew literally says that she "gazes (וַתַּבֵּט)." This was no quick glance. She turned back around, longing for the old life. Just as the children of Israel in the wilderness (Numbers 11:1-5), she returned to Sodom in her heart (Numbers 14:4, Acts 7:39). In her heart she returned to Sodom/Egypt after the Passover seder, and then God turns her into a pillar of salt. Why salt? The salt is what He wanted her to come get. The salt is the "covenant of God (Leviticus 2:13)," which is filled with

God's commandments and how to serve Him. God didn't save them from Sodom, or save Israel from Egypt, or us from sin on Passover so that we can abide or return to our old ways, but rather to come and get filled with the Holy Spirit at Pentecost. The salt, God's commandments, is the cure, after all, this is the entire reason for the unleavened bread on Passover, for "unleavened bread (מצות)" in Hebrew is the same exact word as "commandments (מצות)." The feast of Unleavened Bread is really the feast of turning to God's commandments, which is the salt of the covenant (Leviticus 2:13), hence Jesus' words in Matthew 5:13-14 "be the salt of the earth," and its context is all about Torah and God's commandments (Matthew 5:13-19). The blood of Jesus, the Passover Lamb of God, isn't meant to be trampled or taken lightly, as many have done, as it is written in Hebrews 6:1-6:

> "Therefore, let us leave the basics of the Word of the Messiah, and continue on to its perfection. Or will you again lay another foundation for the repentance which is from dead works and for the faith in God, and for the doctrine of baptism, and for the laying on of a hand, and for the resurrection from the dead, and for the eternal judgement? We will do this, if the LORD permits. But they who have once descended to baptism, and have tasted the gift from heaven, and have received the Holy Spirit, and have tasted the good Word of God and the power of the world to come, cannot again sin and a second time be renewed to repentance, or a second time crucify the Son of God and to shame Him."

The blood of Jesus is meant to be feared, and regarded as holy, righteous, and the power of God unto salvation (Romans 1:16), leading us to be filled with the power of the Holy Spirit.

If we look back, may it only be in praises to God for what He has taken us from, but never for longing or gazing at the past with covetousness. For our God, whose name is Jealous, is a jealous God (Exodus 34:14), and He is an all-consuming fire (Hebrews 12:29). God is the One who tests the hearts and minds (Jeremiah 17:10, 20:12, Psalms 7:10, Revelation 2:23). If you continually look back, those are seeds that will take root, and eventually, you will turn back. I have seen it time and time again, like a dog who returns to its vomit, and a fool who returns to his folly (Proverbs 26:11, 2 Peter 2:22).

If you continually keep those temptations around you, or those people in your life, you are setting yourself up for failure. In Luke 13:6-9 there was a tree, which for three years did not bear fruit, so the owner of the vineyard says to the vinedresser, "I am cutting down this tree. All it does is take up space, and it has not given me the fruit I desire for three years." The vinedresser responds and says "let this tree remain for one more year. I will tend it and fertilize it, perhaps it will bear fruit, and if not, after that year, then cut it down." We must examine our lives, and the soil around us, and make sure it is continually weeded from evil, but also fertilized with an atmosphere that feeds the Holy Spirit. I work with a garden up in Iowa, and one thing I know is, those weeds will choke out that holy root, and it will be destroyed. You'll never bear that proper fruit you are called too. This could be music, TV shows, girlfriend or boyfriend, friends, workplace-remove it.

Let us fulfill everything Jesus paid for on the cross. As He hung on the cross, He desired that we would come to it daily, and carry our cross and follow Him (Luke 9:23). In fact, there is an incredible insight given to us by Paul in Colossians 2:10-13:

> "And in Him you are also complete because He is the head of all principalities and authorities. And in Him

you have been circumcised with a circumcision without hands, by casting off the flesh of sins by a circumcision of the Messiah. And you have been buried with Him by baptism, and by it you have risen with Him while you believed in the power of God who raised Him from the dead. And you who were dead in your sins and by the uncircumcision of your flesh, he has resurrected with Him, and He has forgiven us of all of our sins."

Notice, verses 12-13 do not say that you will be buried and resurrected, but rather, that you were already buried, and were already resurrected. Paul is talking to people who were currently alive on the earth, and to us who are still currently alive on this earth, meaning, right now, we have access to live a resurrected lifestyle of power in the Holy Spirit, as he says again in Colossians 3:1 "therefore, if you have risen with the Messiah, seek that which is above in the place that the Messiah sits at the right hand of God." Paul says again in Romans 6:3-4:

"Or do you not know that we who are baptized into Yeshua the Messiah are baptized into His death? For, we were buried with Him in baptism to death in order that as Yeshua the Messiah rose from the dead in the glory of His Father, so too, we also walk in new life."

Paul makes it clear that as new creations in the Messiah, coming out of the Egyptian bondage of sin, we are to walk in righteousness and power in the Holy Spirit. The same power that Jesus walked in, and even greater (John 14:12). I wrote a blog for Revelation Church on this very topic:

John 7:37-39 "In the last great day of the feast, Yeshua stood and proclaimed, saying, 'A man who will thirst, let him come to Me and drink. The one who believes in Me, as it is written, from his belly will flow rivers of living water.' This He said concerning the Holy Spirit which all who believe in Him would receive, because the Holy Spirit was not yet given because Yeshua had not yet been glorified."

Yeshua continually, especially in the book of John in great detail, makes references to the Holy Spirit, and how necessary it is for believers to be in a deep intimacy with the Holy Spirit. The Holy Spirit is who purifies us, convicts us of sin, reminds us of the Word of God in its proper time, reveals the depths of the Word of God and Yeshua's teaching's, enables us to walk in power and in the gifts of the Holy Spirit, etc. Without the Holy Spirit, being sensitive to His nudges, and walking as one totally consumed by the Holy Spirit, the walk becomes powerless in every way.

There needs to be a hunger and a thirst for the things of the Holy Spirit, and not only a hunger and thirst, but an expectancy. Faith breeds expectancy. Yeshua said in John 14:12 that we would do even greater things than He did because He was going to be with the Father and there is still work to be done. Just because you haven't seen greater maybe, have you lost expectancy for it? Have we made Him out to be a liar? Power and new wine can only come through a new wineskin (Matthew 9:16-17) and a continually submitted and sanctified vessel, and through that, one will attain deep intimacies with the Holy Spirit. As this takes place, you will ignite the fire in those around you, and the rivers of life that flow from your belly will begin to refresh all whom you come across so as imitators of the Messiah, you will say, "come and drink."

We now have availability, through the blood of Jesus, the Passover Lamb of God, to walk according to the resurrected lifestyle of the Holy Spirit. We have the right to groan to God with expectancy for these things to take place in our lives. This is the purpose of the blood. Pentecost. The baptism of the Holy Spirit and fire. To finish what the Messiah started (John 14:12). What is the leaven that is holding you back from fully serving Him, and getting baptized in the Holy Spirit? Is it family ties? Past relationships? Certain traditions? Fear of man? What is it that is hindering you from walking in power, righteousness, to be that burnt offering ready for the fire of God, so that you can fulfill your ministry (2 Timothy 4:5)? What is hindering you from being a Tree Of Fire?

CHAPTER 3

What Is A Christian?

Have you ever wondered what it means to be a Christian? What is a Christian? I believe that if we asked this question with one another, we would actually realize this can be answered quickly, but the revelations contained within the answer can be spoken of until Messiah returns. It is so deep and profound. I don't mean "what is a Christian" from some theological or traditional perspective, or from this person or that person's opinion. I want to tackle this and dig deep on it as it is spoken of and defined out of the Word of God, with its true understanding linguistically, historically, and Scripturally.

In English Bibles, the word "Christian" is only found three times (Acts 11:26, Acts 26:28, 1 Peter 4:16). As I was studying the book of Acts in Hebrew and Aramaic, as I had many times before, there came a time I was struck when I came across it in Acts 11:26, and I began asking myself, "what does this really mean?" In English, it doesn't seem to carry a ton of revelation within the word "Christian" itself, but when seen in Hebrew, it is nothing short of mind-blowing.

In Acts 11, we see that there are certain disciples of Jesus that get scattered from Jerusalem, because of Stephen being murdered back in Acts 7, and they migrate to different towns, one of which, is Antioch. In Antioch, the people there receive the Word of the LORD and receive Jesus as the Messiah. During this time, Barnabas, who is one of Paul's right hand men, and a crucial, yet undervalued figure for Paul's successes, is sent to Antioch. Barnabas is described as a good man, full of the Holy Spirit (Acts 11:24), and when he finds out that Antioch has received the Word of God, He goes to Tarsus in order to pick up Saul (Apostle Paul). Acts 11:19-26:

> "And those who were scattered by the persecution that happened on account of Stephen were reaching all the way to Phenice, and even to the country of Cyprus, and to Antioch, while they were not speaking with anyone, except only a word with the Jews. Now there were men among them from Cyprus and Cyrene. They were entering Antioch and were speaking with Greeks and were preaching concerning our Master Yeshua. And the hand of the LORD was among them, and many believed and turned towards the LORD. And this was heard by the men of the congregation that was in Jerusalem, and they sent Barnabas to Antioch. And when he came there, he saw the grace of God. He rejoiced and sought from them to cleave to our Master with all their heart. He was a good man, full of the Holy Spirit and faith, and many people were added to our Master. And he went to Tarsus in order to seek Saul, and when he found him, he brought him to Antioch. And they were dwelling with the congregation a full year and teaching many people. From then, for the first time, the disciples were called Christians."

Notice, I have translated verse 26 according to the common English translation, which says, it was in Antioch that the disciples were first called "Christians." However, in Hebrew, we do not have this word "Christian." The word "Christian" comes from the Greek, but with Jesus and His followers speaking Hebrew and Aramaic, this is not the language or lens we should be viewing this word through. The term for "Christians" in Hebrew is משיחי׳ם, pronounced, "m'shichi'im, which is plural for the word Mashiach (משיח), which means "Messiah"! Literally, what we see in the text is that we were first called "messiahs" in Antioch! Or was Antioch actually the first place? No, but rather, ever since Abraham, Isaac, and Jacob, God's people have been called "messiah's," which continued through the New Testament to Yeshua's followers, as it is written in Psalms 105:8-15:

> "He remembered His covenant forever, the word He commanded to the thousandth generation, which He made with Abraham, and His oath to Isaac. He established it to Jacob for a statute, and to Israel as an eternal covenant, saying, 'to you I will give the land of Canaan, the possession of your inheritance.' When they were few in number, according to a few, and dwellers in it, and they walked from nation to nation, from kingdom to another people, He did not allow a man to oppress them, and He rebuked kings because of them, 'do not touch My messiah's, and do no evil to My prophets.'"

Now it is important to understand, the Aramaic Peshitta, an ancient Aramaic manuscript of the New Testament, is the oldest manuscript for the New Testament that we have, also being older than ancient Greek manuscripts. There are only five books (2 Peter, 2 John, 3 John, Jude, and Revelation) in the New Testament where the Greek is actually older, although, within those five books, the Aramaic still has a better flow and consistency with all of Scripture in the Aramaic Peshitta, as well as its Hebrew equivalent. So, the Aramaic is the oldest we have of 1 John, and even in 1 John 2:20 in the Aramaic it says, "you have an anointing from the Holy One." In Hebrew, the word "anointing" is Mashichah (מְשִׁיחָה), which is "Messiah," but in the feminine, meaning, we are to be just like the Messiah as His bride in the earth, the feminine version of Messiah, but nonetheless, messiahs in this world. At the wedding it as though God will say, "I now present to you, Mr. and Mrs. Yeshua Messiah." Also, in Aramaic it is Mashichutah (מְשִׁיחוּתָה), which is denominative from the word Mashiach (מְשִׁיח), which is "Messiah." We are being called messiah's, the feminine version of Messiah Himself mirrors the Garden of Eden, as it is written in Genesis 2:23 "and Adam said, 'this time, it is the bone of my bone, and the flesh of my flesh, for this one will be called woman (אִשָּׁה), because this one was taken from man (אִישׁ).'" "Woman" in Hebrew is the same word as "man," the only difference is "woman" is the feminine version of the word, just as we are called messiah, but in the feminine.

We have written in 1 John, but also in Acts 11:26, where it says they first were called "Christians (Messiah's)" in the New Testament. Now, we are talking in context about the Greek believers, so we are talking about Gentiles, and they are being called Messiah's. So, Gentile believers are being called Messiah's, but also the Jews since Abraham, as I showed above from Psalms 105, those who walked in the footsteps of the Messiah were also called "messiahs." Now it is important to not pervert my words here. Jesus is THE Messiah (הַמָּשִׁיח), but nevertheless, we are called messiahs as His disciples. This goes in complete harmony with everything Jesus taught us in the Gospels, and like I said, the original marriage in the Garden of Eden.

There was a time I was asked, "what is the most powerful verse in the New Testament that Jesus said?" For me, that's easy. John 20:21 "as the Father sent Me, so I am sending you." Then, we find it twice in the book of John where Jesus says that we as His students are not above Him, but that we need to be like Him (John 13:16, 15:20). Paul also says in

Galatians 2:20 "it is no longer I who live but Messiah within me." Us being called messiahs should be of no surprise. We could, and should, study this revelation for the rest of our lives. "As the Father sent Me, so I am sending you." Everything Jesus was sent to do in the earth, now we are to do. Every aspect of His life is now ours, and all the potential and authority that's carried within that. So, what does it mean to be like Messiah, or to be a Christian?

This is really the fullness of the Gospel message. The Gospel is not just that Jesus went to the cross for our sins, died, and resurrected. That is what the Passover is. As we have already seen, the Passover was given in Exodus 12 in order to bring the children of Israel out, so that they can serve God at Sinai and come to Pentecost (Exodus 5:1, 7:16). Jesus' going to the cross was so that we can come out of Egypt, come to Pentecost, and be baptized in the Holy Spirit and fire. That is the reason for the Passover. So then, the fullness of the Gospel, is that we as messiah's would be restored by what Jesus did on the cross, and His pouring out the Holy Spirit, that we would be restored back into the image of which we were originally created in the Garden of Eden, which is the image of God, as it is written in Genesis 1:26 "in Our Image, according to Our likeness (בְּצַלְמֵנוּ כִּדְמוּתֵנוּ)," which in gematria is equivalent to 744, which is equivalent to "Messiah Yeshua (משיח ישוע)." It is in the image of Yeshua that we were originally created in the Garden of Eden, and the image to which we are being restored by the Holy Spirit (Romans 8:29).

Similarly, Paul says in Colossians 3:9-10 "and do not lie to one another, but put off the old man with all his practices, and put on the new that is being renewed in knowledge, and in the likeness of his Creator," and Paul says the One Who all things were created through is none other than Yeshua, as it is written in Colossians 1:13-16:

"And has rescued us from the dominion of darkness and transferred us to the kingdom of His beloved Son, by whom we have redemption and forgiveness of sins, who is the likeness of the invisible God, and the firstborn of all creatures, and by Him was everything created that is in heavens and on earth, all that is visible and all that is invisible, whether thrones, or dominions, or principalities, or powers, everything was through Him and was created by Him."

We were made in Yeshua's/Jesus' image, we fell from it, and now, by the Holy Spirit, we are being continually conformed back into the image of the Son of God (Romans 8:29). Because just as He was sent by the Father, so are we sent, just as He was sent as Messiah, so are we sent as messiahs in this world, to be His representatives of everything He walked out (2 Corinthians 5:20), in righteousness, in power, in love, kindness, fruit, identity, etc. He wants to continue to live His ministry through us in our daily lives. This is a major revelation, because when we talk about being like Messiah, to heal people like Messiah, to cast out devils like Messiah, to raise the dead like Messiah, to love people like Messiah, to give our lives for others like Messiah, to be about the Father's business like Messiah, to wash peoples feet like Messiah, etc., we can go on and on and on, which is why I say we can sit on this revelation, that we are called messiah's/Christians, for the rest of our lives. Study Him deeply, and that's what we are sent to do. "As the Father sent Me, so I am sending you (John 20:21)."

When the Holy Spirit showed me this, that we are literally called to be messiah's in this generation as He lives through us and He receives all the glory, this struck me because that same week I had a memory on my Facebook pop up of a post I made within the last couple years where I

WHAT IS A CHRISTIAN?

said "if we are made in the image of God, how are you making Him look today?" I remember the day I saw all this I said, "Father, Messiah Himself is the ultimate standard. He is the Word of God. He is the standard. Not this pastor, or this servant, or this midwife, but Messiah is the standard." I can't compare to doing better than this person or that person, but rather, how do I look in the mirror reflection of Jesus, because that is the standard. When I came to the LORD with this, He immediately started revealing areas of my life that needed to come to Him and get straightened out, confessed, and repented of (Proverbs 28:13). He started working on me in these deep areas with tenderness. I fell on my face, and said, "Father, I am so sorry, help me. In the reflection of Jesus, I didn't realize how far off these certain areas are. Baptize these areas in then Holy Spirit and transform these areas of my life." I do this in the presence of the Holy Spirit every single day, however, knowing we are called messiah's, it now just took a whole new level of not only revelation, but also expectancy of the power and purity we have access to walk in.

The Author and Finisher of our faith (Hebrews 12:2), and He who began a good work in us will continue it until the day of the coming of the Messiah (Philippians 1:6). Until He returns, I will never come to the destination of sanctification. He is perfecting submitted vessels continually to be transformed into the image of the Messiah (2 Timothy 2:21). Teaching the understanding that we are called messiahs, and are to be like King Messiah, just as He was sent so are we, and what that revelation entails, should be the essence of the teachings and true discipleship every week, moving on from the basics of milk, as it is written in Hebrews 6:1-3:

> "Therefore, let us leave the basics of the Word of the
> Messiah, and continue on to its perfection. Or will you
> again lay another foundation for the repentance which is

from dead works and for the faith in God, and for the doctrine of baptism, and for the laying on of a hand, and for the resurrection from the dead, and for eternal judgement? We will do this, if the LORD permits."

We need to teach how to truly study the Scriptures deeply, how to receive an anointing in the Holy Spirit, how to walk with power, how to know which spirit you are warring against, what it means to train our hands for war, and how to move fully in the things of the Spirit of God, which will be spoken of at great length not only in this book, but in the other volumes that come out as well. This is the fullness of the Gospel because it is all about the fullness of Jesus, and not just one part. It is the essence of the identity that is found in Him, and the good news that by the Holy Spirit, we can not only be partakers, but we are expected to be such. This is the mission of every sermon, every prayer time, and every gathering: how can I better bear the image of Messiah, and honor Him with fear and trembling, so that I carry on the very ministry He walked out on the earth, and everything that was contained within it. Jesus said in John 15:8 "in this the Father is glorified: that you bear much fruit, and you will be My disciples," meaning, if you do not bear much fruit, you do not glorify the Father, and therefore, you are not My disciples. Being His disciple means, we abide in Him, and He abides in us, and people see Him in our lives (John 15:9-10). A Christian is one who is like Christ, not only in Word, but in power (1 Corinthians 2:4, 4:20).

There was a time the Holy Spirit sent me to Peru by myself back in 2018. Before I got ordained as a Pastor, I was a traveling solo evangelist. I remember being in Peru and seeing person after person come to Jesus, one of which was a man from Australia with his family. I was walking down the street, and I ran into this man who had his wife and kids with him. When he asked me about my business in Peru, I shared that I was about the Father's business, and when I asked him if he was a believer, he said:

> "No. I left that over 20 years ago. My father was a pastor all of my life, and I was tired of seeing him shove things down my throat, as well as the hypocrisy of not walking out what was being preached."

As I began to speak with him and his family, I remember he stops me and says, "Nick, what is this love and peace in you? I see it in your eyes. Is this Jesus?" I said, "This is Jesus." He said, "I want this." That man repented and gave his life to Jesus in front of his family right there on the sidewalk in Lima, Peru. The fire of Messiah's eyes burned in mine (Revelation 2:18), and he felt it pierce his heart as it did with the two disciples of Jesus on the road to Emmaus, as it is written in Luke 24:32 "and they said to each other, 'were not our hearts burning within us as He spoke to us on the way, and when He revealed the Scriptures to us?'" That man in Peru didn't encounter me, he encountered Jesus, and after I got baptized in the Holy Spirit and fire, the words I spoke now carried such a weight, people began to listen wherever I went, believers and unbelievers alike. Two people can speak the same word and say the same prayer, while one will uproot a mountain, and the other will sound like a clanging cymbal, depending on who is carrying the anointing. God's power manifests as we said, not only with signs and wonders, but in teaching and leading.

With all of this said, I now want to dive deep into the understanding of "what the Messiah is." Jesus is the Messiah, but what is the role of Messiah, because only then, can we know what it means to carry out the mission as messiah's or Christians. We have all these things that Jesus did, such as, He healed the sick, casted out devils, raised the dead, cleansed the lepers, preached the gospel, gave to the poor, loved people, served people, gave His life for others, forgave people, brought reconciliation, etc. The list goes on and on, and we don't even have everything He did in the Scriptures, as it is written in John 20:30 "and behold, Yeshua did many other signs before His disciples, which are not written in this book," and again, in John 21:25 "and there are still many other works that Yeshua did, and if they were all written one by one, I suppose the world would not have enough books that could be written. Amen."

Nevertheless, I want to talk on the role of Messiah. I have continually taught that whenever we want to learn about a specific word or phrase, we need to find the very first place it is used in the Scripture, and study its context in that given spot, because that moment will set the tone and Biblical understanding for that given word or phrase going forward. Well, the word Messiah, which we translate from the Greek as the word "Christ," is first used in Leviticus 4:3. In English, it generally says "the anointed priest," however, the phrase literally reads "the priest, the Messiah (הַכֹּהֵן הַמָּשִׁיחַ)," pronounced, "hacohen hamashiach." The word Messiah means to be anointed, and it is being translated as an attributive adjective as "the anointed priest," but in English, this can cause us to miss a foundational understanding of the Messiah's role. This is the reason why in the New Testament, the Messiah is continually connected to the role as a High Priest, because its defining moment in Leviticus 4:3 has to do with the Messiah and High Priest being one and the same.

In order to understand Messiah's role, and therefore, our role as messiah's, we have to understand the role of the High Priest, and the priests in general, because we too, are called priests, as it is written in Exodus 19:6 "and you will be to Me a kingdom of priests and a holy nation. These are the words which you shall speak to the children of Israel," and again, the prophet says in Isaiah 61:6 "and you shall be called 'priests of the LORD, servants of our God.' It shall be said to you, 'you shall consume the wealth of the nations, and you shall boast in their glory,'" and twice, John says in Revelation 1:6 "and He has made us a kingdom of priests to God His Father, to Whom belong glory and power forever and ever, amen," and again in Revelation 20:6:

> "Blessed and holy is he who has a portion in the first resurrection, the second death has no power over these, these will be priests to God and to the Messiah, and they will reign with Him a thousand years."

The role of the priest was to bring the offerings of the people to God, and by their offerings, they drew near to God, as the word "offering (קרבן)" literally comes from the word qarav (קרב), which means "to draw near." Through the offerings, one draws near to God, however, one could not do this without the priest, so the role of the priest was to be a reconciler of the people back to God, which is literally the essence of Jesus's ministry of reconciliation, teaching the people how to offer themselves to the LORD. We are the offerings. Jesus ALWAYS turned people to the Father, as it is written in John 17:1 "Yeshua spoke these things, and He lifted up His eyes to the heavens and He said, 'My Father, the time has come. Glorify Your Son, so that Your Son may glorify You.'" The essence of all of this as it pertains to the ministry of reconciliation, and therefore, what has been given to us is found in Paul's words in 2 Corinthians 5:17-20:

> "Whoever, therefore, is in the Messiah is a new creature. Old things have passed away, and all things are made new by God who has reconciled us to Himself by the Messiah and has given us the ministry of reconciliation. For God was in the Messiah, who has reconciled the world with His majesty and did not reckon to them their sins, and who has placed in us the Word of reconciliation. We are therefore ambassadors for the Messiah, and it is as if God

was pleading you by us on behalf of the Messiah, therefore, we plead to you to be reconciled to God."

Notice, just as Leviticus 4 with the Messiah being a High Priest who reconciles the people to God, Paul makes the same connection, and carries it down to us as messiah's and priests to carry this same ministry of reconciliation between God and people. Paul says, "God was pleading to you by us," just as Paul says God was pleading to us by the Messiah. This is our job as messiah's and followers of King Jesus the Messiah. In order to carry the ministry of reconciliation, we have to carry the ministry of revelation, meaning, there has to be an overflowing revelation of Messiah within us, as there was an overflowing revelation of God within the Messiah, as the man and his family saw within me in Peru, so that people no longer see us, but Messiah within us (Galatians 2:20), because we must decrease, and He must increase (John 3:30). This is why we must continually, through intimacy with the Holy Spirit, receive things that we need to repent of, because these things can hinder the flow of the Messiah's revelation within us, which will also hinder the flowing power of the Holy Spirit within us as well. It is our job to walk in His footsteps (1 John 2:6). People became reconciled to God by the mercy He showed people (Romans 2:4), such as with the adulterous woman in John 8, also His willingness to sit with sinners, even if other righteous people condemned Him for it, such as Luke 5 and Luke 15, but also, people came back to God and praised God because of the signs and wonders He did. We are expected to walk in all of it. This ministry of reconciliation has many avenues, whether it was through preaching, acts of kindness, power, etc., but all were done within the footsteps of the Messiah.

When I first moved to Iowa in 2022, I was working with a videography and photography team from Cedar Rapids as I was about to launch footage for the Lifestyle Of Eden YouTube and its social media's.

The team was throwing a big party for rappers and music artists at this bar in Cedar Rapids that they would rent and end up selling out pretty regularly. Well, I remember when we first began filming, the first day started at 4am, which is when I wake up daily to be with Abba, and by 8am, the two videographers said, "you are the most inspirational person we have ever met." This team is about my age as well, and I could connect with them on many things. We spent 32 hours together that week alone filming. They began wanting to know more about God, as they both were unbelievers.

We ended up getting pretty close, and they asked me if I wanted to show up at the bar for their party they were throwing. Keep in mind, I hadn't been to a bar in years, and for the first few years of my walk, this would have been a stumbling block for me, given that I had a serious drug and alcohol problem. I heard the Spirit of God tell me to go, so I told them yes, and they said "really? We want you to come, but we were surprised because you are a pastor, and no other pastor would come and hang out with us like that." I said, "I will be there." That night, as I sipped on my lemon water, the videographers had me stand with them at the front and had people coming up to me all night. Because of my tattoos, my physique, and my clear interest in fashion, they were asking if I was a rapper, a model, and all these other things. The LORD used this simply as a magnet to draw them in as He did in Peru, to draw them near as an offering, because then I would tell them I am a full time pastor and talk to them in some way shape or form about the LORD, and they all felt comfortable with me. Even if I didn't speak to them about the LORD, they now trusted me, they drew near, and my words carried weight in their life. They got my card, social media's, etc.

Shortly after this, I began hearing my videography team using phrases I was using, such as, "God willing," and months later I was told that they not only looked to me as a mentor, but that they began praying to

God, and the working of the Holy Spirit and increase in their lives still continues today. They began connecting me with other people in the Kingdom and were starting to draw near on their own. They also got to see a demon manifest around me when I walked with them in downtown Cedar Rapids, and they saw how I handled it. Seeds were being planted and watered. The self-righteous pharisees caught word in Houston that I went to a bar, and began condemning me, and I responded to them, "Is it not written in Luke 5:27-32:

> After these things, Yeshua went out and saw a tax collector whose name was Levi who was sitting at the house of customs. And He said to him, 'come, follow after Me.' And he left everything and arose and went after Him and followed. And Levi made a great feast for Him in his house, and there was a large crowd of tax collectors and others reclining with them. And the scribes and Pharisees were arguing, and they said to His disciples, 'why are tax collectors and sinners eating and drinking among you?' And Yeshua answered and said to them, 'the physician is not needed by the healthy, rather by those who are severely ill.'"

I asked the ones who questioned me, what do you think this passage would have looked like in modern times? There was silence and change of perspective. I don't advertise going to bars, as I said, I hadn't been to one in years. I stay in my lane that God has me in, however, the Holy Spirit told me to go, and clearly did a work without me compromising my position in Him. The righteous don't need reconciliation, but the unrighteous do. However, I have noticed in ministry that the pride of the "righteous" actually cause them to be further from God than those who seem unrighteous (Psalms 138:6). I am a tatted up, muscular, veiny, bold individual who was jumped into a gang at 13 years old, faced 2-20 years of being locked up at seventeen years old, has done just about every drug in extreme amounts, was first shot at by the age of 14 and then continued after that, used to sleep with woman after woman, has broken into houses, cars, and put people in the hospital fighting for their life, and had been close to putting hits on people that did me wrong if they did not come up with my money or things needed, and have done countless things that one can hardly even speak of.

I am not ashamed to sit with people who are doing the same, just as Jesus was not ashamed to come sit with me when I was there. He who has been forgiven much, loves much (Luke 7:46-50). He didn't call me to Him from afar, He came to me and pulled me out. Those people in the bars and clubs are my people, and I am not ashamed of them, just as Jesus was not ashamed to sit with sinners and tax collectors, while eating and drinking, and even the Messiah was called a glutton and a wine bibber (Matthew 11:19). Jacob gave Laban the unblemished flocks and preferred the ones who were brown, spotted, and speckled, and yet God multiplied them for Jacob, so too, I prefer to sit with the ones Laban and the self-righteous leaders throw away. They are my people. There has to be such a revelation and a power flowing through us that people go "that is the Messiah." Even in unbelievers, deep calls unto deep (Psalms 42:8), and they will know.

When we talk about teaching people to draw near to God, we must view this through the proper lens. John 4:23-24 and Isaiah 31:3 tell us God is not physical, but Spirit, and those who draw near or worship Him must do so in Spirit and in truth, so when we talk about drawing near, we aren't talking about a physical drawing near as Jesus says very clearly in John 4:21:

"Yeshua said to her, 'woman, believe Me. The hour is coming that not in this mountain nor in Jerusalem will they worship the Father. You worship something you do not know, but we worship what we know, for life is from the Jews. But the hour is coming, and now is when the true worshippers will worship the Father in Spirit and in truth, indeed. For the Father, He seeks worshippers as these. For God is Spirit, and those who worship Him must worship in Spirit and in truth.'"

Worship and drawing near to a spiritual God isn't about physical things, so you can and should throw out the idols, break down the statues, and even the pictures that put an image in your mind of God and Jesus. What it means to draw near to God, is to imitate His attributes, to look like Him as Yeshua was the very expressed image of the attributes of God in the flesh (Hebrews 1:1-3). One who is very close to God is one who is very close in resemblance of Him, and they are One. They are simply a conduit of God's nature and heart by bearing His image and reputation. When people see us they say, "that is the Father's heart, I see Jesus." They will recognize Him by the fruits. The Holy Spirit begins to do a work, and you come from being a tree of bad fruit, to a tree of good fruit, and a tree of fire for Him, and everyone around you either gets scorched, or catches flame, but you and everyone will be touched somehow, because our God is an all-consuming fire (Hebrews 12:29). Although King Jesus is THE Messiah for all generations, we see serious Messiah-like figures in every generation that God will find and use as a conduit. Enoch, Noah, Abraham, Isaac, Jacob, Joseph, Moses, Joshua, David, Solomon, Jeremiah, Isaiah, the rest of the prophets, Paul, etc., all the way until today. God is looking for individuals that He can use in this way (2 Chronicles 16:9). Sold out, living flames and Trees Of Fire that will start a forest fire for Him. Those who are willing to raise the spiritual temperature for their surroundings and raise the bar of what is really expected of us, and what we should expect of the Father through us.

As messiah's, we need to measure ourselves line for line with Messiah Yeshua Himself, gazing at Him continually with complete obsession, and in this, we will see who we are called to be, and press into the Holy Spirit to receive the full revelation of the identity that Jesus paid the price for us to walk into. We have accepted too little, and set the bar too low, because we have lost sight of being called messiahs, as He is King Messiah. We have lost sight of not only the calling as messiahs, but we have lost sight of the Messiah Himself, as we have compared ourselves to the person to our right or to our left, or to this preacher or that preacher, and as long as we are doing better than they, or at least within the same ballpark, we call it good enough. We have to get back to focusing on the Root, which is Yeshua (Revelation 22:16). He is the standard. It is written in John 14:12 "Amen, amen, I say to you, the one who believes in Me will do the works which I am doing, and he will do greater works than these, because I am going to the Father." I am here to tell you, if you are a Christian/ messiah, there's more.

CHAPTER 4

The Interpreter

We've seen extensively so far in this book the necessity for the baptism of the Holy Spirit, as we will see even deeper throughout the rest of this book. However, one of the key reasons is so that we can properly understand the Scriptures, because the true spiritual concepts embedded within the letters on the pages are only revealed by the Messiah Himself through the Holy Spirit, as Paul emphasizes the necessity of the Holy Spirit in order to understand Scripture in 1 Corinthians 2:13-15:

> "Which things we also speak, not in the teaching of the words of man's wisdom, but in the teaching of the Spirit, and we teach spiritual matters to those with spiritual focus. For a man in his natural self does not receive spiritual concepts, for they are foolishness to him. Neither can he know them, for they are discerned by the Spirit."

Again, Paul says in 2 Corinthians 3:15-17:

> "And to this day, when Moses is read, a veil is thrown upon their hearts. But when any of them is turned to the LORD, the veil is taken from him. Now, the LORD Himself is the Spirit, and where the Spirit of the LORD is there is freedom."

The Scriptures have to be truly understood by the Holy Spirit when one comes to the Messiah, with the understanding beginning in the Torah of Moses, the Prophets, and the Writings (Psalms, Proverbs, Ecclesiastes etc.). The understanding of the Holy Spirit's role in our lives is no different. Its role is best understood in the Torah of Moses, however, apart from the Spirit revealing Himself, one will not see the precious jewels hidden within the Torah of Moses, especially some of the references Jesus Himself makes in the New Testament that have to do with this need for the Holy Spirit in order to understand His words.

After Jesus resurrects from the dead in Luke 24, there are two disciples that are on the road, headed to Emmaus, and they are downcast because Jesus was just crucified, and they didn't know He resurrected from the dead, nor did they understand all of the prophecies regarding this event in order to give them hope. They don't know what to do. As they are walking, Jesus, while concealing His actually identity after He had been resurrected, comes alongside them and they have no idea that during this entire journey they are actually walking with the King of kings. Jesus says to them in Luke 24:26-27:

"Is it not necessary that the Messiah would suffer these things, and to enter into His glory? And He began from Moses and from all the prophets, and He expounded about Himself from all the Scriptures."

Then in verse 32 it is written, "and they said to each other, 'were our hearts not burning within us as He spoke with us on the way and expounded to us the Scriptures?'"

Later He reveals Himself to all the disciples in Luke 24:44-45:

"And He said to them, 'these are the things which I spoke with you when I was with you, that it was necessary for all things that are written about Me in the Torah of Moses and in the Prophets and in the Psalms to be fulfilled.' Then, He opened the eyes of their understanding in order to understand the Scriptures."

Jesus, again, says in John 5:39 "seek the Scriptures, which you think that by them you have eternal life, but they testify of Me." Jesus confronts the Jewish people and His disciples, saying, although they think there is security for them in the Scriptures to have eternal life, all the Scriptures BEGINNING from the Torah of Moses, the Prophets, and the Writings all testify about Him. Anytime Jesus spoke about Himself as the Messiah, He would always expound from the Torah of Moses, then the Prophets, then the writings, as Paul also did (Acts 28:23).

Why am I bringing all of this up? Because I believe we as Christians/ messiah's have missed the mark and watered down the wine of understanding that every letter, word, and verse beginning from Genesis 1:1 is about the Messiah Himself, and the Holy Spirit. No Scripture is legalistic, it's Messiah, Who Himself, is freedom. To speak about the Father's Word in such a degrading way is simply unacceptable. It is just a matter of whether or not the eyes of your understanding are opened in a given portion of Scripture to see Messiah and the Holy Spirit, yes, including Leviticus. Yes, the Torah of Moses is continually about the anointing and the Holy Spirit. I remember when I was invited to teach doctors and pastors in the faith at a Houston seminary, and when I mentioned that I teach about the power of the Holy Spirit and the Messiah from Leviticus, they just about lost their minds. Later in this book, we will see the Holy Spirit from Leviticus.

The revelations of the Messiah, the Holy Spirit, the baptism of the Holy Spirit, the sufferings and resurrection of the Messiah, and our relationship with Messiah through the Holy Spirit is found so deeply in the Torah, as the Torah is the very place Jesus based His teachings on in the New Testament. Wouldn't it be great if we can understand Scripture like

Him? We can. By the Holy Spirit, we have access to be like Him, and have the mind of Messiah (1 Corinthians 2:9-16). I have asked people before, if we were going to do what Jesus or Paul did, expound about the Messiah and the Holy Spirit, how many of us could actually begin from Genesis 1 and do this extensively, or even at all? I have found that even leaders in the body of Messiah are not equipped for this, because we miss the mark of what true discipleship looks like as it was in Scripture. Once a week group training or Bible studies is not the extensive discipleship required to be able to do what they did, and what they did in their ability to expound from the Scriptures should all be our aim. How many can go through Genesis, Exodus, Leviticus, Numbers, and Deuteronomy, the Prophets, and the Writings and extensively talk about the Messiah and the Holy Spirit?

Jesus did this, and 1 John 2:6 says that we are also called to walk as He walked, and John 20:21 says as the Father sent Him, so is He sending us. As we dive deeper into true discipleship, the Holy Spirit will begin to teach us all these things (John 14:26), bring all things into remembrance (John 14:26), and cause us to say the right things at the right time (Matthew 10:19-20). We also need the proper apostles, prophets, evangelists, pastors, and teachers to enable and equip the saints to do such things (Ephesians 4:11-14).

I say all of this to say, I want to discuss something Jesus says in the book of John, which the English Bibles translate as the "Advocate, Comforter, or Helper," but really, as we will see in Hebrew is "ha'meilitz (המליץ)" and Aramaic "park'leitah (פרקליטה)," which can mean "advocate/intercessor," but really, it means "the interpreter," especially if we look at the fluency of the Scriptures from beginning to end, beginning in Genesis. If we do not have the baptism of the Holy Spirit and the lenses of the Holy Spirit, we will only see on natural lines, the letter of the law, and what is on the surface of the page, and we will miss the revelations that we are required to have in order to move with authority, power, and true revelatory understanding in our Father's Word, and the knowledge of the Messiah (Ephesians 1:17-18).

Romans 7:14 in many English Bibles says, "we know that the law is spiritual," however, in Hebrew and Aramaic, the text says, "we know that the Torah is of the Spirit," meaning, apart from the Holy Spirit, you will not understand the Torah or any of the Scriptures. Any person, even an unbeliever can read the Bible and see what's on the page, but it is by the Spirit of God that we can see the hidden treasures, the things that will allow us to see on heavenly planes. It is not as many thought, that there is the Torah, and now the Spirit, as if the Torah is apart from the Spirit and is legalistic. Torah is not apart from the Spirit, but rather, it is OF the Spirit, as Paul says (Romans 7:14), and it is holy, and the commandment is holy, and just, and good (Romans 7:12). The Torah of Moses is a spiritual book, and the greatest book on prophecy that we have access to (Deuteronomy 34:10), and its beauty has been concealed until such a time as this (Daniel 12:4).

The Holy Spirit didn't just show up in the New Testament. We have a Bible of divinely written Scriptures by Spirit filled men (2 Peter 1:21), speaking on spiritual concepts (1 Corinthians 2:13), to be understood by a spiritual people (Exodus 19:6). Deep calls unto deep (Psalms 42:8). Now, I want to discuss something from Genesis, as it pertains directly to Jesus' words in John 16 about the Holy Spirit, or "the Interpreter." In Genesis 42, this is after Joseph goes from the prison to the palace and sits at the right hand of Pharaoh in Genesis 41, which is prophetic insight of Jesus going from the grave to the heavenly palace, sitting at the right hand of God. As God placed all that He has in Jesus' authority (Matthew 28:18-20, Luke 10:22), so too, Pharaoh has placed all that he has in Joseph's authority (Genesis 41:40), including all the grain throughout the great famine. Joseph's brothers have to come to the land of Egypt from the land of Canaan in order to buy grain. Throughout this process, Joseph, while concealing himself from His brothers, begins testing them with things regarding their youngest brother, Benjamin (Genesis 41-45). The Torah tells us as the brothers spoke with Joseph in Genesis 42:23 "and they (the brothers) did not know that Joseph understood them, because the interpreter (ha'meilitz, such as John 14:26) was between them." The Torah tells us that Joseph would not speak to them directly. They didn't understand Joseph, because they didn't understand the language, as Joseph spoke Egyptian, the language of Pharaoh, which would be like Jesus speaking the language of God, a spiritual language, and the brothers/disciples spoke Hebrew and Aramaic, an earthly language.

There must be an interpreter between us and Joseph (Messiah). This was the leader of Joseph's house interpreting, which was actually Joseph's firstborn son, Manasheh. Joseph would speak, Manasheh would interpret, and the brothers would understand, because Joseph's words are in a language not our own. Without the Interpreter, Manasheh/Holy Spirit, they could not understand the words of Joseph, so too, without the Interpreter, the Holy Spirit, we cannot understand the words of Jesus. Joseph is like the Messiah! Just as Joseph was kicked out by his brothers and sold to Gentiles, so too, Jesus was kicked out by His Jewish brothers and sold to the Gentiles. Joseph goes down into a pit and ascends to the right hand of Pharaoh, so too, Jesus goes down into the pit and ascends to the right hand of God. Joseph, while in the pit, comes across two men of Pharaoh's, one condemned to death, and one exalted. While Jesus is on the cross, He is surrounded by two criminals, one of which is condemned, and one exalted to Paradise. Joseph then reigns amongst Gentiles for a time, so too, Jesus is now reigning amongst Gentiles until their fullness (Genesis 48:19, Romans 11:25). Joseph is line by line a picture of Jesus' first coming, and just as the brothers cannot speak with Joseph without the interpreter, Manasheh, neither can we truly understand all the depths of the Word of God, beginning from the Torah of Moses, and Jesus' words without the Interpreter, the Holy Spirit. Genesis 42:23 "and they did not know that Joseph understood them, because the interpreter was between them (וְהֵם לֹא יָדְעוּ כִּי שֹׁמֵעַ יוֹסֵף כִּי הַמֵּלִיץ בֵּינֹתָם)."

Apart from the Advocate or Interpreter, the Holy Spirit, we do not know what Jesus is saying. This is the context and framework of Jesus' words in John 14-16. We have to understand the fluency of Scripture, because as we have discussed, nothing is new under the sun (Ecclesiastes 1:9-10). We have to connect these things in order to get the full picture, but even connecting it all comes by the Holy Spirit! Jesus says in John 16:12 "there are still many things for Me to say to you, but you are not able to understand them now." Now think about the book of Acts. It was only after they were baptized in the Holy Spirit in Acts 2, "then they understood Jesus' words." They walked with Jesus for 3.5 years and couldn't understand Him, but they receive the Holy Spirit, and they now understand His words fluently. The Interpreter came and revealed to them Joseph's/Jesus' words. I don't care how much seminary you have or how many years in the faith you have. I will take five minutes with the Holy Spirit over all of it.

What can this be compared too? There was a certain city with a bunch of villages surrounding it, and in these surrounding villages were Jewish families. The Jews were unable to read Hebrew, the language they spoke. They loved God but were unable to read the Scriptures since they were illiterate. So, the parents of the Jewish families in these surrounding villages decided to come together to the central city, because they want their kids to not only be raised up loving God, but also able to read the Scriptures. So, they decided, since they were poor and unable to pay for their own private tutors in each village, they joined finances and paid for a tutor in the central city for their children to go learn from every day, in order to learn how to read Hebrew and the Scriptures.

One day, a father of one of these kids receives a letter that is written in Hebrew; therefore, he was unable to read or understand it. He decides to go to his child's tutor, so that the tutor would interpret the letter for him. When he gets to the tutor, he says, "please interpret this letter for me." The tutor opens it up, looks at it, hands it back to him with no emotion, saying, "your father died," then goes back about his business. The father of the child who just found out his father died begins to weep. Why am I sharing this? Many of us today are trying to read our Father's letter without the Interpreter, and we don't understand it, and because of this, there's no weeping, there's no emotion, no intimacy, and now, there's thousands of interpretations dividing the body of Messiah into thousands of denominations, who all claim to be moving by the Holy Spirit, the Interpreter. We need the real Interpreter. We need to weep. We need to be moved by our Father's letter, our sin, and the death of His Son.

We need the baptism of the Holy Spirit. Many people read today and do not understand the Word of God, and I even know many baptized in the Holy Spirit, but they are still so analytical, they are thinking on natural planes, trying to rationalize every detail of God's ways. This will quench the Spirit of God. Being baptized isn't enough. You have to also believe all things (1 Corinthians 13:7). We need intimacy. It is not enough to read the Bible casually on your chair while your kids run around in the living room, or while patients and chaos are moving about in the waiting room at the doctor's office. It is meant to be as Jesus said, a time of un-rushed and un-disturbed intimacy, where you close the door behind you, and it is an intimate date with you and the Holy Spirit (Matthew 6:6-7).

Many today are teaching that the Holy Spirit and the gifts are not for today. Around 2018 or 2019, I was speaking with a pastor in the Dallas area who was visiting from North Carolina where he pastors a church. He had a problem because he knew that I speak in tongues, and he told me the gifts stopped with the apostles, so I asked him, when did there cease to be apostles? He said, "2,000 years ago with Paul and those apostles." I said, "oh, really? Because Ephesians 4:11-12 says that Jesus gave some to be apostles, prophets, evangelists, pastors, and teachers, so if apostles are no more today, neither are pastors, and you sir, are not a pastor." That conversation ended quickly.

Apostles are here today, prophets are here today, as well as the other three, along with the Holy Spirit, speaking in tongues, the prophetic anointing, healing the sick, raising the dead, and casting out devils. He is the same yesterday, today, and forever (Malachi 3:6, Hebrews 13:8). I don't even want to know the stale atmosphere of that church if they reflect that pastor's teaching. As I mentioned in Chapter 1, I have encountered these things. I am already ruined to the world and bad theology. God marked me and sanctified me by His glory (Exodus 29:43).

We have to hunger and thirst for the Holy Spirit. Joseph's brothers couldn't understand Joseph without the interpreter, so how can we understand Jesus without the Interpreter? Jesus said in John 15:26 "when the Interpreter will come, whom I will send to you from My Father, the Spirit of Truth that goes out from My Father, He will testify of Me." The Holy Spirit will testify of Jesus, just as Manasheh would testify of the words of Joseph, or as Aaron would testify of the words of Moses (Exodus 4:14-16) because Israel also couldn't understand Moses! We must understand these principles from the spiritual framework and patterns of the Torah, as well as it being the basis for all prophecy (Deuteronomy 34:10). The Torah at its very essence is a book of prophecy, not only for the times of the New Testament, but prophecy that reigns even until today in circular motion, because nothing is new under the sun, and whatever has been, will be, and whatever has been done, will be done. Someone will come and say that something is new, but this has been since long ago (Ecclesiastes 1:9-10).

As we mentioned from John 16:12, Jesus still has many things to tell us, but we are not able to understand them yet, but then in verses 13-14 He tells us that the Spirit will come and reveal these things and the hidden treasures of the Messiah! What is Jesus saying? He is saying, "My son, My daughter, I want to speak with you. Yes, you. I don't want to just speak with you through someone else, I want to speak with you personally. Will you hunger and thirst for the things of the Holy Spirit?" It is written in John 16:13 "when the Spirit of Truth comes, He will guide you into all truth, because He will not speak of Himself, but rather, what He hears He will speak, and He will tell you of things to come." What is Jesus saying? He is talking about Genesis 42, Manasheh (as well as Aaron with Moses), the interpreter, never spoke his own words, but only what he heard from Joseph. The Holy Spirit only testifies of the words of the Messiah and never speaks on His own accord.

The same thing in Exodus 4, as Moses, who is a picture of the Messiah, is not a good speaker because of his speech impediment and the language barrier, as he was raised amongst the Egyptians. What does God do? Exodus 4:14-16:

"And the anger of the LORD was kindled against Moses, and He said, 'Is Aaron the Levite not your brother? I know he speaks. And also, behold, he is coming out to meet you, and he will see you and rejoice in his heart. And you will speak to him, and you will place the words in his mouth, and I will be with your mouth and with his mouth, and I will teach you what you will do. And he will speak for you to the people, and he will be a mouth for you, and you will be God to him.'"

Once again, Moses, being a type of Messiah, and now we have Aaron having to be the interpreter because of the same situation with Joseph with the language barrier, and people not being able to understand Moses very well, and once again, nothing is new under the sun, and now we are beginning to touch the surface of understanding the Messiah and the Holy Spirit beginning from the Torah, just as Jesus and Paul both expounded. But notice Jesus' words above in John 16:13, when Jesus says about the Holy Spirit "He will tell you of things to come." King Messiah Himself says:

> "I have many things I want to tell you, but you aren't
> able to receive them right now, however, when the Spirit
> of Truth comes, He will lead you into all truth, He will
> not speak of Himself, but rather He will speak My words,
> and He will tell you of things....to come."

What does that sound like? What is Jesus saying? The Holy Spirit will tell us of things to come? He is saying, "when the Holy Spirit comes, you are going to prophesy!"

You, as a believer, have access, to partake to some degree, of the prophetic anointing, each person according to their anointing from God, nevertheless, this is part of the nature of the Holy Spirit is for us to prophesy. He isn't necessarily talking about the gift of prophecy or the gift of speaking in tongues, but to some degree, the nature of God's Spirit within a believer is to know things to come, as Moses said to Joshua in Numbers 11:29 "and Moses said to him, 'are you zealous for me? If only all of the people of the LORD were prophets, that the LORD would place His Spirit upon them.'" Prophesying isn't a separate gift, it is part of the package deal for those in the Messiah, and a by-product of being full of the Holy Spirit. Each person can taste the prophetic anointing to differing degrees. Just because you have had a prophetic dream or prophetic word doesn't make you a prophet, although there are prophets, neither does it mean you have the gift of prophecy. The Holy Spirit wants to operate through prophecy in your life. It is written in Joel 3:1-2 (Joel 2:28-29 in English Bibles), which Peter quotes in Acts 2:16-18:

> "And it shall come to pass afterward that I will pour out My Spirit upon all flesh, and your sons and your daughters shall prophesy. Your old men shall dream dreams and your young men shall see visions. And also, upon the servants and upon the handmaids I will pour out My Spirit in those days."

These things are for the here and now. The LORD longs that we all move under the influence of the Interpreter, the Holy Spirit. He wants us to all move in the power of the Holy Spirit, but first you have to want the Holy Spirit, and secondly, expect. You have to be desperate, as I explained I was desperate in Chapter 1. There is power in desperation. Show me a desperate man, I will show you a powerful one. Do not be complacent in saying, "I just don't understand my Father's letter." That Jewish man in the story I spoke on earlier in this chapter was not complacent. He didn't care how far he had to walk to the central city. His thought was, "I will get the interpreter." So too, I also didn't care that I had to drive to Dallas to get the baptism of the Holy Spirit and fire. I was going to do whatever it took. I was desperate, and I still am. Only by the Interpreter can we truly become one with the LORD and team up with Him. By the Holy Spirit you can "taste and see that the LORD is good (Psalms 34:9)."

Everything Jesus is saying about the Interpreter, the Holy Spirit, is directly from Genesis 42:23 and Exodus 4, as well as previous passages that I won't go into here. Context is key, and these understandings will come to life by the Spirit of God. What if we could understand Jesus' words as He meant them when He said it? Just as there had to be an interpreter between Joseph and the brothers, so too, there must be One between Messiah and us. Jesus says in John 14:25-26:

> "I have spoken these things to you while I am still with you. But the Interpreter, the Holy Spirit whom My Father will send in My name, He will teach you all things and cause you to remember all things that I have told you."

This is why I said in the book of Acts, it says the disciples would all of the sudden remember Jesus' words and understand them, which is why Jesus said things like He did in John 13:7 "and Yeshua answered him, 'what I am doing you do not know at this time, but afterwards you will know.'" We must notice though, the Holy Spirit is to REMIND us of all things, meaning, He reminds us of the things we have already studied and dove into. Reminding means, something you have already come across, something you have already studied. It is our job to study Scripture, and His job to reveal it, and then to remind us of it in its proper time (Matthew 10:19-20), so that we can properly divide the Word of Truth (2 Timothy 2:15). It is our job to put the tools on our tool belt, but His job to tell us which tool to use in its proper time. We must be prepared, and we must have the guidance of the Holy Spirit. If you don't understand what you are reading, it's okay, keep going. It will come out when it is supposed too.

When you receive things of the Holy Spirit and begin moving in such, it is not just about being able to lay hands on the sick and seeing them healed. There is power in revelation, and in rightly dividing the Word of God with authority (2 Timothy 2:15), because this is how you move in impartation to others. You can't give what you don't have, but by the Spirit of God, the revelation now becomes a part of you, transforming your essence into the essence and revelation of the Messiah (Romans

8:29), so that now when you speak and move, it will pierce the hearts of people like a double edged sword (Luke 24:32). Your enemy will fall before you (Leviticus 26:7), devils will be cast out, and your property and dwellings will be cleansed.

There must be true impartation. True impartation means you become a candle that has the flame, and because you have the flame, you can impart it to others and light others on fire, just like a tree of fire. Don't just speak about the revelation, be the revelation as it is imparted to you by the Holy Spirit, the Flame of God. Impartation from us to others cannot come by an intellectual knowing, or going ahead of what the Holy Spirit has done in our lives, but it can only be given or imparted by our being totally consumed by Him in that given area. It is why I never have to use notes to preach and quote Scripture left and right. I don't speak, preach, and teach from head knowledge, I do it from an overflow of revelation that permeates me from the inside out. As I said in the foreword, Jesus is the walking Word of God, and we are called to walk as He walked (1 John 2:6), therefore, due to my deep study of Scripture and surrender to the Holy Spirit, it is no longer I who live, but Messiah within me (Galatians 2:20), and in Him, I too, am the walking Word of God. Through this, I impart.

In Numbers 11:16-30, Moses was so consumed by the Spirit of God, the LORD took some of that Spirit that was upon him to be upon the elders, without it diminishing Moses' anointing, just as a candle that lights another candle doesn't diminish no matter how many other candles it kindles. A revelation or gifting can't just be knowledge of the mind, but some knowledge by revelation of the Holy Spirit that transforms you from the inside, because it now becomes a part of your nature (Galatians 2:20). Because it is one with you, and you can now explain it in seven different ways. Think about when you are following directions to get to a specific location. At first, you have to follow notes or Siri, but eventually, not only do you not need Siri and can get there on your own, but now, even if you had to come from the north, east, south, or west, you can get there seven different ways because it overflows within you. It is yours. The same goes with preaching. I must not preach from restrictive notes forever, but from an overflow of revelation that consumes me by the Holy Spirit on a given matter.

If you are desperate, if you cry out, if you hunger and thirst, you will be filled (Matthew 5:6). Listen to the words of Jesus in Luke 11:5-13:

> "And He said to them, 'who among you has a friend and would go to him in the middle of the night and say to him, my friend, lend me three loaves, because a friend of mine has come to me from a journey, and I have nothing to set before him. And his friend from within would answer and say to him, do not bother me, for behold, the door is closed, and my children are with me in bed. I am not able to get up and give to you. I say to you that if he does not give to him because of friendship, he will arise because of his urgency and give to him as much as is required by him. I also say to you, ask and it will be given to you, seek and you will find, knock and it will be opened to you. For everyone who asks will receive and who seeks will find and who knocks it will be opened to him. For which one among you who is a father, if his son asks bread from him would hand him a stone? And if he asks a fish from him would hand him a snake instead of a fish? And if he asks an egg from him, would he hand a scorpion to him? And if you who are evil know how

to give good gifts to your children, how much more will your Father from heaven give the Holy Spirit to those who ask Him?'"

CHAPTER 5

Partaking In The
Divine Nature Of God

As I am sure you can tell from everything so far, from the time I came to the LORD in September of 2017, I thank the LORD and give Him the glory that I have walked very intimately with the Holy Spirit, however, starting about October or November of 2021, this intimacy reached new heights. God began pouring into me in a new way with the Holy Spirit. He began pouring into me His heart for the necessity of the baptism of the Holy Spirit and fire, and that He so longingly desires for His people to begin to really move in the Holy Spirit. He imparted to me His heart that He wants to raise the hunger and thirst, and even the desperation of Him within the hearts of His people. Jesus says in Matthew 5:6 "blessed are those who hunger and thirst for righteousness, for they shall be filled."

I never told many people, but back in 2020, the Holy Spirit took me on a very interesting journey. I was not to read a single book of the Bible that was not in the Torah of Moses (the first five books of the Bible) for a year, and it was to be done only in Hebrew. After a year passed, due to the intensity of the revelations, I decided to keep going for almost two years. I only read the Torah in Hebrew for almost two years, studying it very deeply and exhaustively, some days being only four verses. The Holy

Spirit was wanting to re-train my mind, so that I began seeing Scripture as a Jew, as Jesus, Peter, or Paul would have understood Scripture. I began to see the Torah through the lens of the Holy Spirit about the Spirit and the Messiah in a way I had never seen, as you will see in this chapter, and have probably already noticed thus far.

I started getting so much revelation in Torah in Hebrew, that when I came back to the rest of the Tanach (Old Testament) and the New Testament, I was blown away at how without realizing it for those two years, the authors of the New Testament and I were getting all of the same revelations. I could explain things inside and out in the New Testament, including the book of Revelation in a way nobody around me had seen. I literally had pastors of large churches, evangelists, and doctors of the faith simply mind blown at the ability to interpret and see the things of the Holy Spirit, and I was showing where Jesus and Paul would get their teachings from, and the foundation of those teachings, as well as simply explaining all of the mysterious symbolism of the book of Revelation.

I began teaching on the Holy Spirit from Leviticus in a way that now people wanted to actually study Leviticus. As all of this had already been brewing in 2020 and 2021, it wasn't until 2022, the hardest time of my life and when I stepped back from ministry for over four months that it began to be fully birthed within me, and I felt like a wild dog that God was about to let loose in the Holy Spirit. It was right when He let me loose that I released over 120 teachings in about six or seven months, including writing this book and putting together other books as well. I felt like if He didn't let me loose, I was going to explode. With all of this said, I want to talk about the Divine Nature of God, and how we become partakers of the Divine Nature of God. As we get into this, I want to start from 2 Peter 1:1-4:

"Simon Peter, a servant, and apostle of Yeshua the Messiah, to those who have obtained equally precious faith with us through the righteousness of our Master and Redeemer, Yeshua the Messiah. May grace and peace abound to you through the recognition of our Master Yeshua the Messiah, as the giver to us of all things that be of the power of God to life and the fear of God, through the recognition of Him who has called us to His own glory and moral excellence. Which, by them, He has given us great and precious promises, so that by these you will be partakers of the Divine Nature, while you flee from the corruption of the lusts that are in the world."

In Hebrew and Aramaic, the word for "Divine" is literally coming from where we get the word "God (אלהים)." So, the text can be rendered as "partakers of the nature of God/Godly nature." Divine is simply another word we use for God. Notice in the last verse (4), it states "which, by them," them, being, all things that are given to us by the power of God, "so that by these you will be partakers of the Nature of God (or Divine Nature) while you flee from the corruption of the lusts that are in the world." Peter is saying that there are certain promises that have been given to us, and these promises are really the theme of the entire Torah. Torah was not only about the promise of the Messiah (Acts 13:32-33, John 12:34), but the promise of the Holy Spirit so that we could walk in the image of the Messiah, which I could show over and over again. In other words, the promise in the Torah was for us to be filled with the Holy Spirit through the Promised Messiah, to enable us to walk in the Divine Nature of God, as Jesus walked in the Divine Nature of God (Hebrews 1:1-3), and as God sent Jesus, so too, is Jesus sending us (John

20:21), and we who abide in Him are also expected to walk as He walked (1 John 2:6).

We all know that the Messiah is Divine. Jesus walked on the earth as the very expressed image of God Himself, not a physical image, but His very attributes and heart. Just as kids tend to look similar in appearance to their fathers, Jesus looks identical to His. God being embodied fully in the very person of Jesus, as it is written in Hebrews 1:1-3:

> "In many ways and many forms, God anciently conversed with our fathers by the prophets. But in these latter days, He has conversed with us by His Son whom He has constituted heir of all things, and by whom He made the worlds, who is the splendor of His glory and the exact image of His nature, and upholds all by the power of His Word, and by Himself He made a purification of sins and sat down on the right hand of the Majesty on high."

And again, in Colossians 1:13-17:

> "And has rescued us from the dominion of darkness and transferred us to the Kingdom of His beloved Son, by whom we have redemption and forgiveness of sins, who is the likeness of the invisible God and the firstborn of all creatures, and by Him everything was created that is in heaven and on earth, all that is visible and all that is invisible, whether thrones or dominions or principalities or powers. Everything was through Him and was created by Him, and He was prior to all, and by Him everything exists."

All of this can be very clearly shown in the Torah of Moses; however, I won't go into all of the details on this from there. So, as we have seen, the Divine Messiah walked the earth as God embodied in the flesh and the very person of Jesus with power, in word, and in righteous acts. Jesus said in John 14:8-9 "if you have seen Me, you have seen the Father." But the verse that forever grips me with this understanding is Jesus' words in John 20:21 "as the Father sent Me, so I am sending you," meaning, so too, when people see us, they should see the Father. We too, as children of our Father, should look like Him, as Paul said in Ephesians 5:1 "be imitators of God, as dear children." He says again in Matthew 10:25 that it is good for a disciple to be like his Master. 1 John 2:6 says, "whoever says 'I am in him,' it is upon him to walk as He walked."

Jesus says in Mark 16:17-18:

> "These signs will follow them that believe: in My name they will cast out devils, they will speak with new tongues, they will lift up serpents, if they drink deadly poison it will not hurt them, and they will place their hands on the sick and they will recover."

Jesus made things quite clear. We are not only called to, but EXPECTED to walk in righteousness in word, in deed, and in the power of the Holy Spirit, but the key is we walk in power as Peter says in our above verses "while you flee from the corruption of the lusts that are in the world." Power in the Holy Spirit will cost you everything. Jesus is saying, as He walked in the Divine Nature of God, we are expected to walk in the Divine Nature of God. This is why Jesus says to stay in Jerusalem "until the power of the Holy Spirit has come upon you (Luke 24:49, Acts 1:4-8)." Only then, when you have been baptized from on high can you be His witnesses and be partakers of the Divine Nature with our words, our actions, and with power. So that when people encounter Pastor Nick, they really encounter the Messiah who lives in me (Galatians 2:20). Through their seeing Him in us so abundantly, the Spirit of

God begins to stir up a Godly jealousy within others to want what we have, or better yet, Who we have. Even believers need to be stirred up to a greater jealousy to walk in such an intimacy with Him.

I want to dedicate this chapter to what is available to us with this high calling, and how we can tap into this Divine Nature of God as believers in Jesus, because as I mentioned, it is expected of us to walk in power. Jesus was disappointed in His disciples when they didn't cast out a devil or heal someone (Matthew 17:16-17). As I moved to Iowa in 2022, I had made a lengthy Houston trip from about mid-September through the end of October (roughly six weeks), and while I was in Houston for that trip, the Holy Spirit began revealing to me a new availability in Him, and what I got to see in the Holy Spirit was absolutely incredible jaw-dropping even. The trip was so full of the Holy Spirit, I kid you not, with everything I was going through at the time, it was like for those six or so weeks, the more I was oppressed, the more fruit and supernatural miracles I began to see before my eyes, as it is written in Exodus 1:12 "and as they (the Egyptians) afflicted them (Israel), the more they (Israel) multiplied and broke forth, and they loathed the children of Israel."

With the healings, prophecy, words of knowledge, etc., that I had already experienced up until this point, this surpassed it. I knew the new season of my vision from April of 2022 of the Trees Of Fire was beginning, or at least a taste of it. This is the thing about impartation, it was no longer about what I have heard about through others or even read about in the Scriptures, but now what I have encountered. It was now mine to give unto others, as Jesus said in Luke 7:22 "go and tell John that which you have seen and heard," meaning, don't tell anyone something that is hearsay, but what you have personally seen and personally heard, and as you freely received, freely give (Matthew 10:8).

The same thing takes place in Exodus 18:1-12, as Jethro comes to Moses, Moses tells Jethro everything he had just personally encountered with the LORD. He told his own testimony, and Jethro converted. Why? Because this is impartation. We cannot give to someone that which we have not received. We have to stay in our lane, which is a problem for people today, everyone is trying to switch lanes and enter into an authority that is not theirs, not honoring another's anointing, as Proverbs 27:8 says, "as a bird wanders from its nest, so is a man who wanders from his place."

We need to live from a place of impartation. Impartation gives of what one has without diminishing it from oneself, as we said, a candle that lights another candle, a tree that lights another on fire. Impartation is an overflow in the public place of your intimacy with the Holy Spirit in the secret place. So now I want to share a couple stories about this Houston trip that goes along with partaking in the Divine Nature of God. It seemed the Presence of God was favoring coffee shops, because multiple of these encounters took place when I was at a couple different ones. I was at one coffee shop in Magnolia, called HeBrews, and two young men in their early 20's decide to move tables, and the table they moved to was the one I was sitting alone at studying, and we immediately started talking. These young men were young believers, filled with zeal and love for God.

As we go back and forth, the Spirit began to flow through me like a river, quoting Scripture and pouring out revelation. These two began to just sit as hungry disciples, absorbing everything. The atmosphere shifted as Holy Spirit gripped me. This is one of the busiest coffee shops in the state of Texas, and the place was slammed with lines out the door, but it was like we were the only ones in the room. I began telling these men that we cannot just walk in Word, but we must also walk in power (1 Corinthians 2:4, 4:20). Acts 8:5-6 tells us it was because of the miracles that the Samaritans heeded Phillip. The signs confirm the validity that God is with us (John 3:2), as it says in Mark 16:20 "and they went out and preached in every place, and our Master helped them, confirming their words with the signs that they did," and Jesus says in John 14:11 "believe that I am in My Father, and My Father is in Me. And if not, believe for the sake of the works."

They knew I was on sabbatical and that the LORD had been showing me some things, and they asked, "what is He showing you?" I told them that He is stressing how badly we need to walk in power, alongside righteousness. So, they asked, "how do we walk in the power, and the things of Jesus, and the anointing that breaks the yokes and chains (Isaiah 10:27)? Does this come by walking more obedient with Him?" I said, "100%." The closer we are with God, the more obedient, and the more we look like the Messiah in our lives, the more the anointing will flow, because the power is part of who the Messiah is, it is a package deal. But this isn't my opinion, this is what the Scripture says. So, I took them back to Leviticus.

I want to share about the Holy Spirit from the book of Leviticus, which I know you may have never heard before. I have shared continually thus far that the Scriptures can only be understood by the Spirit of God, and that the Torah is OF the Spirit (1 Corinthians 2:9-16, Romans 7:14). If you read the Scriptures, then an unbeliever reads it, and that unbeliever gets the same thing from it that you did, you read it in the flesh. Anyone can read Scripture and read Torah and get what seems to be on the surface of the page, but only by the Holy Spirit will the things of the Spirit be revealed, and will the Messiah be unveiled in a way that you had never seen before.

Let's dive deep now into Leviticus 26:3-9:

> "If you will walk in My statutes and keep My commandments and do them, I will give your rain in its season, and the land will give its produce, and the tree of the field

will give its fruit. The threshing for you will overtake the vintage, and the vintage will overtake the sowing, and you will eat your bread to satisfaction, and you will dwell securely in your land. And I will give peace in your land, and you will lie down and there will be none to cause fear, and I will cause the evil beast to cease from the land, and the sword will not pass through your land. You will pursue your enemies and they will fall before you by the sword. And five of you will pursue a hundred, and a hundred of you will pursue ten thousand, and your enemies will fall before you by the sword. And I will turn to you, and I will make you fruitful, and I will multiply you, and I will establish My covenant with you."

Let's start from the beginning, as the Scripture says, "if you will walk in My statutes (אִם־בְּחֻקֹּתַי תֵּלֵכוּ)." The phrase "you will walk (תֵּלֵכוּ)" in Biblical Hebrew is what we call the Qal, Imperfect, 2nd person, masculine, plural. According to the rules of Biblical Hebrew grammar, the Imperfect conjugation means "habitual or customary" action, so what it is saying is "if you will continually walk in My statutes and in My commandments," then you get all these promises following it. The promises take place IF we habitually, day by day, walk in His ways, and the promise I want to focus on is:

> "You will pursue your enemies and they will fall before you by the sword. And five of you will pursue a hundred, and a hundred of you will pursue ten thousand, and your enemies will fall before you by the sword."

I began sharing with these young men at the coffee shop these promises right here and began to expound on it (Deuteronomy 1:5). If we walk in His ways, our enemies will fall at our sword, but we have to read this by the Holy Spirit, because we don't war against flesh and blood (Ephesians 6:12, 2 Corinthians 10:3-5). The passage is not talking about a person falling before us, because we don't war with people, but rather, with principalities, powers, rulers of darkness of this age, and spiritual hosts of wickedness in heavenly places (Ephesians 6:12). The enemy that the Torah is telling us about here who will fall before us is the Enemy, Satan himself, and demonic spirits. Jesus didn't come warring against people, but He was defeating the works of the devil, and disarming the power that the devil had over people, so that when He healed someone, He was breaking the yokes and chains of the enemy (Isaiah 10:27).

Paul says in Ephesians 6:17 that the "sword" of the Spirit is every word of God, and here in Leviticus, the Torah says the enemy will fall at your sword. We have to see this by the spiritual lens Jesus, Paul, and the other disciples saw Torah through, the same lenses I received when for almost two years I only studied Torah in Hebrew. The Torah is saying that when you walk very closely with God in obedience and intimacy with Him day by day, when you speak a word, it will pierce through the enemy camp and the power of the enemy, and demons will fall before you at your word/sword. You will carry an anointing that allows you to further walk in the Divine Nature of God. When you command that sickness to be gone, the enemy strength will fall and they will be healed, and when you break a chain that is upon someone, it will shatter before you. There is power upon our tongues in these promises (Proverbs 18:21), which is the sword, because it is the sword of the Spirit of God upon our tongue as we first walk in obedience with Him.

Now, all of the sudden, we are reading this in Leviticus in the coffee shop, and now we are talking about the power of the Holy Spirit and the anointing that breaks the yokes and chains. As I said, during those two years of only reading Torah in Hebrew, I began seeing things in the

Spirit of everything the disciples were speaking of in the New Testament. Torah says, because of your obedience, we can now be entrusted with the anointing! Power, signs, and wonders are convincing, and if it falls into the wrong hands, it can be used to lead people in an improper path (Matthew 24:24, 2 Thessalonians 2:9-11). The anointing doesn't come easy or free of charge, it requires everything of who you are. If you want more of Him, you have to give up more of you, and more of the things that are found by those who live in the world.

Through this revelation of Leviticus 26:3-9, we can now tap into the gifts of the Holy Spirit, because walking in that deep intimacy with God brings about an overflow, including, the enemy camp falling at your sword/word. I don't try to heal, I am not the healer, the Father is. Healing is simply a fruit of overflow as He operates through me. There can be no disconnect, because a branch apart from the root can bear nothing (John 15). The branch must be fully connected and intimate at all times. Power flows not from a power hungry people, but rather from an intimate people walking in such love for Him, that we simply become supernatural vessels of honor, prepared for the Master's work (2 Timothy 2:19-21). Power is not a separate thing we seek, but rather it is an overflow from intimacy with the One we become One with. When this becomes an overflow from sonship, it is so healthy. Meanwhile, when we seek power, it becomes witchcraft.

As I sit there with these young men, I began telling them about a story from about one week before I met with them at a different coffee shop, where I was with a woman and her daughter. I had actually baptized this woman's daughter a few years earlier, and also laid hands upon her and she got baptized in the Holy Spirit that night. She said from then on, she has never been the same, praise be to God. As we are at the coffee shop, the daughter has this eczema like rash all over her arm, clearly visible. As she was telling me about the pains and things she was going through in life, my heart was rent in two with compassion, the same way Jesus looks to the people as sheep with no shepherd and has compassion on them (Mark 6:34). This supernatural compassion from heaven consumed me. It was by no means earthly. The Holy Spirit gave me the heart of the Father in that moment, not wanting to see her in pain not only physically, but also the other things she was sharing with me that she had to experience and was going through that she warred with mentally and emotionally. Out of that compassion I wanted to see her healed. I could care less about being involved; it wasn't about me. This was the overflow of sonship with Him, so I told her right there in the coffee shop, "I want to pray. You, your mother, and I right now."

I took the young woman's hand as her mom sits there with us, and the Holy Spirit began showing me the word curses that had been spoken over her and different things that had happened to her, and why these curses were able to hit her, because a curse without a cause cannot come (Proverbs 26:2). I immediately started breaking things off as Leviticus 26 says that our word/sword will cause the enemy to fall before us. I broke it all off and commanded healing over her, and as I am praying, she yells out, "Mom! Look at my arm!" Her arm healed right before her. So, as I kept praying, I heard the Holy Spirit say, "stop praying, pray in tongues quietly," and I sat there quietly with them both in the middle of the coffee shop, and I was praying in tongues quietly, but loud enough that they could hear me pray in tongues. As I began praying in tongues, I started getting images, like a slideshow, going across my eyes, and after I was done praying in tongues, I began speaking in English everything that was in that "slideshow" that I saw, because I knew it was the interpretation of my tongues. This is one of the gifts of the Holy Spirit (1 Corinthians 12), not only speaking in tongues, but that we pray to be able to interpret the tongues (1 Corinthians 14:13).

As I began speaking what I saw over her, she starts weeping right there in the coffee shop. She turned towards her mom in shock, and then her mom looks at me, and her mother says to me, "everything you just said, she told me before we came here. Everything you just said, she has told me. There is no way you could have known what you just said." So, I asked them both if they heard me speaking in tongues, and they both said yes. I told them that when I was doing so, I was getting a slideshow in the Spirit of what I was saying in tongues as the interpretation, and so that is what I spoke, and that is how I knew everything I said.

Right there they got to encounter the Holy Spirit, and there was a fire that was ignited. The same thing happens the next time I meet them as I get a word for the mother as soon as she walks in the door, and she started crying as we sat down because of the word of knowledge the Holy Spirit gave me for her as she walked in the coffee shop. They messaged me afterwards how much that time impacted them. In fact, usually, it will be me messaging the daughter as a big brother and mentor, and we will schedule times to get coffee and catch up, and her mom will say "I am coming. Every time I have been around Nick the Holy Spirit moves, and I need to be around it." It's an addiction to Him and His presence. We as partakers in the Divine Nature get to be carriers of the glory.

I always notice, there will be some atmospheres I walk into, and it is like words of knowledge and prophecy begin to flow through me like a mighty river. Literally, one after the other. The atmosphere has hunger, and it draws the living water from the well of the Spirit right out of me. Then, there are other atmospheres of believers, and it is like trying to give water from a dry well. I can do nothing there in the Spirit because the atmosphere just has no hunger or thirst for these things, and I began to have a revelation of when on one hand, the power literally is pulled out of Jesus because a woman who is hungry for Him touches His garment, as it is written in Luke 8:43-46:

"And a certain woman whose blood was flowing for twelve years who among the doctors had spent all her money but was not able to be healed by man. She approached from behind Him and touched the wing of His garment, and immediately the flow of her blood stopped. And Yeshua said, 'who touched Me?' And while all were denying it, Simon Peter and those with Him said to Him, 'our Master, the crowds are pressing you and thronging you, and you say who touched me?' And He said, 'someone touched Me. For I know that power went out of Me.'"

But then, around others, it is written in Mark 6:5-6:

"And He was not able to do even one miracle there, except that upon a few sick He laid His hands and healed them. And He was amazed by their lack of faith and would go around the villages while teaching."

So, I am still sharing all of this with these two young men in He-Brews coffee shop, and I said to them that anywhere we go, it is not that we are trying to carry the Divine Nature, but rather, it is because we are living from a place of "abiding" in Him (John 15:1-7). We are people of Presence. We are being sons and daughters and filled with expectancy. We are being partakers of the Divine Nature. It is no longer I who live, but the Messiah within me (Galatians 2:20). It is who we are called to be, it is simply who we are. In the Kingdom, as a son and daughter, it is actually unnatural not to carry such things. We have allowed the world to consume our minds that doing these things is not ordinary, but I argue that not doing them is actually not ordinary. A dog barks and a cat meows, so too, a believer walks in the overflow of sonship and power. I am walking as a co-heir with the Messiah in the Divine nature and promises of God (Romans 8:17). As a co-heir with Messiah, everything the Father wants to give unto the Son, so does He give unto us as sons and daughters. "As the Father sent me, so I am sending you (John 20:21)." We have access to these things in the Spirit IF we will continually walk in His ways as it says in Leviticus 26:3 above.

I can't walk in His power if I won't walk in His image or with His heart. The gifts of the Spirit are a means of edification and for gathering the lost, in order to show His love for others and to distinguish between the real and the counterfeit. If my staff turns into a snake by the power of God and so does another's staff who walks in a deceptive power, my snake will eat his (Exodus 7:9-12). If they claim to be a prophet, and I tell you I am a prophet, then let's see who really brings fire from heaven (1 Kings 18). The signs and wonders of God takes things from a theological debate to proof by power. These things come from a place of intimacy and expectancy. Faith breeds expectancy. I expect my Father to move. I always tell people, I don't believe God visits me in dreams almost every night and gives me encounters by accident. God is no respecter of persons (Deuteronomy 16:19, Romans 2:11, Galatians 2:6, Colossians 3:25, Ephesians 6:9, 1 Timothy 5:21). I expect Him to move. I know He will. I tell people, "let me pray. God will come and show me." Or I tell them I know God will come to me in a dream. I don't walk on the waters of wishful thinking when it comes to my relationship with my Father. I know my Father and I walk very closely with Him. That may trigger the insecurities of the insecure and self-righteous, and I may be accused as being prideful, but God forbid that we don't carry such confidence in our relationship with the Father and as co-heirs with the Messiah.

There are a few gyms I go too in the Houston area, but one specifically that I have gone to since 2016. This gym has been a harvest for the LORD in my life that I have continually labored in. This gym specifically is a bodybuilding gym where people dress half naked, cussing, and lustful music plays on the speakers, and honestly, it is in no way a place for the Holy Spirit within you to be fed, or at least as what may meet the eye. Yet, it is at this place I encounter God's power over and over again, which makes sense, because Jesus wasn't found amongst the righteous, but rather, eating and drinking with sinners and tax collectors (Luke 5/15). I cannot tell you how many supernatural stories I have of God flowing through me at this gym.

One day, I walk in the gym, and I am going straight to the water fountain which is right in front of me, and there is a man in front of me at the fountain that I have never spoken to before, nor have I ever even seen before this moment. The man starts backing up and I am right behind him, and not seeing I am behind him, he is about to walk right into to me. All I did was put my hand out so he would back into my hand, and my hand was placed upon his lower back. As he backs into my hand, he turns around quickly and looks at me, and I just walk right around him to fill up my water bottle. As I finish filling it up, I am walking off and he stops me immediately, and says, "hey man, are you close to God or something?" I said, "I am, and I am actually a pastor." He said, "when you touched me, I felt it go through my whole body." So, I told him, "I have been with the LORD all day in His Presence, and the Scripture says that when Moses was with the LORD, Moses' face began to shine and all Israel saw it (Exodus 34:29-35), and the same thing with Jesus as He was transfigured (Matthew 17:1-12). Just as this time at the gym, and as the time that I shared when I preached in Iowa, two pastors approached me afterwards because gold dust manifested on my forehead.

We can be carriers of the glory, but only by being very close to Him, and One with Him. It is so that people don't experience us, but Him through us. So right when this happens at the gym, now I have validity in this man's eyes, and a door was opened for me to minister and pray.

Now from this second forward, I don't have to speak with persuasive words. He just encountered the Holy Spirit. Now everything I say begins to pierce his heart. The soil is prepared for me to labor in. The Spirit of God made my job easy. There was no trying or striving, just being, just abiding (John 15:1-7).

During this same Houston trip, I was at the gym and there was a man there who looked so familiar, but I couldn't remember how I knew him or encountered him. I was on the second to last set of my workout and he walks up to me, saying, "do you remember me?" I told him I had been trying to recall who he was my entire workout. He said:

> "About six months ago I saw you here at the gym. My hand was in a brace because I had anger issues and punched through a wall, completely shattering my hand. I couldn't afford the procedure to get my hand worked on, and due to this, I lost my job as a physical therapist. You prayed for me, and a couple days later, I didn't even realize but my hand had been healed and I was using it for days. I got my job back and now I am on fire for God. He has been showing me things in the Spirit realm ever since."

I completely forgot that this took place when he initially approached me. This man now follows me on social media, and the signs and wonders brought him to the Living God. Something similar happened with a young man who apparently had terrible knee issues at this gym. He never limped, so I never knew, but the LORD came to me in a dream and showed me issues with his right knee. The next day, I kid you not, the moment I am walking in the gym, he is walking out. The LORD set up the scene. I said "do you have pain in your right knee? God showed me in a dream." He said yes. I prayed for it right there. Days later he sees me at the gym with someone else, leaping in excitement that his knee is healed, and now he is wanting to get into full time ministry.

I have story after story of this going on in that gym, which I would probably have to have a book dedicated just to those stories to even relate them. Healing, words of knowledge, people being baptized in the Holy Spirit and fire, power, and mighty, mighty deeds at a gym the church would shun, and a gym that would never walk into the church. It is a place of harvest for the LORD in my life. A place many might say like a pharisee, "why does Pastor Nick workout at this place with this terrible music and these half naked men and women?" Because I am not afraid to sit with sinners and tax collectors (Luke 5/15), and I will leave the 99 on the hill, in order to go into the valley to get the 1 (Matthew 18). The power gets the attention of others to give you room to bring them to Jesus and disciple them. Leviticus 26 is clear now in the Holy Spirit. If we will walk continually in His ways and be so intimate with Him, the enemy will fall at our sword, the sword of the Spirit upon our tongues. Jesus says you will trample serpents and scorpions, and over all the power of the enemy (Luke 10:19). Every morning I am generally up at 4am, and I usually don't even open the Bible until about 5 or 5:30am, because for 1-2 hours, I am literally just sitting or walking outside in the dark, conversing with my Father (Mark 1:35). He loves dialogue, communication, un-rushed and un-disturbed intimacy. I can't wait to get up every morning.

Finishing the story with these two men at the coffee shop, one of them asks me, "how can we transform people like this to want to have more?" So, I answer and said, "well, you two have been sitting before me for almost an hour now. Why are you two still here?" One of them said, "honestly, the wisdom, revelation, and the power of God is just flowing out of you. His presence here with you is heavy." So, I said, "that really kept you here all this time?" They both said yes. I told them, "then go and do the same thing to others, freely you received, freely give (Matthew 10:8)." So just as the women at the other coffee shop, one of these young men reached out to me weeks later. Not only did it keep them there in the first place, but it kept them coming back, as they still keep up with me and my teachings.

They want His presence. This is how revival takes place. True movement with the real Spirit of God, not just in word, but in power. So, I told them, go forth and do what you encountered today for others. Be so filled with the Holy Spirit that it just flows through you. Devour the Word of God (Jeremiah 15:16) daily from Genesis to Revelation, yes, including Leviticus. Devour it all, because it is all holy (Romans 7:12), it is all the power of God, it is all Jesus (John 1:1-5). Hunger and thirst. See the way Jesus moved, how He spoke, how He walked, and how He EXPECTED not only from His Father, but also from His disciples.

Jesus expected His Father to move, and so too, as I said earlier, I expect Him to move. Jesus also expected us to move in these things. I think many of us expect the Father to move, but we do so without expecting the prerequisites from ourselves as the Leviticus 26 passage states, which is our continual obedience to Him not just as Savior, but as LORD and Master, as Jesus said in Luke 6:46 "why do you call me, 'Master, Master,' but you do not do what I say?" If we expect the power of God, He first expects an obedient vessel, cleansed and ready for every good work, and most importantly, in deep intimacy and relationship with Him. We may look foolish at first, we may look foolish too many, including our families and friends (1 Corinthians 2:14). Be bold. Look foolish. I have seen God move at restaurants, grocery stores, churches, synagogues, airports, planes, bars, gyms, etc. In all of these places I have seen, due to the Divine Nature, lifeless trees become Trees Of Fire, and dry bones come to life (Ezekiel 37:1-10).

CHAPTER 6

The Fear Of The LORD

The fear of the LORD is one of the most important concepts in the Scriptures. Not only this, as we will see later in this chapter, it is one of the fruits of Pentecost and the baptism of the Holy Spirit and fire. One thing people who are baptized in the Holy Spirit have in common, or people who have had deep encounters with the LORD, is they all fear Him, and that fear keeps them close to Him. One may view fearing God and the baptism as totally separate things, but is the fruit that the farmer reaped totally separate from the seed that he plants? No, but one is simply the fruit of the other. So too, the fear of the LORD is a fruit of the baptism of the Holy Spirit and fire and is also one of the seven Spirits of God (Isaiah 11:1-3). I also want to say, before diving deep into this topic, the fear of man and religious spirits of the day can sometimes be called the fear of the LORD, when really, this is nothing but a gaslighting tactic of the evil one, and a form of witchcraft, in order to get you to conform to the doctrines of man, and it must not be confused with the pure Spirit of the fear of the LORD as it is written in Isaiah 29:13:

> "The Lord said, 'because this people has drawn close with its mouth, and with its lips it has honored Me, yet, it has distanced its heart from Me. Their fear of Me is according to the learning of the commandments of men.'"

Let's dive into not only why the fear of the LORD is crucial for moving in the power of the Spirit, but also why moving in the Spirit will cause someone to be in the fear of the LORD. They feed each other. In Exodus 1 the children of Israel are in Egypt after Jacob and his twelve sons have died, but the descendants of Jacob are now in Egypt in bondage as it was prophesied to Abraham in Genesis 15. Long story short, the children of Israel become so strong and numerous that Pharaoh becomes intimidated (Exodus 1:7-10), and Pharaoh says that due to how strong and numerous they have become, if the children of Israel went to war with Egypt, they would win and leave the land. He was afraid that the children of Israel would realize this, so in order distract them, he commands physical burdens to come upon them. I won't go into this revelation here specifically in this chapter, but this is actually a picture of the evil one seeing how mighty someone is in the Spirit of God, and then attacks their life physically in order to distract them. In other words, the evil one knows the mighty ones in the Spirit by name as the demons in Acts 19:15, saying, they knew Jesus and Paul due to how mighty they were in the Spirit. Some people become known in the spirit realm, and even feared, because they are powerhouses in the Holy Spirit.

However, due to all of this, Pharaoh goes to two of the Hebrew midwives, Shifrah and Puah (Exodus 1:15). Shifrah is actually Jochebed (Moses' mom) and Puah is Miriam (Moses' sister), which is not only understood through rabbinic literature, but is quite obvious when you study the passages carefully in Exodus 1-2. Pharaoh tells them in Exodus 1:16-17:

> "And he (Pharaoh) said, 'when you are midwifing the Hebrew women, and you see upon the birth stones that it be a son, you shall kill it, but if it is a daughter, you shall keep it alive.' The midwives feared God, and they

did not do as the king of Egypt spoke to them, and they saved the children."

When I read this, it hit me very deeply. The fear of the LORD is not something that is spoken of enough, and I don't think its purpose is actually even very well known, which by the end of this chapter, I believe you will view it completely different than ever before. I have even heard it, over and over again, that the fear of the LORD isn't for today. As I mentioned, the fear of the LORD is one of the seven Spirits of God (Isaiah 11:1-3), which are also spoken of again in Revelation 4:5. So, notice, the midwives didn't listen to Pharaoh, BECAUSE they feared God. Whom you fear, you obey. Then Exodus 1:21 is key, "and because the midwives feared God, He made houses for them (וַיְהִי כִּי־יָרְאוּ הַמְיַלְּדֹת אֶת־הָאֱלֹהִים וַיַּעַשׂ לָהֶם בָּתִּים)." The Scripture says "because (כִּי)" they feared God, He made them houses. The blessing was BECAUSE of their fear of the LORD, because their fear of the LORD brought obedience to Him, and not to man. Psalms 34:8 says, "the angel of the LORD encamps around those who fear Him and delivers them," and Psalms 25:14 "the secret of the LORD is to those who fear Him, and His covenant He makes known to them."

These midwives didn't just ignore someone at the gas station or a random comment on their Facebook, but rather the Pharaoh, the king of Egypt who may or may not kill them for their actions. The fear of the LORD shows no bounds or favoritism of man but sees only the King of kings who sits upon the Throne. Proverbs 29:25 says, "the fear of man brings a snare, but one who trusts in the LORD will be exalted." Jesus, the Messiah Himself, says in Matthew 10:28 "do not fear those who can kill the body, but they are not able to kill the soul, but rather fear Whom is able to destroy the soul and body in hell." Jesus says to fear God, and the fear of the LORD is literally found all throughout the New Testament. John 9:31 says "we know that God does not hear the voice of sinners, but rather He hears those who fear Him and do His will." In English Bibles, this verse may read "He hears those who worship Him," however, the Hebrew and Aramaic, as well as a Hebrew manuscript translated from the Greek clarifies and says, "those who fear Him." The term "worship" is very vague. Acts 10:34-35 also says, "and Simon (Peter) opened his mouth and said, 'in truth I perceive that God does not show favoritism, but among all people, he who fears Him and works righteousness is acceptable to Him.'"

As I was studying one day, there was a verse in 2 Timothy that really spoke to me on this topic that I ended up sharing with my leaders as follows:

"2 Timothy 3:5 says, 'having a form of godliness but denying its power. And from such people turn away!'

This is the NKJV translation of this verse, and is unfortunately, very vague with very little impact due to that, in my opinion. What is godliness? What does it mean denying its power? We need to know because Paul says we need to flee from these individuals. Does this mean people that portray godliness but deny the gifts and power of the spirit? See, it's very vague. It's a prophecy about times we are living in now and couldn't be more relevant. In the Aramaic Peshitta Manuscript and Hebrew Text, this verse is as clear as day. The verse should read, 'who have for themselves an agreement/form of the fear of God, but they are far from its power. Of these, reject them from you.' People will have a robe, or profession that they fear God, but they are really far from the fruits of the power of the fear of God. Fear of God is not professed by lips, but by very visible fruit in their actions and the way they speak, not what they speak. Jeremiah 32:40, Exodus 20:17-21, Proverbs 16:6, Matthew 10:28-31 etc., show us that the fear of God turns us from sin. It makes sin very uncomfortable, and it purges out even the THOUGHT of rebellion or pride. Fear of God makes sin impossible to live with. Those who profess it, but they are far from its power is something we can see in their lives, as they have no fear of when slandering, tale bearing, talking of future plans with pride (James 4:13-16), etc. Many people have a fear of man cloaked in the fear of God. They don't fear God, but they fear a person, church, or institution, because they have been brought into thinking if they stand against it, it will be them rebelling against God. Or thinking apart from a person, church, or institution, how will they get to their 'calling.' This is idolatry. It's a compromise of our convictions and it is falling into the fear of man, which brings a snare. This is where people have now been our conduit to God, rather than us being intimate with God Himself. This verse in 2 Timothy 3:5 is crucial in leadership. I have seen many "godly" people, but I've watched what really takes place. These are they. Never judge with favoritism (Deuteronomy 16:19, Romans 2:11, Galatians 2:6, Ephesians 6:9, Colossians 3:25, 1 Timothy 5:21) based off your nearness to someone or their words, but by their fruits you will know them. Do all things in the fear of the LORD, a reverence that doesn't seek to please man on any lines, but Him alone (Galatians 1:10, 1 Thessalonians 2:4).

Out of the seven Spirits of God, it is the fear of the LORD that Isaiah 33:6 says is God's "treasure." Wisdom, understanding, and knowledge are likened to gold and silver (Proverbs 3:13-14), but the fear of the LORD is His treasure. He who fears man obeys man, but he who fears God obeys God. I have personally, with my own ears and eyes, seen many people who simply fear man and deceive themselves. I have literally had someone tell me that they know they are being disobedient to God, but they are afraid to be obedient because of the fear of a certain person or people or what will happen. The fear of man is a deadly chain that many fall under today, even those who don't think they do, but really, in one way or another, they fear man. They are afraid of what people will think of them, or afraid to walk alone, afraid to be made fun of, lose friends, family, or even be removed from their church or synagogue. Personally, I would be willing to lose any job or relationship when it comes to radical obedience to the Holy Spirit, and not only would I be willing, but I have multiple times. John 9 and John 12 tell us of people who were afraid to speak up because they would be kicked out or ostracized, and assuredly I tell you, there is nothing new under the sun (Ecclesiastes 1:9-10), for the same thing is happening today, not over there, but near and dear to all of us.

Personally, I do not know anyone who continually lives in the Holy Spirit and can also live in rebellion against God or tolerate sin in their lives. I do know people who have been baptized in the Holy Spirit, but they have left the things of the Spirit for the doctrines of men, or, like Demas, "for the love this present world (Colossians 4:14, 2 Timothy 4:10)." Jeremiah 32:40 says, "I will make an eternal covenant for them, where I will not turn away from them to do them good, and I will place My fear in their hearts in order to not turn away from Me." Proverbs 16:6 says, "by the fear of the LORD, depart from evil." Solomon, in all of his great wisdom sums up life on earth and his entire book of Ecclesiastes by saying in Ecclesiastes 12:13 "the end of the matter of all that is heard is to fear God and keep His commandments. This is all of man."

The fear of the LORD prepares us to be vessels that can receive things from Him, because He knows that what we receive will be used with fear and trembling for His glory, and not squandered. Why would God give something to anyone who fears man? If God gives you any authority, and you fear man, now all that was given to you is not subject to God, but rather submitted to the man you fear. If God wanted them to have that authority, he would just give it to them. When we serve God, it doesn't matter what he or she has to say, but rather, what does God have to say, as Paul said in Galatians 1:15-17:

> "But when He willed it, He who set me apart from the womb and from my mother, called me to His grace, in order to reveal the manifestation of His Son that I preached to the nations, I did not explain this to flesh and blood. Nor did I even go to Jerusalem to the apostles who were there before me, but instead, I went to Arabia and then returned to Damascus."

Paul didn't submit his revelations nor his calling to flesh and blood approval. The fear of the LORD prepares the soil to receive the seeds of wisdom. Peter says before the leaders of the day, with all boldness, in Acts 4:19-20:

> "Simon Peter and John answered and said to them, 'if it is right before God that we obey you more than God, you judge. For we are not able to not speak about that which we have seen and heard.'"

Paul says in Galatians 1:10 "do I persuade men or God? Do I seek to please the sons of men? If so, I should not be a servant of Messiah." The two midwives, Shifrah and Puah in Exodus 1 feared God at all costs, even if they had to lose their lives, and God entrusted them with great blessing because of it. God built them houses and thought "they are worthy of My blessing, and if I build them houses, they will use those houses to bring people in and teach them My ways." Out of our love for the LORD, we fear doing anything that is displeasing to Him, and anything that can hinder intimacy with Him and grieve the Holy Spirit (Ephesians 4:30, 1 Thessalonians 5:19).

What I really want to dive into is the fear of the LORD as it is related to the promise land, Pentecost, and the baptism of the Holy Spirit and fire, because as we will see, we can't even get to the promise land without the fear of the LORD, and if we get there without it, we can't abide in it without the fear of the LORD. In Exodus 20, which is the day of Pentecost when the Torah was given, and just as on Pentecost Torah was given on Tablets of Stone, so too, in Acts 2 the Torah was written on the Tablet of our heart (Jeremiah 31:31-34, Ezekiel 36:26-27, Hebrews 10:16). Nothing is new under the sun. It is important to see Pentecost and the baptism of the Holy Spirit through Exodus 20 lenses, as we saw in Chapter 1 on the baptism of the Holy Spirit, because it sets the framework for Pentecost in Acts 2. In Exodus 20 on Pentecost, God is coming to give Torah, but before He gives them the Tablets, God speaks the Ten Words on the Tablets of Stone out loud for all of Israel to hear His voice. Because of this, and due to the great and fearful scene of Sinai at that time, the people are in great fear, for it is a fearful thing to fall into the hands of the Living God (Hebrews 10:31).

Notice, the Torah is wisdom, but before God gives them all of Torah wisdom, He speaks to them out loud, and notice what happens on Pentecost as He speaks. Exodus 20:15-17:

"And all the people saw the voices, and the torches, and the voice of the shofar, and the mountain was smoking, and the people feared, and trembled, and stood afar off. And they said to Moses, 'you speak with us, and we will hear, but do not let God speak with us, lest we die.' And Moses said to the people, 'do not fear, for God has come in order to test you, and so that His fear will be upon your faces so that you will not sin."

The Hebrew tells us plainly, God came for two reasons: to test Israel and SO THAT His fear will be upon their faces so that they won't sin. God's encountering them on Pentecost is for the sake of bringing the fear of God upon and in someone, also, so they won't sin. Pentecost and the baptism of the Holy Spirit is an encounter that brings the fear of the LORD, so the baptism and the fear of the LORD cannot be separated, as I said earlier, the fear is the fruit of the baptism of the Holy Spirit and the Pentecost experience. Once again, the fear of the LORD is keeping one from sin. But my point is this, Pentecost had a purpose, and it is the fear of the LORD. God couldn't give them Torah, teaching, guidance, revelation, etc., until they first had the fear of Him. Now that they fear Him, the soil is prepared for the Farmer to plant the seeds of wisdom. Now that they fear Him, He has their attention, and their posture is "whatever He wants we will do it (Exodus 24:7). We are ready to walk in His ways. We don't want His wrath. We are ready to receive His instruction. He has our attention."

The fear of the LORD prepares you to receive the things of God with fear and trembling and extreme diligence. Why do we need this? Because we can't enter the promise land without receiving His wisdom and instruction. The children of Israel could not enter the promise land unless they received Torah and God's ways. The Torah tells us eight times just in Deuteronomy alone (Deuteronomy 4:26, 40, 5:33, 11:9, 17:20, 22:7, 30:18, 32:47) that the children of Israel will either be kicked out of the land or prolong their days based off of their obedience to Him and His Torah. One prepares their heart to be obedient through the fear of the LORD, but one learns how to be obedient by the instruction one receives after they have the fear of the LORD. The fear of the LORD makes you attentive to learn God's ways. The fear of the LORD causes us to steward God's blessings properly, otherwise, the land will vomit you out (Leviticus 18:28, 20:22, Revelation 3:16).

We need the wisdom, revelation, and discipleship first so that we can enter into our promise lands, but first we need the fear of the LORD on Pentecost through a deep encounter with God. When I got baptized in the Holy Spirit and the glory fell upon me and I was paralyzed from the neck down under the weightiness of the glory, I learned something that day. There is judgement in the glory (Leviticus 10:1-3). When you step into that encounter and into His Presence, there is judgement, responsibility, and great fear and trembling, as it is written in Luke 12:47-48:

> "And that servant who knows the will of his Master and does not prepare for Him according to His will, he will be beaten with many stripes. But he who does not know and does the thing that is worthy of stripes will be beaten with fewer stripes. For anyone who is given much, much is required from him, and to he whom they have committed much to him, much more they will require by his hand."

Many people have been walking in circles in the wilderness for years, and yet, they still have not come to Pentecost. You still have not received the proper discipleship and wisdom, and it is because you have no fear of God upon your face that is given at Pentecost as it was given to the children of Israel at Sinai. When one gets finances, how does one operate with finances? When one gets a wife, or husband, or kids, how does one steward these things? When one becomes a boss, king, or CEO, how does one steward this position? All of it is found in the Scriptures, but one will only run to them and dissect them with great fervency based upon their level of fear for Him, and that will determine how prepared their soil is and how much they care to be attentive to learning His ways, and walking as one with His Spirit. The spirit of the fear of the LORD is literally one of the seven spirits of God (Isaiah 11:1-12, Revelation 4:5), so when one gets baptized in the Holy Spirit, the fear of the LORD is part of the package deal. One must come to Pentecost, get baptized in the Holy Spirit, and be discipled, so that you can be equipped with the wisdom to steward His promises. Pentecost, the baptism of the Holy Spirit and fire, and the fear of the LORD are to take place simultaneously.

Solomon, and all of his wisdom, says in Ecclesiastes 7:11 "wisdom is good with an inheritance." What is he saying? He is talking about the first five books of the Bible, the Torah of Moses, this is the wisdom. The entire Torah talks about the inheritance being the promise land! Solomon says, "wisdom is good WITH an inheritance," meaning, you have to have the wisdom to know how to steward that promise land or inheritance. It is not good to have an inheritance with no wisdom, as this would be like a beautiful woman without understanding (Proverbs 11:22). Remember how in Exodus 20 God couldn't even give them the wisdom/Torah until they had His fear upon their faces? This is the meaning of Psalm 111:10 and Proverbs 9:10, which says, "the fear of the LORD is the beginning of wisdom." This is a direct reference to the Exodus 20 Pentecost narrative. One wants wisdom, but there is a prerequisite-the fear of the LORD (James 1:5). This is what the baptism of the Holy Spirit should be doing, and the continual walk of intimacy with the Spirit of God.

In 2 Kings 17, God drives out Israel from the land because of sexual immorality, idolatry, and murder, or in other words, not keeping His ways as He continually promised in the Torah of Prophecy/Moses (Exodus 34:10). But notice what happens after they get driven out, and the king of Assyria causes others to settle there. 2 Kings 17:22-28:

> "And the children of Israel followed all the sins of Jeroboam that he committed. They did not turn away from it until the LORD removed Israel from His Presence, as He had spoken through all His servants, the prophets, and Israel went into exile from their land to Assyria until this day. And the king of Assyria brought from Babylon and from Cutha and from Avva and from Hamath and from Sepharvaim, and he settled them in the cities of Samaria instead of the children of Israel, and they took possession of Samaria and dwelt in its cities. And it was in the beginning of their dwelling there, that they did not fear the LORD, and then the LORD incited lions against them, and they were killing them. And they said to the king of Assyria, saying, 'the nations that you exiled and settled in the cities of Samaria, do not know the law of the God of the land, and He has incited lions against them, and behold they are killing them, as they do not know the law of the God of the land.' And the king of Assyria commanded, saying, 'bring one of the priests there whom you have exiled from there, and they will go and dwell there, and teach them the law of the God of the land.' And one of the priests whom they had exiled from Samaria came and settled in Bethel, and he would teach them how they should fear the LORD."

Notice, due to disobedience, God drives out the children of Israel, and has others dwell there in their place. Then, Scripture says that "in the beginning of their dwelling there, that they did not fear the LORD" God incites lions. With no baptism and fear of the LORD, God will remove us quicker than we came in. The Scripture says that they did not fear God, and because of this, they didn't even care to learn God's ways. It wasn't until they had the fear of the LORD due to God bringing lions that they now care to learn His ways. His bringing lions is like God speaking personally to Israel at Sinai and them encountering such a fearful thing (Hebrews 10:31).

The fear of the LORD is the beginning of wisdom (Psalm 111:10, Proverbs 9:10), meaning, the fear of the LORD prepares the soil to be ready to receive the seeds of wisdom. No Pentecost/baptism of the Holy Spirit=no fear of the LORD=no wisdom=no inheritance/promise land. If you have not had the baptism, and yet you say there is a fear of the LORD in you, I would encourage you to really confront that, as it may or may not be the fear of man cloaked in the garment of the fear of the LORD. Also, if you say you have had the baptism, but you do not have the fear of the LORD, I will bet you never really got the baptism. The fear of the LORD is a by-product of the baptism of the Holy Spirit and fire. The fear of the LORD produces availability within us to receive the wisdom, so that we may properly dwell in the inheritance, as Solomon said in Ecclesiastes 7:11 "wisdom is good with an inheritance." All of this, the fear of the LORD and the wisdom comes on Pentecost through the baptism of the Holy Spirit and fire, and the continual immersion and intimacy with the Holy Spirit, which will, in turn, bring you into the promise land.

So not only on Pentecost and by the baptism of the Holy Spirit and fire do we receive an initial fear of the LORD, but how do we nurture this so that it increases daily? As I will show us, it is by reading the Word of God, and reading it apart from the doctrines of men. Don't read it through man's lenses which are usually in bondage to the chains of traditional theology, whether Jewish or Christian, but come as a clean slate with no preconceived thoughts, as a blank tablet for the Holy Spirit to write His Torah on. I know people that will read Torah and all of Scripture, and they will read a commentary on every single line. You are reading Scripture only according to what man has to say, rather than allowing Holy Spirit to saturate you. Having teachers and reading commentaries can be good, but God sees who depends on the Spirit and simply visits commentaries, rather than somebody who depends on commentaries and only visits the Holy Spirit. The Holy Spirit always comes first and will take you deeper, as it is written in Ezekiel 47:3-5:

> "When the man went out eastward with a cord in his hand, he measured one thousand cubits, and he led me through the water, waters reaching the ankles. And he measured one thousand and he led me through the water, water reaching the knees, and he measured one thousand, and he led me through waters that reached the loins. And he measured one thousand, a stream that I could not cross, for the water was so high, that it was water for swimming, a stream that could not be crossed."

Man will lead you to places of limitation, but when led by the Holy Spirit and Messiah Himself, you will walk upon the water of the great deep (Matthew 14:22-33). The commentaries and doctrines of man will fill you with the fear of man, because it will cause you to fear if you get a different interpretation by the Spirit. I have had the Spirit of God show me things that are directly against other pastors and rabbis, and when I prove my point with power, there is no rebuttal. The mouths of the lions are shut (Daniel 6, 2 Timothy 4:17). If I fear man or certain authorities,

I now submit to them over the Spirit of God. Always remain humble, remain teachable, but fear God.

As I said, the fear of the LORD will grow the more you study and hear the Word of God, as it is written in Deuteronomy 31:10-13:

> "And Moses commanded them, saying, 'at the end of seven years, in the appointed time, the year of the release (Sh'mittah), in the festival of Sukkot (feast of Tabernacles), when all Israel will come to appear before the LORD your God in the place that He will choose, you shall read this Torah before all Israel in their ears. Gather the people, the men, the women, the children, and your sojourner which is in your gates, so that they will hear, and so that they will learn, and they will fear the LORD your God, and they will be careful to do all of this Torah. And their children which do not know, they will hear, and they will learn to fear the LORD your God all the days that you live upon the land that you are crossing over the Jordan there to possess."

Moses says that by reading and hearing the Word of God, the fear of the LORD is imparted to us. Moses repeats the same things to the kings of Israel as they sit upon their throne, as it is written in Deuteronomy 17:18-20:

> "And it will be as he sits upon the throne of his kingdom, he shall write for himself upon a scroll a copy of this Torah from before the priests, the Levites. And it shall be with him, and he shall read it all the days of his life, so that he will learn to fear the LORD his God, to guard all the words of this Torah, and these statutes by doing

them, to not exalt his heart above his brethren, and to not turn aside from the commandment to the right or to the left, so that he will prolong the days upon his kingdom, he and his sons in the midst of Israel."

Once again, by reading Torah, fear is a by-product that gets instilled in you more and more, and this commandment is for us in the Messiah, not just physical kings of Israel, for we too are called "kings and priests to God" through Messiah (Revelation 1:6).

For myself, there is no way I can read the Torah of Moses, or the book of Revelation, Jesus' words (Matthew 7:21-23), or literally any of the Scriptures and see the powerful God we serve, as well as certain consequences of rebelling against Him (Leviticus 26/Deuteronomy 28), and not be filled with dread before Him. As Paul says in Hebrews 10:31, "it is a fearful thing to fall into the hands of the Living God." Not only that, the phrase in Deuteronomy 31:13 above, which says, "they will learn to fear the LORD your God (לְמְדוּ לְיִרְאָה אֶת־יְהוָה אֱלֹהֵיכֶם)," can actually be read as "they will learn IN ORDER to fear the LORD your God." The letter lamed (ל) that is prefixed to the word "fear (יִרְאָה!)" can be seen in Biblical Hebrew grammar as creating a "purpose clause," which is rather common with this prefix. So, regardless of how it is read, Deuteronomy says that the reading of Scripture and hearing it will increase the fear of the LORD, which will prepare our hearts to be in a student posture to want to learn, as it was with the children of Israel on Pentecost at Sinai, as the fear prepared them to be hungry for God's wisdom and His ways in order to not grieve Him/Holy Spirit (Ephesians 4:30, 1 Thessalonians 5:19). In fact, the LORD says this very thing again about the day of Pentecost from Exodus 20 in Deuteronomy 4:10:

"The day when you stood before the LORD your God in Horeb, when He said to me, 'gather the people to Me, and I will cause them to hear My Words which they will learn, in order to fear Me all the days that they are living upon the land, and they will teach their children.'"

There is no way we can truly study the Word of God without receiving the fear of Him. You will see how mighty He is, how righteous He is, the justice He requires, because it says in Psalms 89:15 and Psalms 97:2 that righteousness and justice are the foundation of His Throne. We read in Acts 5 about Ananias and Saphira, who both lie to the apostles about their finances, and the LORD slays them on the spot. As I said, there is judgement in the glory. How can one read these things and not tremble?

When one comes to Pentecost, and receives the fear of the LORD, your soil becomes so prepared, and the revelation and entrustment from God will begin to flow at a pace you never thought possible. Those who fear Him can be entrusted, as it says in Psalms 25:14, "the secret of the LORD is with those who fear Him." The fear of the LORD in and of itself is a purging fire, as the Holy Spirit and fire, removing sin from your life, setting you like a tree of fire, as it is written in Jeremiah 23:29 "is not My Word like a fire, and like a hammer that will shatter a rock?"

Once you have the fear of Him, and you are hungry to learn His ways, eventually, you will be brought into the promise land, and you will prolong your days within it. Only through the fear of God will He build our house, as He did with Shifrah and Puah in Exodus 1. Provisions come with the fear of the LORD, because they will be stewarded properly. Exaltation comes with the fear of the LORD, because one will stay humble. Honor comes with the fear of the LORD, because one will push the glory to God (John 17:1, Acts 12:20-23).

CHAPTER 7

Embracing The Spirit In Each Season

On January 27, 2023, a dear brother and sister of mine in the faith got married. At their wedding reception party, my friend who got married had a close friend of his in ministry come up to me and introduced himself. I had never met this man, but he had heard some things about me in regard to the prophetic anointing, of which I still do not know how. As he walked up, I was in conversation with some other ministry leaders, and one of his first words to me were, "Pastor Nick, it is very nice to meet you. I hear you are a prophet. What season is the body of Messiah currently in? What is God doing right now?" I told him:

> "I will tell you exactly where God has us. God showed me a dream where He placed His people in a pressure cooker, and its pressure would be used to sift the body of Messiah. He has shown me very clearly starting one week before the Covid mask mandate and quarantine in early 2020, one week before Passover in 2020, God brought the body of Messiah into a sifting season. Not only a sifting of the individual to cleanse their life, but also God is bringing a sifting and separation within congregations, business partners, and even with marriages as it was with Lot and his wife in Genesis 19. Lot kept chasing God in

the fiery trials, and his wife turned back to Sodom, which brought about a sifting or separation. God hates divorce, but He has allowed us to be in such a season that peoples choices are clearly made known, and they are not sitting on the fence anymore. It has been moment of gather or scatter, for or against (Matthew 12:30). Through His sifting, it has caused much pain emotionally, relationally, financially, and ministerially, but God in the midst of it all is truly equipping those who are going to be brought out in the next season for Him, and exposing those who are not really His in the long term. He is revealing the ones who simply go to a church or synagogue service, or use His Name, or have "God first" in their Instagram or Facebook bio's. This new season will begin after this year's Passover (2023), where He reveals Himself in a new way through His true apostles and prophets. Three years of sifting. That's what God is doing."

With that said, I want to talk about submitting to the work of the Holy Spirit in our lives, and the sifting and pruning that He has to do with us in order to receive the anointing, the power, the revelation, etc. Many people are trying to rush through seasons, but we can't rush through them. One shouldn't be focused on doing the work in order to get out of that season, but rather, allowing the Holy Spirit to have that season do a work within us. Rather than rush through the season, we have to embrace the season, and be pliable to the work the Holy Spirit is wanting to do within and around us, even when it is tough and uncomfortable.

We can choose to either go through the seasons as a sheep, or as a goat. On the farm, I learn a lot about Torah and the Holy Spirit. A sheep will go wherever it is told with no argument. It is pliable, but a goat is very stubborn. In fact, when we have to move the goats, if they are the older goats with long enough horns, I literally have to grab them by their horns and drag them to where they need to be, or if they are young goats with short horns that I can't grab, I have to pick them up and hold down their neck as they kick and scream in order to bring them where I need them to be. Don't kick and scream, and when you find yourself doing so, stop, pray, and submit to the LORD's sovereign work. Once again, every season is not for us to do work in order to get out of it, but it is to allow that season to do a work in us, to bear certain fruits through us, so then, at the LORD's appointed time, He can bring us out into the next one, as it is written in Ecclesiastes 3:1-8:

> "Everything has an appointed season, and there is a time for every matter under heaven. A time to give birth and a time to die, a time to plant, and a time to uproot that which is planted, a time to kill, and a time to heal, a time to break, and a time to build, a time to weep, and a time to laugh, a time of wailing, and a time of dancing, a time to cast stones, and a time to gather stones, a time to embrace, and a time to refrain from embracing, a time to seek, and a time to lose, a time to keep, and a time to cast away, a time to rend, and a time to sew, a time to be silent, and a time to speak, a time to love, and a time to hate, a time for war, and a time for peace."

I want to start discussing this concept of seasons and times from Leviticus 19, and how we can't rush them. As you can see by now, I truly love speaking on the Holy Spirit from the book of Leviticus. Isn't it interesting, the most neglected book in the Bible in Christianity is the same book that contains the most insight about what Christianity loves most (Holy Spirit)? Walking with God can be such a paradox. God loves putting diamonds in the rough. Leviticus 19:23-25:

> "And when you come to the land, and you plant any food tree, you shall consider its fruit uncircumcised for three years. It is uncircumcised to you; it shall not be eaten. But in the fourth year all of its fruit will be holy for rejoicing to the LORD. And in the fifth year you shall eat its fruit, in order to add its produce to you. I am the LORD your God."

The Hebrew text literally says that the fruit is "uncircumcised" for the first three years, however, what Scripture is really saying is that the fruit is just simply not ripe to be used or eaten yet. It is not bad fruit; it is good fruit that is just simply not ripe yet. Think about when you buy green bananas. They are good bananas, but they aren't ripe or as sweet, and won't provide as much value to the one eating them. There is a greater flavor or fullness that the fruit has to get to first before it can be used in a beneficial way for the public. In the fourth year one can use the fruit from the tree ONLY in praises to God, meaning, for the three festivals of Exodus 23:14-16 and Deuteronomy 16:16 (Passover, Pentecost, Tabernacles). But in the fifth year, you can use this fruit for your own increase, and others. Notice, there are set times by God. Three years of no eating, the fourth year eating only during the three festivals, and in the fifth year you can have it for your own increase.

One thing we have to understand about Torah, is every Scripture is for us, and about us, and about Messiah. When we talk about cattle, we aren't really talking about cattle, as Paul states very clearly in 1 Corinthians 9:8-11 about ministers living from their work in the Gospel:

"Is it as a man I say these things? Behold, Torah also says the same, for it is written in the Torah of Moses 'do not muzzle an ox while it threshes." Does God have regard for oxen? But it is revealed to us for whose sake He said it, and indeed, for our sakes it was written, because the farmer should plough in hope, and the thresher in hope of fruit. If we have sown among you the things of the Spirit, is it a great matter if we reap from you the things of the body?"

Cattle always has to do with disciples and people. God used the oxen or cattle in Torah simply as a parable for us in practical daily life, but we have to read Torah by the Holy Spirit. The same goes for trees, which is why in Mark 8:22-24, Jesus heals a man that is blind and before the man sees physically, he tells Jesus, "I see people like trees walking," which as you may remember from the foreword of this book, is actually where my heavenly vision came from for Trees Of Fire is that very story in April of 2022 on Shiloh farm in Chelsea, Iowa. That story was showing us how Jesus sees us in the Spirit. We are all trees that either bear good fruit or bad fruit, as it is written in Luke 6:43-45:

"There is not a good tree which produces bad fruit. There is also no bad tree which produces good fruit. For every tree is known by its fruit. For they do not gather thorns from figs, nor do they gather grapes from a thorn bush. From a good man the treasures that are in his good heart brings forth good things, and an evil man the evil treasures that are in his heart brings forth evil things. For from the abundance of the heart does the mouth speak."

Contrary to the translations, Deuteronomy 20:19 literally says "for man is the tree of the field (כִּי הָאָדָם עֵץ הַשָּׂדֶה)." So then, this Leviticus 19 passage about the tree within its first three years, fourth year, and fifth year, is actually talking about people, ministries, businesses, callings, etc. The Torah is actually telling us that when you plant a tree IN the Promise Land, meaning, when you come into the Messiah and at whatever point you start to step into your calling, the fruit you bear for the first three years is not bad fruit, it's just not ripe yet to be beneficial for others. There is still great pruning, ripening, refining of oneself, theology, vision, etc. needing to be had. In the fourth year you will start to get glimpses of the fruit being used, especially as it pertains to the appointed times, such as Passover, Pentecost, and Sukkot/Tabernacles, and then in the fifth year you will start to see doors open up, because whatever it is that you are producing has gotten to a point that it will edify the body.

For example, in October of 2022 I had begun my fifth year in ministry. I was ordained and began my ministry Revelation Church October 28, 2018, but it wasn't until the following year that I got a revelation of Torah by the Holy Spirit and began learning Hebrew. For the first three years, God kept me and my revelations of Torah and Hebrew very contained. I wasn't doing any guest speaking hardly, broadcasts, raising up leaders and teachers, but was speaking to a small body of believers in my parents' home every single week. But in the fourth year God started bringing me upon other ministries broadcasts that reached about sixty different countries and brought me into some other ministries as a guest speaker, but rarely, and actually, it would be for the appointed times, such as Passover. But in the fifth year, the LORD started bringing pastors, evangelists, and teachers of other churches underneath our ministry as an apostolic ministry. I started getting invited to teach doctor's and church leaders at seminaries, and more and more doors began to open in every way, including financially. In fact, the fifth year is when this book was written.

It is important to notice about the tree described in Leviticus 19 that there is a set time for all of it-three years, then the fourth, then the fifth. One couldn't rush those three years. You can't water the tree more, and give it more sunlight, and speed up the process. The Holy Spirit has to do a work in our life that continually transforms us in that season more and more, but us trying to do more work, or work faster in order to rush it is manipulation and control, which is a form of witchcraft. Rushing through school won't cause your next season to open up quicker. It is not about rushing through the school, but rather allowing the information from that school to transform you. Head knowledge is not fruit bearing and transformation. When one becomes pregnant with a seed of wisdom, you can't rush the pregnancy of understanding to produce the childbearing revelation. There is a set time for these things. We can't rush the seasons in our lives that the Holy Spirit has us in, but we can delay them. If God has us in a given season, it is because God has a certain fruit of the Spirit (Galatians 5:22-23) or understanding that He is wanting us to be pregnant with. Pregnancy, if rushed, will only cause pain and detriment, or even death, God forbid. The baby isn't "ripe" yet to be given into the world. There is still development to be had.

During my third year in ministry, I remember there were two things specifically that I said, "if I can just finish these two things, the next doors will open, and we will enter into these promises." I did every ounce of work I possibly could, and all that it brought was stress and heartache, but during that four month sabbatical in 2022 I mentioned earlier in this book, God downloaded these revelations into me as well, showing me that there was no work I was going to be able to do to rush the process of ripening the fruit of a tree. If God said it will take three years, it will take three years, or maybe ten years, or twenty. God decided in Genesis 15 that it would take 430 years until the Exodus for the children of Israel. The three years doesn't need to be taken so literally. It took Abraham decades before he had Isaac. It took Joseph 22 years before he saw his dreams from Genesis 37 realized. A rabbi once told me a famous story:

> "Nick, there was a story about a man that wanted to study so much that he asked his teacher, 'how long will it take me to get to that calling if I study for four hours a day?' The teacher said, 'if you study for four hours a day, it will take five years.' So then, the student asks his teacher, 'what if I study ten hours a day?' The teacher answers him, and says, 'seven years.' The student was puzzled. The teacher explains, 'you can't rush the process. It is not about receiving more seed, but rather producing its fruit, which is a process that cannot be rushed.'"

Our job is not to rush the process, but to be diligent within the process. With our diligence there is a set time. Here is the thing, you must continually remain diligent and water the tree, and give it sunlight and proper airflow, while also weeding and fertilizing around it. In Iowa, I work in a garden, and with the garden you have to water it every day and continually weed around it, as well as putting things into the soil, or the holy, fruit bearing roots will dry up, be choked out, and die. I had to remain diligent. The time it took to get the harvest was only if I was diligent, as it is written in Galatians 6:9 "and let us not be weary now that we are working for good, for in the season of reaping, because if we do not grow weary, we will reap." If I was to stop being diligent and the plant or tree dies, I can't pick up where I left off. I now have to re-start the entire process, which is why I said, we can't rush the process, but we can delay it. That promise of time is only if one is diligent in the first place. So too, you won't get through your seasons by going through them passively, one has to be diligent, while recognizing that diligence doesn't rush it either. But diligence and staying on course is better than causing it to die, and then re-starting again and again, delaying the promise of the fruit.

For me personally, during those years and sabbatical that the LORD had me hidden in the Ark of Noah, I was continually studying Scripture and in prayer. I continually stored up wisdom, understanding, and revelation for the day I would need to pour it out to the hungry as Joseph stored up grain in the cities of Egypt for when the world became hungry. Day after day, night after night I was, and still am devoted to reading, praying, and teaching, as Paul told Timothy in 1 Timothy 4:13 "until I come, be diligent in reading, and prayer, and teaching." If I had been lazy, watching TV all day, not deeply rooted in study, etc., the LORD would have never been able to bring me out into anything because I would have no fruit or revelation to give. I wouldn't have been as equipped as I would have been had I been diligent. The Spirit of Messiah is a Spirit of diligence. We must be a diligent tree in those seasons, or the diligent farmer, as it is written in James 5:7 "but my brothers, be patient until the coming of the LORD, like the farmer who waits for the precious fruits of his ground and is patient as to them until he receives the early and the latter rain," without deceiving ourselves into a thought process of speeding things up. We need to truly receive the revelation that comes through the word "embrace." Embrace the moment, embrace the season, and embrace the work of the Holy Spirit.

I have taught before on the importance of diligence. In Numbers 17 the children of Israel rebel against Moses and Aaron, and God was going to show who He has truly chosen. Moses gathers one rod from every tribe, including the tribe of Levi, which had Aaron's name written on it, and which ever staff bore fruit, that was whom God had chosen. Not only did Aaron's rod bud, revealing that He was chosen by God, but

TREES OF FIRE

it budded almonds (שְׁקֵדִים) specifically. In Hebrew, the word "almond (שָׁקֵד)," pronounced "shakeid" is the same exact word for "diligent/studious (שָׁקַד)," pronounced "shakad." By definition, a shakdan (שַׁקְדָן) is a diligent person or scrupulous student. God chose Aaron because of his diligence and persistence to the LORD.

Diligence, which is the same word as "almond," actually creates an illusion of speed or swiftness, as it is written in Jeremiah 1:11-12 "and the word of the LORD came to me, saying, 'what do you see, Jeremiah?' And I said, 'I see an almond (שָׁקֵד) rod' And the LORD said to me, 'you see well, for I am hastening (שֹׁקֵד) to do My word.'" The word for "hastening" is not only the same as almond, but it really means "diligent" or "eager," however, due to that, it is generally interpreted as "hastening" in this context, because it is giving off this connotation. So many times, we want to speed up our seasons, but what we don't realize is diligence breeds swiftness. Why do I say this? Proverbs 22:29 says "do you see a man quick in his work? He will stand before kings, and he won't stand before ignorant men." This man who is quick in his work, it is not that he rushes through things, but rather that he is diligent in his work in any given season. He stays in his lane, as it is written in Proverbs 27:8 "as a bird wanders from its nest, so is a man who wanders from his place." Be diligent in your season, and rather than rush, evaluate, in order to see what fruit God is trying to bear within you.

An example I use for finding a person "quick" in his work, as Proverbs 22:29 above says is actually the story of how I learned Biblical Hebrew. I began learning Hebrew in July of 2019. People, including orthodox rabbis, have literally been blown away with how quickly I learned and mastered Biblical Hebrew. In 2022 I was at an orthodox deli in Des Moines, Iowa. As I walked in, I began speaking with the rabbi and his wife in Hebrew from the Scriptures and they both asked, "we have studied Hebrew our whole lives, and are still learning. The language is so tough. How did you only start in 2019 and know what you know?"

The truth is it doesn't have to do with me having superpowers. God is no respecter of persons (Deuteronomy 16:19, Acts 10:34, Romans 2:11, Galatians 2:6, Ephesians 6:9, 1 Timothy 5:21). God doesn't favor me over others. Not many know this story, but when I started learning Hebrew, I was diligent with it daily. Some days were so tough that I wanted to quit. I had great days, as well as terrible days. As I was going through Izzy Avraham's *Holy Language Institute* in order to learn Biblical Hebrew, at first, I was diligent, spending about 60-90 mins a day in class learning the letters, vowel markings, and some other aspects of Biblical Hebrew grammar in order to enable me to start sounding out words and verses.

After I had set a foundation for about 4-8 weeks, there was a Jewish woman, who is a believer in the Messiah, and she lived in Florida at the time while I was in Houston, Texas. She took me under her wing while I got on my feet with Hebrew and told me, "Nick, if you will study for ten minutes every day, practicing reading the Scriptures in Hebrew, not fifteen minutes, and not five, but just ten minutes a day, you will be amazed at the results." She told me, "every day I want you to call me, and over the phone we will begin in Genesis 1:1. You will read Hebrew and I will oversee you, correcting you as needed." The first couple days, I didn't even get through one verse in ten minutes. In Hebrew, it isn't just about knowing the letters, but all of the vowel markers as well. It can be overwhelming at first.

For example, the very first word in the Bible is "in the beginning (בְּרֵאשִׁית)," which is pronounced, "b'rei'sheet," and I may have said "b'ro'sheet," and so we would stop, she would correct me and tell me, "look harder at that second vowel." I would correct it, and then we would keep moving. This happened every single day for ten minutes. On my own I would study and focus on the letters and vowels even more, but with her I would read. A few days go by, and now I was able to get through an entire verse, or a few verses in one day. Weeks go by, and now I am reading paragraphs fluently, and she finally says after a few weeks, "Nick, you don't need to call me tomorrow." Within a few months I began a weekly YouTube teaching called "Ta'alumot B'Ivrit (Secrets In Hebrew)," and the LORD began coming to me in dreams, revealing things to me from the Hebrew Scriptures, and speaking to me in ways that would only be understood if one was reading in Hebrew or Aramaic. As time went on, now my entire Bible from Genesis to Revelation is in Hebrew and Aramaic.

In 2021 I was already reading from the Hebrew Bible better than just about anyone around me, including rabbis, but I was not yet a "Hebrew scholar." I remember one time towards the end of 2021, another individual and I were sitting before a rabbi whose first language is Hebrew, and the rabbi told me in front of the other individual "Nick, you know Hebrew very well, but you are not a Hebrew scholar." My competitive nature rose up, and I told the other individual, "he just made a big mistake." From that point on, every day, I spent hours a day, starting in Chapter 1 of the Biblical Hebrew Grammar books, and within nine months I mastered and memorized the 35 chapters of Biblical Hebrew Grammar. I was never going to allow anyone to tell me such a thing again, especially with something I was so passionate about. I was diligent and focused.

A couple years later, all people saw was my successes, and would make ignorant comments such as "you are so lucky you learned Hebrew so fast." No, I am not lucky. I am diligent. They don't know the days I was in tears, frustrated before God, and almost quit. Every day I put in the work. I then read through Genesis, then Exodus, then the entire Torah over and over again, and Jonah, Esther, certain Psalms, Matthew,

Mark, Luke, John, Acts, 1 John, 2 John, 3 John, James, etc. One step and day of diligence at a time. Many days, just doing ten verses a day, but over a few years, that added up. It seemed like three years was quick, but I didn't rush, I was just diligent, and my diligence gave off the illusion of speed.

I am still a student of Hebrew and Aramaic, because my goal is also that when I have kids, I will teach them Hebrew and Aramaic as babies just as they learn English, and God willing, they will never have to touch an English Bible in their lives, because in the original Hebrew and Aramaic will be how they learn to read the Scriptures. In fact, I still have the very first Tanach (Hebrew Bible) that I ever used as a beginner still in its original box, and with God's help, it will be given to my firstborn son as an inheritance and a legacy that is passed down for generations. I am sowing now for the fruit of the children I don't even have yet. One man plants a tree, but its fruit is not there until the next generation. The Spirit of God desires diligence in each season. The Holy Spirit will do a work in you day by day, and eventually, you will walk into the anointing, and you will see the fruit for which you had been laboring.

I have recognized my place (Proverbs 27:8) in the body of Messiah for years now, and I have been diligent in the garden of Eden that God has called me to labor in (Genesis 2:15). I have studied the apostolic anointing from every place in the Scriptures in rigorous details, beginning back in Genesis. I have studied the prophetic anointing, and the anointing in general in great detail, as you have probably seen, but will continue to see throughout this book. I have remained diligent in learning about the Spirit of Messiah, Hebrew, etc. behind closed doors in the secret place that nobody sees, rather, they only see the fruit of it all.

The same thing in my life has happened with fitness and nutrition. When I competed for Mr. Texas at 22 years old and placed top five, people were amazed at my progress in three years and how I got their so quickly. I went from starting out as a men's physique competitor at the age of 19, to being a top heavyweight bodybuilder in the state of Texas by the age of 22. They also never saw the diligence. Each day, I never missed a meal, a workout, a vitamin, a supplement, a cardio session, and I sacrificed everything, day in and day out. Over time, my diligence gave off the illusion of speed. Proverbs 22:29 "do you see a man quick in his work? He will stand before kings, and he won't stand before ignorant men." His speed was a reflection of his diligence in a given area of his life. Our job is not necessarily to do the work in order to get out of that season, but rather to allow the Holy Spirit in that season to do a work within us through the circumstances of that season.

We will notice that in certain seasons the Holy Spirit will continually put us in the same circumstances, no matter where we go or who we are around, every few days or weeks we will feel a certain way or see a certain thing that is on repeat like a broken record. This is because God has us in a season where we are needing that circumstance to prune us to bear a certain fruit or rectify a certain character trait or habit, and when we team up with Holy Spirit submissively, diligently, and faithfully, there will be a set time that God has for that circumstance to perfect a certain attribute within us that causes us to be conformed more and more into the image of the Son of God (Romans 8:29). We will see in a later chapter how we are to yield to that circumstance in a given season, and how to hear the voice of the Holy Spirit within these seasons and circumstances, because that circumstance is the work of the Spirit of God, and actually the voice of God. Our ability to submit to the season, as we will discuss in Chapter 8, will enable us to receive the anointing to walk in the authority and power of the Holy Spirit as we will discuss in Chapter 9.

To sum up the matter, as the tree in Leviticus 19, you have to be diligent in the work that God is giving you in each season, but it is the perspective of your circumstance or season that must change, so that we don't try to do work that rushes us into the next season, and we run through each season blindly to everything else around us. It is not your work that is going to get you out of that season, because works are done on the outside, but really, the Holy Spirit is trying to do work on the inside. Don't focus on doing works to get out of the season, but focus on allowing the work of the Spirit in that season to get into you, so that in the appointed time, you will be naturally bearing the circumcised fruit, and your gifting can feed the world and edify the body of Messiah, as it is written in Proverbs 18:16 "a man's gift will make room for him, and will place him before great men." God forbid that we live every season of our lives rushing, looking continually at the ends of the earth, as it is written in Proverbs 17:24 "wisdom is before the man of understanding, but the eyes of a fool are on the end of the earth," so too, are a fool's eyes continually on the next season. I can only share this now because I have done this so much in my life. A life lived that way would look back twenty, thirty, forty, fifty plus years later, and realize they have lived a rushed life, and never embraced each season with joy, love, and peace. I didn't get this revelation until I turned almost 29, but most don't get this until they are at the end of their days, and some never get it at all.

Be encouraged with this insight. The next season isn't your responsibility, diligence in your current season is, and embracing the work of the Holy Spirit. God will get you into your next season, and He will open and close the right doors at the right time. As a tree, you can't rush your time. With your diligence, there is an appointed time set by God, just as the tree had a set time in Leviticus 19. Remember, with the tree in its first three years, if the farmer quits taking care of it after 2.5 years, the tree will die, and he can't pick back up where he left off, but now he has to start all over with planting. Don't quit, for you will reap in due time if you do not lose hope (Galatians 6:9). As we will see in the next two chapters, the calling can be instant, but receiving the anointing for that calling takes time, for many are called, but few are chosen (Matthew 20:16). That season is meant to prune you into a fruit bearing Tree Of Fire. Team up with the Holy Spirit in this season and ask for His perspective.

CHAPTER 8

Biblical Meekness And The Voice Of God

Before we get into how to receive a greater anointing in the next chapter and its practicalities in the last couple chapters, and true entrustment of the things of the Holy Spirit, which will be a furthered progression of Chapter 5, I want to discuss what I think may be the most precious thing we can experience in our walk-the voice of God. You will notice that I named the chapter "Biblical Meekness And The Voice Of God," and the reason is because when we understand these two concepts, we will realize the former prepares us for the latter, and actually, they become one and the same.

The end of 2021, all of 2022, and much of 2023, the LORD was teaching me so much about meekness. One of the things I had to learn was, one cannot become obedient, until they are placed in a situation that allows them to be disobedient, as it is written in Deuteronomy 30:15-20:

> "Behold, I have placed before you today life and good, and death and evil, in as much as I command you this day to love the LORD your God, to walk in His ways, to observe His commandments, so that you will live and increase, and the LORD your God will bless you in the land which you are coming to possess. But if your heart

deviates and you do not listen, and you will be drawn astray, and you will prostrate yourself to other gods and serve them, I declare to you this day that you will surely perish, and that you will not live long days on the land to which you are crossing the Jordan, in order to come there to possess it. This day I call upon the heavens and the earth to witness against you, I have set before you life and death, the blessing and the curse. You shall choose life so that you and your offspring will live, to love the LORD your God, to listen to His voice, and to cleave to Him, for He is your life, and the length of your days, in order to dwell upon the land, which the LORD your God swore to Abraham, to Isaac, and to Jacob in order to give them."

God places before us good and evil, right and wrong, because one cannot be obedient if you don't have the choice to not be obedient. One can't not eat from the Tree of Knowledge of Good and Evil until they are given a chance or test to eat it. One can't not commit adultery, until they have an opportunity to commit adultery, and one can't become meek, unless they are put in situations that give you the choice of being meek or not. God continually placed me in situations where I knew meekness was the goal of the season. This work continues, as meekness is such a revelation of Jesus, as it is written in Matthew 5:5 "blessed are the meek, for they will inherit the earth."

It is important to note that I said meekness, and not humility. Although humility is important, the two are completely different concepts Biblically. First, we have to ask ourselves what is the Biblical definition of meekness? I have taught many times that we have to find Biblical definitions. One could go to Merriam Webster or some other route and get the definition of meekness, and it's not that it is far off from the Biblical definition of the word, but it doesn't necessary encapsulate the identity of the word. Too many times we can allow earthly or worldly wisdom to saturate our understanding of a Biblical concept. But really, the wisdom of the world is foolishness with God (1 Corinthians 3:18-19). Generally speaking, when looking for a Biblical definition of a word, it won't be found in one sentence, but rather in a greater context, while recognizing its juxtaposition, and the different ways that it is used throughout the Scripture, especially as it is seen in the original Hebrew language. I have an in depth teaching on Biblical Compassion, not worldly compassion, but what the Biblical definition is. I always bring Biblical understanding of a word or phrase, in hopes that we can become transformed by the renewing of our minds (Romans 12:2, Ephesians 4:23).

With Biblical meekness, we will first start to approach this from a horizontal perspective between man and fellow man, but then we will start to tie it in between us and God, and then realize, they too, are actually one and the same, and through this, you will see how it is one of the best ways to hear the voice of God and discerning the voice of God. I want to say, I thank God so, so much, that ever since I came to Him in 2017, I have had a very strong discernment and ability to hear the voice of God. I have heard His voice very well, and although its needing continual improvement, this is simply something, by His grace, that has been very fruitful and evident to all around me. This has happened through dreams and open eyed visions, as many know, I dream almost every night, and when I go to Him in prayer, many times, He will visit me the same night to answer me in a dream. Or maybe through His Word as I study and the Holy Spirit will quicken that Word I read, in order to let me know it's Him speaking in a given moment for a certain circumstance. Or just walking and living daily life and hearing Him in the moment, whether it be at the gym, the airport, the grocery store, etc.

People around me have recognized this very clearly and have continually asked me how to hear the voice of God better. I have been told over and over, "Nick, be thankful, because I don't hear God like that or get dreams." For years this has been somewhat difficult to answer on how to hear Him better.

In some ways I have given helpful insight, but not to the extent that I have desired, nor do I think to the extent of what others are wanting. Now, I do understand that there are apostles and prophets who will hear the voice of God clearer, or a little more frequently than others, and in some contexts that will reach a more public eye due to the roll of those positions, however, God desires to speak to every believer, as we discussed earlier in this book. Although it may look different in practicality, the voice of God, to differing degrees, is for everyone, and that intimate relationship and two way street is for everyone, while still respecting the office of prophets and the heavy prophetic anointing. I tell people, "God wants to speak to you, and you need to hear His voice."

Part of my internal struggle has been, "Father, how do I teach them to hear Your voice?" I have longed continually to see everyone in my life hear His voice. Nehemiah 2:12 says God spoke to Nehemiah in his heart, just as Psalm 37:4 says that if you delight in Him, He will start to place His desires into your heart, and this is one of the many ways God speaks to us, and I might even say the most common way He can and does speak to every believer whether they realize it or not. I cannot tell you how many times God has spoken to me through my father, and my father has no idea. My dad has been baptized in the Holy Spirit and is with the LORD every morning in study and in prayer, and my dad will be guided by Him with His desires, and because my father walks so closely with God, he doesn't realize he is constantly hearing God. But that's the great thing about sonship, God's voice doesn't come as a separate thing all the time, but rather we become fluent with it, step and step together (Genesis 22:6/8) without realizing we are literally being manifestations of His Spirit.

There are so many different ways that God speaks, and the more I have walked with God, the more I have been able to share, especially through the concept of two or three witnesses as it is written in Deuteronomy 19:15, which Christianity commonly calls "confirmations," but getting back to the Biblical root and understanding, these things will help us know His voice. Two or three witnesses in a righteous context is another way God speaks. I have heard the voice of God audibly twice while being awake, but the rest of the time are through many different avenues. It isn't about physical ears, but a spiritual sensitivity. This is why fasting is so critical because it is a crucifying of the flesh, and a heightening of spiritual sensitivity. Jesus says, "My sheep hear My voice (John 10:27)." Not only His apostles, prophets, evangelists, pastors, and teachers, but His sheep, His disciples, the people of His pasture (Psalm 95:7). We also have to recognize that many times God's voice has audible tune to it, but its audibility is manifested through factors and circumstances that are embedded all throughout our lives, rather than a voice as if you and I were in conversation. Meaning, His "audible voice" may manifest through a license plate, or billboard, or a song, or a passing conversation or a phone call you received.

So, as we discuss Biblical meekness, we will immediately flow within the same river to the voice of God and discerning it more clearly. Biblical meekness, if needing to be summed up in one word, which is hard to do, however, if I were to do so, it would be summed up in the word "submission." Submission to what? Submission to one's circumstances. We must have a revelation of the sovereignty of God. Not just in some mere head knowledge, but true revelation that is imparted to us of this fact. Everything going on around you is governed by Divine order, by God Himself. Jesus says that there is not a single sparrow that touches the ground apart from the Father personally ordaining it (Matthew 10:29). Jesus also says that every single hair on your head is numbered (Matthew 10:30). When God created you, He said "this person will have this many hairs on his head, arms, legs, etc." He knows us perfectly, through and through. Your hair doesn't just grow on its own either, I mean, I started balding in my 20's. God Himself brings the increase to every one of those hairs each day. For me, God knows I look better with a bald fade anyways. The sun doesn't rise every morning because that is what it does, the sun won't rise apart from God saying, "rise" every morning. There is not a squirrel that runs across your path apart from God saying, "run." Your heart doesn't beat X number of times every minute because that is what it does. The moment God takes even a single second off of you being on His mind to say "beat, beat, beat" every second, you will die. He governs every minute detail of our lives with intention and focus, as it is written in Job 37:6 "for He says to the snow, 'be upon the earth,' likewise to the shower of rain, and to the showers of His mighty rain." He is our sufficiency, He is our life, and He is the Sovereign One.

Having said all of this, through this revelation, we can more simply accept and submit to our circumstances all around us in every moment. Whether they seem bad or seem good is irrelevant, but recognizing God is in control of it all, as it is written in Ecclesiastes 7:14 "in the day of goodness, be in the good, but in the day of evil, see, God has made this one corresponding to this one, so that man should not know what will happen after him." Isaiah 45:7 also says, "the One who forms light, and the One who creates darkness, the One who makes peace, and the One who creates evil. I am the LORD who does all these things." Keep in mind, I am translating this myself directly from the Hebrew. I say that because I hear people constantly trying to change the words of verses who do not know Hebrew and say "this word really doesn't mean this" or something along those lines. I assure you, what I just translated, is exactly what it means. Think about John 19:10-11, where Pilate tells Jesus that he has the authority to free Jesus or to condemn Him, and Jesus responds, "you would have no authority over Me if it were not given to you from above, therefore, he who handed Me over to you has the greater sin."

Jesus is saying that He is submitting to the circumstances without complaint, although the charges are false, but recognizes that all things are being ordained in the heavens, because He recognizes the sovereignty of God over every detail of His life. God is in control of your blessings and persecutions, as it is written in Psalms 105:25 "He changed their (Egypt) heart to hate His people, to conspire against His servants," and the opposite is seen in Psalm 106:46 "and He made them to be pitied before all of their captors." If we are consumed by looking only at the physical things within our lives, we are blinded to the movement of the Spirit behind the scenes. The physical things are simply manifestations of the spiritual things ordained in the heavens by God Himself.

Jesus didn't waste time on Judas, talking about how everything he is doing is wrong, because it would be missing the point. All of our circumstances are ordained by God, and God trying to get to one goal, which is using our circumstances to bring about the character of the Messiah within us, which is why Hebrews 5:8 says "and though He was a Son, yet from the fear and sufferings He endured, He learned obedience," meaning, by our circumstances, it is like iron sharpening our character that we must learn to submit too. This is meekness. It was said by a rabbi that in Jewish thought, true spiritual maturity is dependent upon one's ability to always recognize our lives are governed by One, God Himself, whether the circumstances seem good or bad.

John the Baptist says the same thing in John 3:27 "no man is able to receive anything according to his own will, but only if it is given to him from heaven," which means, whether good or bad, so instead of fighting against our circumstances, ride the river, and say, "LORD, what are you showing me?" The circumstance is the voice of God, and yet, we miss it continually, as it is written in Job 33:14 "for God speaks once, and twice, but man does not perceive it." God is always speaking, and many times, rather than it being warfare, we find ourselves kicking against the goads, as we will see in this chapter.

As we now go head on to define the term "Biblical meekness," we will look at Psalms 37. Biblical meekness, as we will see, is also defined right out of the Torah of Moses, however, in Psalms 37 David gives us the Biblical definition in a way that not only is incredibly simplified, but there is a phrase from Psalms 37 on the topic of meekness that King Messiah Yeshua quotes directly in the Beatitudes (Matthew 5:5). Jesus says in Matthew 5:5 "blessed are the meek, for they shall inherit the earth." In these Beatitudes, Jesus wasn't giving something of His own accord, but rather, Jesus got these concepts in the Matthew 5 Beatitudes directly from the Psalms, and was simply summarizing them, assuming, we would know the background to each line and study it ourselves.

The same thing goes for the LORD's prayer, as it was a compilation of Jewish prayers that were already being prayed, which we won't dive into in this volume. As we will see, Jesus' Beatitude on the meek is a direct quote from Psalms 37, which says the meek shall inherit the earth (Psalms 37:11), which is identical word for word in Hebrew, and the rest of Psalms 37 discusses what it means to be meek, and how they will inherit the earth. Who are the ones defined as being meek? What was the standard Jesus was giving here for this precious, blessed Beatitude? Although Psalms 37 has 40 verses, we will only look at the first 15 verses, but I am doing this simply so we can get the idea and understanding of the definition for meekness, however, I cannot emphasize enough to go and read the entire chapter very, very carefully. Psalms 37:1-15:

"Of David. Do not compete with evildoers, do not envy those who commit injustice. For they will be speedily cut off like grass and wither like green vegetation. Trust in the LORD and do good. Dwell in the land and feed on faith. So shall you delight in the LORD, and He will give you the desires of your heart. Commit your way to the LORD, and trust in Him, and He will act. He will bring out your righteousness as the light, and your justice as noon. Wait for the LORD and hope for Him. Do not compete with one who prospers his way, with a man who executes malicious plans. Desist from anger and forsake wrath, do not compete only to do evil. For evildoers shall be cut off, and those who hope for the LORD, they shall inherit the earth. A short while longer, and the wicked man is not here, and you shall look at his place, and he is not there. But the meek shall inherit the earth, and they shall delight upon an abundance of peace. The wicked man plots against the righteous and gnashes his teeth at him. The LORD will laugh at him because He saw that his day will come. The wicked have pulled out their sword and bent their bow to cast down the poor and needy, to slay those who walk on a straight path. Their sword shall enter into their own heart, and their bows shall be broken."

Notice, multiple times, directly translated from the Hebrew, the Scripture tells the righteous and meek not to "compete" when someone does you wrong, and the context of the chapter continually has to do with the meek being ones who can accept wickedness being done to them, and although not "agreeing" with it as Jesus didn't agree with

Pilate condemning Him, but still putting their hope and expectancy in the LORD to come and execute His justice in its proper time. David makes it clear in this chapter that the meek are the ones who can submit to the hard circumstances, and accept these things that transpire in their life, and God will vindicate you and bring forth your righteousness and justice as the noon day for all to see in plain sight (also see Ezekiel 34 on the lean and fat sheep).

Think about David, the one writing the Psalm, as His life continually defines meekness. Did he fight back against Saul? No. Even though He was already anointed as king, David submitted to the circumstance and hid in the cave of meekness. Did he fight back against his son, Absalom? No, but even as king he submitted to his circumstances and prayed to God, and every time God would vindicate Him. So then, Biblical meekness is all about being able to submit to one's circumstances, whether good or bad. Think about Jesus' continual submission to the wrong being done to Him, without complaint, because David and Jesus both recognize that the LORD is the one fully in charge, the Sovereign One. Jesus didn't agree with the wickedness, but He accepted it knowing that nothing could happen unless it was the Father granting it (John 3:27, 19:11). This is revealed very clearly through Psalms 39:1-14:

> "For the conductor, to Jeduthun, a song of David. I said, 'I will guard my ways from sinning with my tongue, I will guard my mouth as with a muzzle while the wicked man is still before me.' I made myself dumb in silence; I was silent from good although my pain was intense. My heart is hot within me, in my thoughts fire burns. I spoke with my tongue, 'O LORD let me know my end, and the measure of my days, what it is, I will know when I will cease. Behold, You made my days as handbreadths, and

my old age is as nought before You. But all of man is but vapor. Selah. Man walks but in darkness, all that they stir is but vanity. He gathers, but he does not know who will bring them in. And now, what have I hoped, O Lord? My hope is to You. Save me from all of my transgressions. Do not make me the reproach of a wicked man. I have become mute. I will not open my mouth because You have done it. Remove Your affliction from me, I am destroyed from the quarrel of Your hand. With the rebukes of iniquity, You have chastised man. You have caused his flesh to decay as a moth. But all of man is vapor. Selah. Hear my prayer, O LORD, and hearken to my cry. Do not be silent to my tears, for I am a stranger with you, a dweller as all of my fathers. Turn away from me that I may recover before I go and am no more.'"

David himself says very clearly, his hard times and punishments were from God, and the difficulties that he faced were directly from God, as he says above "I will not open my mouth because You have done it." Believers, as an easy way out always blame others and the devil, as Adam blamed Eve, then Eve blamed Satan, rather than taking responsibility and reflecting inwardly first, we always point the finger, especially at "warfare." As I said, Eve did this in the garden. She blamed the devil for her hardship and temptation, and the bride is still doing the same thing constantly today, because nothing is new under the sun (Ecclesiastes 1:9-10). It was wrong then, and it is wrong now. The truth is, everything is divinely orchestrated, and I mean everything, even something as simple as the tearing of a garment, as it is written in 1 Samuel 15:26-28:

"And Samuel said to Saul, 'I shall not return with you, for you have rejected the word of the LORD, and the

LORD has rejected you from being a king over Israel.' And Samuel turned to go, and he seized the corner of his robe, and it tore. And Samuel said to him, 'the LORD has torn the kingdom of Israel from you today, and He has given it to your friend who is better than you."

We need a revelation of the sovereignty of God and submitting to His overseeing and orchestrating every nuance of our lives through meekness and submission to the circumstances. Humans have such a problem with meekness because we have such a problem with needing to control everything and justify ourselves. So, when Numbers 12:3 says that Moses was the meekest man (ענו) who was upon the entire earth, the Torah is saying that Moses is actually the most submissive man upon the face of the earth, which if you just read the Torah of Moses, you will know that is 100% true, with Abraham being second.

Moses is continually being wronged and complained against, and yet, he always goes to his face (Numbers 16:4) and doesn't retaliate. He submits to His circumstances, recognizing the LORD is in charge, and the LORD always vindicates he and Aaron. He never competes or fights back, but always hopes in the LORD as Psalms 37 states. All of these meek and righteous individuals recognize the sovereignty of God, while recognizing that they won't miss their calling or their vindication. They know, somehow God will get them to where they need to be. His hand is not shortened (Numbers 11:23, Isaiah 59:1). Joseph continually submitted to his circumstances and didn't agree with the wrong being done to him, however, he recognized that God will be the One to vindicate him (Genesis 45:5-8). Meekness isn't just submission, but a willingness to be wronged. It is a realization that one's circumstance has the voice of God embedded within it, and that He is always teaching, but rather than learning, we fight back and actually kick against the goads. Each circumstance has God's voice teaching us a lesson, even when you are doing something as simple as checking out at the grocery store, as we said, even the tear of a garment is the voice of God according to Samuel. One cannot be meek unless they are in situations that give them the opportunity to be meek, which is always the tough part of bearing its fruit.

In 2021, 2022, and continuing in 2023, I cannot tell you how badly I was being wronged. So much so, that if I was to put the details in this book, your jaw would drop because some of these things were actually illegal that were being done unto me. It was honestly hard to comprehend how and why these things were taking place. In the natural, it made no sense. There was truly no explanation….in the natural. The few people that even heard a few of the details would give me responses like "Nick, if you could only see that my jaw is dropped right now. I am speechless when I hear these things."

The Holy Spirit showed me early on in 2022 that He was wanting to breed the fruit of meekness within me to a whole new level, and how would I be able to bear that fruit if I am not in a position where I can choose to be meek or not? In order to bear that type of meekness that we see with Abraham, Isaac, Jacob, Joseph, Moses, Jeremiah, David, Jesus, Paul, etc., I had to be in situations of being totally wronged. I could have fought back, in fact, I had family, friends, and even mentors telling me to, but the LORD had me read Psalms 37 and Psalms 18 I cannot tell you how many times in 2022. The Father kept me silent with meekness and to be as harmless as a dove (Matthew 10:16), and had me walking in David's footsteps, as it is written in Psalms 38:13-16:

> "And those who seek my life lay traps, and those who seek
> my harm speak treachery, and all day long they think of
> deceits. But I am as a deaf person, I do not hear, and like
> a mute, who does not open his mouth. And I was as a

man who does not understand and in whose mouth there are no arguments. Because I hoped for You, O LORD, You shall answer, O Lord my God."

Day and night I kept myself under the shadow of Psalms 109:4 "in the place of my love, they persecute me. But I pray." I knew what the LORD was doing, and I thank God I remained within my convictions and revelations of Psalms 37. I submitted to my circumstances, but in that, I was really submitting to the Holy Spirit and what He was doing in my life, because it is the voice of God.

If God is not bringing the finances you need, or the views, or the right people, submit. Stop trying to do it in your flesh. Ask Him what He is trying to teach you, because the circumstance carries the voice of God. To emphasize this point, I want us to really focus on two verses in the New Testament. James 1:21 "and so throw all that is defiled and the myriads of evil things far away from yourselves, and with meekness receive the Word that is implanted in our nature, which is able to resurrect your souls." When James says that we are to receive the Word with meekness, he is not just implying reading the Bible, and saying, "wow, that is a hard word to swallow, but I need to submit to its authority," although, that is true, and we need to do that as the Word of God is the standard. James is talking about more than that when he says to receive with meekness the implanted word, meaning, submit to your circumstances because God's Word is not just on pages, but it is alive and active all around us (Hebrews 4:12), and everything going on around us is by the Word and decrees of God (John 1:1-3). Jesus Himself says to Pilate that Pilate only has authority over that circumstance because it was given to him from above (John 19:11), and that no bird can hit the ground apart from the will of God (Matthew 10:29-31). Therefore, anything in my life is being ordained by God in one way or another (Isaiah 45:7, Ecclesiastes 7:14).

God doesn't delight in evil, but our perspective is so shallow and low (Isaiah 55:8-9) that what we think is evil or unrighteous around us may be the very thing pushing us into our calling, or pruning us to bear a certain fruit, or humbling us, etc., as Joseph's brothers selling him was a catapult in order to get him to where he was meant to go. God can use those circumstances to prune good fruits in our lives and thrust us into our calling. It is by these things that we become transformed into the image of the Messiah and learn obedience to His ways (Hebrews 5:8). I tell people all the time, if it wasn't for 2021-2023 that I was so wronged, I would have never learned the meekness I know today, nor would I have ever gotten the abundance of revelation and faith that I now walk in. I thank God for everything I have gone through. Five years prior, I would have broken down every door and wall like the juggernaut bodybuilder I was, but now, I let those circumstances do a work within me, as my full dependence is upon God. People who know me can tell you, I have an utter dependency upon Him for everything. It isn't just something I say.

As James says, the Word of God is going on around us all the time and it needs to be submitted too. God's spiritual voice is embedded in the physical circumstances, which brings us now to Romans 1:20 "for from the foundations of the world, the hidden things of God are seen by the mind in the things He created, even His eternal power and divinity, so that they might be without excuse." Paul says the HIDDEN things of God, and His divinity are seen in the PHYSICAL things that He created, meaning, when God speaks in the Spirit, it manifests with the clothing of the physical world, as Jesus said that His will is done on earth as it is in the heavens (Matthew 6:10). The physical world and physical circumstances should not be what our minds hone in on, but rather, the physical things are a parable for something greater, that is, God's voice and will in the Spirit realm, as the tearing of Samuel's garment, was as God's tearing Saul's kingdom from him. When we fight our circumstances, as we will see, we fight against what God is trying to do within us. This revelation is explained crystal clear in the Torah of Moses in Exodus 16 where God brings down manna from heaven for the children of Israel in the wilderness. Day by day they must go and gather, and on Friday (the sixth day) they gather twice as much for Shabbat/Sabbath (Saturday). Exodus 16:1-8:

> "And they journeyed from Elim and all of the congregation of the children of Israel came to the wilderness of Sin, which is between Elim and Sinai, in the fifteenth day of the second month of their going out from the land of Egypt. And all of the assembly of the children of Israel complained against Moses and against Aaron in the wilderness. And the children of Israel said to them, 'if only we would have died by the hand of the LORD in the land of Egypt, when we sat by pots of meat, and we ate bread to the full, for you have brought us out to this wilderness in order to kill this congregation with hunger.' And the LORD said to Moses, 'behold, I am raining bread for you from heaven, and the people will go out and collect a day's worth each day, so that I may test them, whether they will walk in My Torah or not. And on the sixth day they will prepare that which they bring in, and it shall be double of what they collect each day.' And Moses and Aaron said to all the children of Israel, 'at evening you will know that the LORD brought you out from the land of Egypt, and in the morning, you will see the glory of the LORD in that He heard your complaints against the LORD, and what are we that you complain against us?' And Moses said, 'when the LORD gives you

flesh in the evening to eat, and bread in the morning to the full, in the LORD's hearing your complaints which you are complaining against Him, and what are we? Your complaints are not against us, but against the LORD.'"

The children of Israel are hungry and complain against Moses and Aaron, saying, not only did Moses and Aaron make a mistake by bringing them out of Egypt, but that they are also to blame for their circumstance of not having the food they want. In the physical, they see Moses and Aaron as the ones who took them out, and who are responsible for their being fed, protected, and taken care of, or lack thereof. They are only seeing their circumstances in the physical world, without realizing, they are missing the point. They complain against Moses and Aaron, which happens continually against Moses, and literally happened one chapter earlier (Exodus 15) because they went three days without water. But remember, Romans 1:20 says that the hidden things of God and His divinity are seen in the physical things, meaning, the physical is just a manifestation of God's will. Moses and Aaron aren't the Source, nor should they be the focus, rather, they are the parable or physical expression of One greater behind the scenes. Because they blame Moses for taking them out of Egypt, he answers and says, "you will know that the LORD brought you out of Egypt, and your complaints aren't really against us, but they are actually against the LORD." They didn't realize, their "problems" were not warfare, and it was not the enemy hindering their finances in the spirit realm, but it was all the LORD. Many say, "the devil is holding back my finances," just as the children of Israel thought about the bread, but it was the LORD. The same thing is in Numbers 26:9:

"And the children of Eliav, and N'muel, and Datan, and Aviram, which is the Datan and Aviram who were chosen of the assembly who quarreled against Moses and against Aaron in the assembly of Korah when they quarreled against the LORD."

Once again, by quarreling against Moses and Aaron, they are actually quarreling against the LORD. This is not to just be viewed as rebelling against leadership, but more so just rebelling against your circumstances in general, and not recognizing God is in control. Unfortunately, I have also seen wolves take this concept and abuse their authority and leadership, saying to people, "by rebelling against me, you rebel against the LORD and have a problem with pride and authority."

The truth is, Christianity's continual blame of Satan is a cheap and easy way out, just as Adam and Eve blaming each other, and then Satan, and it's always the go-to. There is such a lack of discernment between warfare and kicking against the goads. It is a lack of taking responsibility and evaluating that we, many times, are the root of our issues. It doesn't mean there isn't warfare, as I will share later in this book, and in another volume, but there needs to be some perspective on our part. All of our circumstances are actually a manifestation of His hand, somehow, in some way. God says in Exodus 15 and Exodus 16 that He is doing what He does in order to test us, which He repeats again in Deuteronomy 8:2:

"And you shall remember all of this way that the LORD your God has led you these forty years in the wilderness in order to afflict you, in order to test you, in order to know what is in your heart, whether you would keep His commandments or not."

There was no meekness or submission to the circumstances. They didn't get the provisions they wanted when they wanted. Many people are not getting the spouse just yet, or the finances, or the job opportunity, or whatever it may be. Every single thing, every person we come across, every circumstance has the voice of God embedded into it. In 2023, I had a woman tell me one time how much she appreciated how calm I was in certain situations, and the reason is, I had to learn that everything is from Him. I would have people literally walk into my office in the Woodlands and say, "I just came in for a moment because the peace of God always fills your office," and then walk right out. Jesus told us not to worry, and that we can't add one cubit to our stature by worry (Matthew 6:27). My peace and acceptance have come through learning how to walk with the Spirit of God. It has not always been this way, believe me. I have peace in the midst of the storm because it is God behind it all. This revelation of meekness within the Exodus 16 narrative above literally changed my life and how I view everything around me in my daily life.

Moses and Aaron say, "your complaints aren't against us, but against the LORD. You think we are the problem because you are stuck seeing the physical things, but you need to think bigger, think spiritual, be heavenly minded," as Paul says in Colossians 3:2 that we need to keep our minds on the things above, and not on the things of the earth. Your husband/wife is not the problem, neither are your kids, or your boss, your financial situation, etc. God is always speaking and teaching, trying to prune a certain fruit within us through our circumstance. Let God deal with you, then He will also deal with them. This is the job of the Holy Spirit, to sanctify us, and prune us through our circumstances into the image of the Messiah (Romans 8:29).

Moses was emphasizing that it was God who has placed them in the circumstance they are in, and not to shoot the messenger. If one could keep Exodus 16 on their mind at all times, your life will change. It will help you walk in a Biblical meekness, to submit to your circumstances, because the horizontal issues or delights are just a manifestation of the vertical will from God, and therefore, the voice of God. As I said at the beginning of this chapter, I would show us how meekness to the circumstances, especially on horizontal lines, and the voice of God are really one and the same. It just depends on if we can see it through the lens of the Spirit and understand the fruit that we can bear in that moment. Through this Exodus 16 revelation, there will be a new intimacy in walking with the Holy Spirit, as well as new revelations of peace.

Now think about the very next chapter in Exodus 17 when Amalek came to fight with Israel (Exodus 17:8-16). God was the one who brought them to fight Israel because of their complaints in the first seven verses, as it is shown clearly in Hebrew in verse 8 that God brought them. The physical trouble was a manifestation of God's design. When I went through everything, I went through during 2021-2023, sure, it was wrong as Psalms 37 states, and God was teaching me meekness, but I would be a fool if I wasn't honest and saying it was also God working a humbling within my character, pruning my perspective, and continually performing a repentant work within me. No man can stand self-righteous before God, and my hands have had to be continually washed from the sins of the flesh (Job 32-33). In faithfulness God had afflicted me (Psalms 119:67/71/75). It doesn't have to be an either/or, was this person wrong, or was I wrong, or is God just wanting me to learn, or is this a correction. It doesn't need to be an either/or, but rather, it is probably an and/also, and God doing multiple things at once. The co-existence of these things is taking place more times than not.

In the Exodus 16 narrative God said He was testing Israel and trying to teach them faith and obedience. He was trying to grow in relationship with them by wanting to teach them the nature of their Father in heaven. Our Father is so mighty, miraculous, and all-powerful, and unless we are put into stretching circumstances, we won't see these attributes of Him. The entire concept is a paradox, that what seems to be, is really not, and what seems not, really is. The physical problem is not really the problem. The problem only seems like the problem when it is viewed in isolation, but when viewed on the 35,000 foot scale and the greater scheme of things, we see the problem is not a problem at all, but a tool by which the LORD is embodying His will and voice, in order to prune us into the image of His Son (Romans 8:29). We have to see above the paradox, but the only way to see the higher things of God, is for us to go lower with meekness, just as Moses wouldn't fight back, but would go lower onto his face (Numbers 16:4). This concept of meekness and the revelation of Exodus 16 is the essence of our above verses: James 1:21 and Romans 1:20.

Stephen also says in Acts 7:51 "alas, oh stiff necked and uncircumcised of heart and ear. You continually rise up against the Holy Spirit, as your forefathers, so are you." Notice, Stephen says the forefathers in the wilderness, by their rebellion against their circumstances, were actually warring against the Holy Spirit! Like I said, what seems to be warfare, isn't always warfare, and is many times, kicking against the goads and the Holy Spirit Himself. We point the finger at Israel in the wilderness, without realizing, they are us, as it is written in 1 Corinthians 10:11 "all these things which befell them, were for an example to us, and they are written for our instruction, on whom the end of the world has come."

We are so quick to blame the devil, when in reality, the devil himself is a vessel created and used by God. As David said in Psalms 37, Stephen is saying that submission to the circumstance could very well be walking with the Holy Spirit. We fight against the pruning work of the Spirit of God in our lives, especially if it brings us out of our comfort zones. Every single work He wants to do begins with our meekness and submission to the circumstance God has created. As we read in Job 33:14, so many times we miss the voice of God right in front of us, because we are so busy in our lives, and we are constantly fighting, rather than coming to the LORD over and over with a posture of "Father, what are you showing me?"

There was something in my life that I began to notice in 2022 that the LORD was continually orchestrating. I think I would be foolish to say it was in 2022 that He began doing it, but it would be more accurate to say that is when I started recognizing it, and now I recognize it every time, and quite frequently. For example, in 2017 I bought a new charcoal grey Dodge Challenger, and before I got it, I never (or, so it seemed) saw them on the road, however, after I bought it, it seemed like everyone and their mom had a charcoal grey Dodge Challenger. I am sure this was the case before, I just didn't recognize it, so too, with the story I will tell of what I began to recognize God doing in my life in 2022. In fact, what I am about to tell you, within about 3-4 months of me catching on, this happened at least a very distinct 3-4x in those first 3-4 months alone of me recognizing it.

It was December of 2022. I was in Iowa as I am on the farm, and generally, somewhere on the property, and usually within the same building, is Todd, Maria, myself, their workers, etc. There was a situation that had not really come up since I had been living there, or at least that I remember. On Thursday, December 8th, 2022, I had taken Todd and Maria to the airport for their trip to Israel. Then the next day, their workers did not come in, and I remember by about 9am I started thinking, "where is everyone?" Usually people are there by 7am, and on this Friday absolutely nobody was there but Kaia (my pit-bull) and myself.

Later in the morning I realized that the workers were at a job site that day off of the property. Then I am making certain phone calls and people aren't answering their phones. I remember sitting back, saying, "what is going on?" It wasn't just in the physical, but something in the spirit shifted. There was this isolation that was not just physical, but an isolation that could be felt, as it is written in Exodus 10:21 "and the LORD said to Moses, 'stretch out your hand to the heavens, and there will be a darkness upon the earth, and the darkness will be felt.'" This isolation was an isolation I could literally feel in the physical, an isolation from heaven. This very thing still happens to this day. This isn't just a time of being alone. I am alone a lot, as I am continually in my office day to day. This, like I said, was spiritual. God had my attention.

In the past, I think I would have complained about being isolated, alone, or someone not answering their phone etc., but this day was different. That day the LORD showed me isolation in the Scriptures. In Leviticus 13-14, when one had leprosy, they would get isolated, and although I wasn't like a leper, the concept of isolation was being revealed through this passage and another passage in Genesis. He began revealing why He was isolating me. In Leviticus 13-14, one is isolated first for seven days (שִׁבְעַת יָמִים), pronounced "shivat yamim." This is why linguistics are so important, because although there may be words that translate the same in English, in Hebrew, we have missing and added letters, even to the same word or phrase, however, when the word or phrase is spelled exactly the same, it means there is a connection between the two passages that they are in, which in rabbinic literature is called a "gizra shava," meaning, an "equivalence of expressions." They carry the same implication within those two passages, and you can adopt the perspective from one place to the other, and now by putting the two passages together like two puzzle pieces, one can gain a fuller understanding for that word, phrase, or the purpose for a given circumstance.

With leprosy, one is isolated for shivat yamim (seven days), the priest checks on the leper, then the leper is isolated for another shivat yamim, and he will come check on the leper again. To be isolated for leprosy, it is also important to note that Leviticus 13:1-4 says one must have a "sei'ar lavan (שער לבן)," which means a "white hair." Lavan (לבן), which means "white," is the same word as "Laban," who was Rachel and Leah's father, and the father-in-law of Jacob. That day when I saw this, I began to ask the LORD, "ok, Father. If you are isolating me like this, what are you wanting to do?" He began to show me that when He isolates us, it is because there is something God is wanting to speak to us about and reveal to us. He has to take drastic measures in order to get our attention. As we saw earlier in this chapter, being too busy is one of the many tools the enemy uses to hinder us from seeing and hearing God in each moment. Many times, out of insecurity, we over busy ourselves because it can give a sense of self-worth, but this is the evil one leading us to find identity in the wrong places. Due to this over busying of ourselves, we miss the voice of God.

I had to submit to these circumstances. The reason I knew God wanted to speak with me was because of what else He showed me with the section on leprosy. As I said, there was a seven day period (shivat yamim) of isolation, but also a hair that had to be white (lavan, which is the same word for Laban). The LORD took me to Genesis 31 where Jacob, his wives, and his kids flee from Laban (white), and Laban pursues Him, and it is written in Genesis 31:23-24:

> "And he (Laban) took his brothers with him, and he pursued him (Jacob) a journey of seven days (shivat yamim), and he overtook him at mount Gilead. And God came to Laban the Aramean in a dream of the night, and He said to him, 'be careful, lest you speak with Jacob either good or evil.'"

So, the two passages of Leviticus 13, where there is an isolation for seven days with a white hair, which "white" is the name of Laban, also connects us to Genesis 31 where Laban (white) is chasing Jacob for seven days (shivat yamim). Laban was so busy pursuing, he missed the voice of God, so God comes to him in a dream. If we put Genesis 31 and

Leviticus 13 together, we see the fuller picture for isolation, which is because God wants to speak with us, but sometimes, we miss the LORD because of our pursuit, even for Godly things. As we see in Job 33:14-18, God speaks in one way or another, yet man doesn't perceive it, so then God will open our ears in a dream while we sleep in order to seal our instruction. Job's insight is directly from this passage and connection I am displaying with Genesis 31 and Leviticus 13-14.

It was that day in Iowa that the Holy Spirit downloaded this entire revelation to me. At that moment, I put everything down, I stopped studying, I stopped working, I stopped calling, and everything else, and I said, "LORD, what do You want me to know? What are You trying to show me? What am I missing? Speak, LORD, for Your servant is listening (1 Samuel 3:9)." The very things I am complaining about, the isolation, unanswered calls, etc., was the hand of God, as the children of Israel complained in the wilderness against the physical circumstances, but it was the LORD, and there fighting against it was them rebelling against the Holy Spirit Stephen says (Acts 7:51). Every detail, even like something I was facing, was Him. So, He said, "stop fighting." I was in between a very important decision and had been stressing and wrestling over it for weeks. It was in that moment that the Father told me, "I want you to go from Iowa back to Houston," as He told Jacob in that same Genesis 31 passage, as it is written in Genesis 31:3 "and the LORD said to Jacob, 'return to the land of your fathers, and to your birthplace, and I will be with you.'"

With this revelation, it is important to know, I don't always look at things in the long term. I walk with God, meaning, today is today, but tomorrow may be something different, as Jesus would show us, or as Paul lived. Today God said go here, but tomorrow may be something different, as it is written in John 3:8 "the wind will blow where it desires and you hear its voice, but you do not know from where it comes or to where it goes. Likewise, is everyone who is born from the Spirit." My thoughts weren't "how long will I be there for?" The LORD tells me that Friday to pack up and leave, and it was Monday, three days later after I packed that I was on my journey back to Houston. This isolation process continually happens in my life because it is a time when God really has my attention. In fact, it was during one of these isolation times where I was being very wronged that God isolated me, I recognized it and dropped everything, and He downloaded this entire concept of Biblical meekness into me as it pertains to hearing the voice of God, and the Exodus 16/ Romans 1:20 understanding that the voice of God is embedded in the physical circumstance. This whole chapter was downloaded and birthed out of one of those times. However, now, due to my understanding of this revelation, I have noticed God does not isolate me as much, because I am more sensitive to Him in every moment.

I was fighting certain circumstances, and I became exhausted and wasn't seeing the fruit. Warfare is one thing where the Spirit sustains you to keep going, and then there's another where you become exhausted in the physical, because your circumstances are out of your control, and you are warring it in the flesh, and you aren't seeing the fruit of what you are fighting for or against. Don't get me wrong, true spiritual warfare is exhausting, too. Now, you have to ask, "Father, is this me fighting in the flesh without Your blessing, and is the very thing I am fighting actually Your hand and voice in my life?" Stop kicking against the goads, because as Stephen said, it is fighting the Holy Spirit (Acts 7:51). Submit to the circumstance, because as Gamaliel said, if it is from God, it will prevail, and if not, it will crumble anyway (Acts 5:33-42).

We can continually look at everything as spiritual warfare, and the enemy camp trying to "stop us," but in reality, a lot of times it is not warfare, but rather kicking against the goads. The voice of God is actually embedded within that physical circumstance, and although it may seem like a trial, it is actually the very hand of God trying to guide us, because we could be going "out of bounds." But one will not recognize this unless there is a grasping and application of the concept of Biblical meekness-a submission to one's circumstances, not only in the horizontal, but the horizontal is a manifestation of the vertical, a manifestation of the things of the Spirit of God (Romans 1:20). You can look at Moses and Aaron and say that they are not providing what they said would happen, but we need to recognize that neither Moses, nor any other person or circumstance before us is what we really need to see or hone in on, but rather recognize those things are just clothing for the will of God in the Spirit, as Paul says in Romans 1:20, that the hidden things of God and His divinity are known by the things which are seen in the physical world.

Then one might argue and say that Moses and Aaron were God-fearing individuals, led by God, however, Pontius Pilate, a wicked man, was actually led by God as well (John 19:11). Scripture says in Revelation 17:16-17:

> "And the ten horns which you saw, and the beast of prey
> will hate the harlot, and they will make her desolate and
> naked, and will eat her flesh, and burn her with fire. For
> God has put it into their hearts to do His will and to ex-
> ecute one purpose, and to give their kingdom to the beast
> of prey until the words of God will be fulfilled."

Again, in Exodus 14:4 "And I (God) will harden the heart of Pharaoh, and he will pursue after them, and I will be glorified by Pharaoh, and by all his army, and Egypt will know that I am the LORD, and they did so." God isn't just in charge of the righteous, God is also in charge of the wicked, and He is always speaking, even though donkeys (Numbers 22:22-35). God is in charge. We give too much credit to "chance" or to Satan. God is the King of kings, the Sovereign One, the LORD of lords,

185

the Creator of heaven and earth, Alpha and Omega, the Beginning and the End, the First and the Last, and there is none other besides Him (Isaiah 45:6).

As I read Scripture through this lens of Biblical meekness, I can't help but realize that it is literally everywhere. In Jeremiah, the children of Israel look at Nebuchadnezzar as the evil one and begin rebelling against him. They see it as warfare, not realizing, TWICE in the book of Jeremiah God calls Nebuchadnezzar "my servant (Jeremiah 25:9, 27:6)," and God is the one bringing Nebuchadnezzar against the land of Israel as a correction against them. God says to submit to Nebuchadnezzar, and it will be well with them, but if they don't, they will die (Jeremiah 27:8-22). What they viewed as warfare, was actually kicking against the LORD's hand. Read the Scriptures, blessing and curses come from God (Genesis 3, Leviticus 26, Deuteronomy 28), so does health and sickness (Exodus 4:11, 15:26, John 5:14), so does leprosy (Leviticus 14:34), so does every plague (Genesis 12, Exodus 1-12, the entire book of Revelation). Our circumstances are divinely orchestrated by God Himself, and only one who walks very, very intimately with Him, with great meekness and humility will recognize such things. In the physical, it is easy to think Nebuchadnezzar is wicked, but in all things, we must see beyond the physical, whether you are at the coffee shop, the gym, the grocery store, texting, or whatever it may be.

As I study carefully, I sit back and go "oh, the sovereignty of the LORD, even with the good and the bad." It isn't that God does evil or orchestrates it for the sake of doing evil, but rather, He allows it so that it can produce good fruit, nevertheless, it is all under His sovereignty, as it is written in Amos 3:6 "will there be evil in a city if the LORD has not done it?" The LORD is the same yesterday, today, and forever (Malachi 3:6, Hebrews 13:8). If we go off course, and evil comes our way, that evil is being used by God to return us to Him in repentance, so in reality, the evil itself is being used for good (Genesis 50:20). When evil is viewed by itself, it looks only evil, but when viewed in the greater scheme of things, we realize, all things work for the good of those who love Him (Romans 8:28). It is a paradox that we must recognize.

Many who know me, know, I am very driven, and laser focused. My dad once told me when I was a child:

> "Nick, because of your drive and determination, you will either be the President of the United States, or the head of a cartel. You choose which route you want to take, whether good or evil, but the drive you have always shown will get you there."

Due to my ASD (Autism Spectrum Disorder, specifically Asperger's, also known as HFA- High Functioning Autism with superior intelligence), when I focus, I hyper focus, and I lose awareness of almost everything around me, including time, in order to focus on the task in front of me. My drive turns me into something that says, "nothing will get in my way." I turn into a machine. God can use this so well for Him, but it can also be detrimental if I don't realize the obstacles could be from God Himself trying to get my attention.

Sometimes, God has to slam the breaks with me and isolate me as I explained, in order to get my attention and speak with me. Every time He isolates me now, I recognize it, and it never fails that He speaks to me very clearly, because I now know how to submit to my circumstances. The ultimate job of the Holy Spirit is to transform you and I into the image of the Messiah (Romans 8:29, 1 John 2:6). That is God's number one concern and top priority for our lives. So, when we are in a circumstance, even if being treated wrong, sure, what they are doing is wrong, and God will deal with them (Amos 1-2), but what about that circumstance can still be used to prune me and help me to bear a certain fruit, such as faith, long-suffering, meekness, humility, learning how to love and bless those who wrong us (Matthew 5:44)? If Jesus tells us to bless and love those who hurt us, how can I be obedient to that unless someone hurts me? The circumstance is always one of pruning.

The last six months or so of 2022, I cannot tell you how many times I read Psalms 37. I honestly cannot tell you. God had me in Psalms 37 and Psalms 18 (and certain other Scriptures) literally all the time. I devoured Psalms 37 (Jeremiah 15:16), and what this did in my life and with my perspective changed my entire life, due to having to go through such a season of meekness and being trampled, while learning, as Psalms 37 says, not to "compete" with these things, but to submit to the circumstances with meekness and the fear of God. Read Psalms 37 very carefully, along with Exodus 16, and even Exodus 15 at the end where the children of Israel continually complain against Moses for no water or food. Get familiar with James 1:21 and Romans 1:20. Also, remember what I said when I put Psalms 37 at the beginning of this chapter, verses 1/7 may translate as "do not fret" in English, however, it really says, "do not compete." Meekness doesn't try and compete, but it submits, and receives the understanding of "stop and know that I am God (Psalms 46:11)." You will now start to see all of these men of God-Abraham, Isaac, Jacob, Joseph, Moses, Aaron, Joshua, David, Jesus, Paul etc., continually submitted to even the toughest of circumstances, and within that, they always saw the hand of God move on their behalf.

There is one last example I will give when it comes to this Biblical meekness, submitting to your circumstances, and how if we don't, it can be kicking against the goads and against the LORD's hand. In Numbers 22-24, Balak tries to hire Balaam the sorcerer in order to come and curse Israel for him. Numbers 22:21-34:

"Balaam arose in the morning, and saddled his she-donkey and went with the leaders of Moab. God's wrath flared because he was going, and an angel of the LORD stood in the way to be an adversary to him, and he was riding on his she-donkey, and his two servants were with him. The she-donkey saw the angel of the LORD standing in the way and his sword drawn in his hand, and the she-donkey turned aside from the road and went into a field. Balaam beat the she-donkey to get it back on the road. The angel of the LORD stood in a path of the vineyards with a fence on this side and a fence on that side. The she-donkey saw the angel of the LORD and she was pressed toward the wall. She pressed Balaam's leg toward the wall, and he beat her again. And the angel passed over again and stood in a narrow place where there was no way to turn right or left. The she-donkey saw the angel of the LORD, and it crouched down under Balaam. Balaam's anger flared, and he beat the she-donkey with a stick. The LORD opened the mouth of the she-donkey, and she said to Balaam, 'what have I done to you that you have struck me these three times?' Balaam said to the she-donkey, 'for you have abused me. If I had a sword in my hand, I would kill you right now.' The she-donkey said to Balaam, 'am I not your she-donkey which you have ridden since you first started until now? Have I been accustomed to do this to you?' He said, 'no.' The LORD opened Balaam's eyes, and he saw the angel of the LORD standing on the road with a sword drawn in his hand. He bowed and worshipped on his face. The angel of the LORD said to him, 'why have you beaten your she-donkey these three times? Behold, I have come out to be an adversary, for you have gone down on this journey against me. When the she-donkey saw me, it turned aside these three times. Had she not turned aside before me, I also would have killed you and spared her.' Balaam said to the angel of the LORD, 'I have sinned for I did not know that you were standing on the road before me. Now if it displeases you, I will return.'"

Something we need to notice, both times that the Scripture says the angel of the LORD is being an "adversary" against Balaam, the word in Hebrew is "satan (שָׂטָן)," whose name means to hinder, accuse, or to be an adversary. God is using Satan, who is called an angel of the LORD to try and stop Balaam from his plans. Balaam's she-donkey sees in the spirit, and is trying to save Balaam, but in Balaam's eyes she seems to go off course, even hurting Balaam's leg as it scrapes against the fence. Balaam begins beating his donkey because he is seeing in the physical, and it seems his donkey is being disobedient, not realizing, the donkey is saving his life, and the very thing that seems to be warfare, hindering him from moving forward, is actually Balaam fighting against the LORD, just as the children of Israel seem to be angry at Moses and Aaron, when in reality, they are complaining against the LORD. Yes, God uses our animals. I cannot tell you how many times God has taught me through my pit-bull, Kaia. God is always teaching, and everything around us is Divine, because the hidden things of God are seen by the physical (Romans 1:20). God can use anything and uses everything. In fact, if He sees fit, He can make these rocks cry out (Luke 19:40).

I cannot tell you how many times we are Balaam. We are so set on our mission, and we think we are doing a work for the kingdom, and we clothe all of our actions in the garment of "it is for the LORD," especially in ministry, but many times, we use it as a crutch for our own desire to be seen, or known, or we will do something without consulting Him. A student of mine in another state called me one morning and said "Pastor, I had a dream I need to tell you. In the dream I was traveling on a narrow road, and I couldn't turn right or left, and before me was a beast, set there to devour me." The Holy Spirit revealed the meaning right there, and I said:

> "The interpretation is from Numbers 22 with Balaam. You are Balaam, who has made a decision with either the wrong heart or not consulting God, and the narrow way with the inability to turn right or left is the road they were on, and the beast is satan before you as an adversary, trying to stop you from proceeding with whatever decision you just made, as it is written 'and the angel passed over again and stood in a narrow place where there was no way to turn right or left. The she-donkey saw the angel of the LORD, and it crouched down under Balaam.'"

The man immediately thanked me and knew exactly what the decision was that he made without consulting the LORD. As I said, many times, we are Balaam, and God is trying to get our attention. I think we would be surprised how many times it is not spiritual warfare at all, but warring against Him and the flow of His Spirit. The meek will always be in tune with the Spirit of God, sensitive to His nudges, and pliable to wherever He is leading, as it is written in John 3:8 "the wind settles where it wishes, and its sound you hear, but you do not know where it comes from or where it is going. So too, is every person who is born from the Spirit." A foundational part of becoming a Tree Of Fire is learning how to walk in unison with the Holy Spirit and fire, who is a cloud by day, and fire by night (Exodus 13:21, Numbers 9:16-21), and submitting to the atmosphere He orchestrates in our lives. In every moment, be postured in meekness, with submission to the circumstance because He is there. For the One who said, "blessed are the meek, for they shall inherit the earth (Matthew 5:5)," is the same One who said, "and he who desires to go to court with you and take your tunic, let him also have your robe (Matthew 5:40)."

CHAPTER 9

The Anointing And
The Menorah Within

In Christianity we are always talking about the anointing. People will continually say, "so and so has an anointing," however, I want to get to the Biblical root of not only what the anointing really is, but also why it is needed, how does one obtain an anointing, how does one maintain the anointing, and how does one increase in the anointing, because as we will see, someone may have an anointing, but the anointing can be taken away, regardless of what ones theology may be or traditional lenses they've received. We will see all of this clearly in this chapter. The anointing has been one of my favorite topics to dive deep into, because not only a growth in the anointing, but also true revelation of its Biblical understanding came to me by the Holy Spirit in 2022 as I was in such a battling and life-changing season.

I love discussing the anointing, as we did earlier in this book from Leviticus 26, because it will cause one to be a spiritual powerhouse. With it, the atmosphere shifts, and everyone will recognize it upon someone. Without it, one is riding on pure talent and "calling," but "calling" without the anointing will not get the job done in the spirit realm, and it is all too common that this is what takes place. We have confused someone's calling with an anointing. One can have a calling, but not yet have the anointing needed to fulfill that calling. I know many people with a calling, but never received the anointing, or still haven't, because the anointing comes through a very specific process laid out in the Scriptures, specifically the Torah of Moses, which we will see is referenced by Paul as well.

One thing we need to understand about the New Testament, which I have taught over and over again, whether it be the words of Jesus, John, Paul, Peter, etc., they are giving a sermon or an interpretation from an understanding or revelation they've received from the Scriptures. We have to understand what I mean when I say the "Scriptures," because in their day, there was no New Testament. The "Scriptures" to them are only what is written in the Tanach (Old Testament). This is Paul's mindset when he says to Timothy in 2 Timothy 3:16-17:

> "All Scripture that was written by the Spirit is profitable
> for instruction and for decisive refutation, and for correc-
> tion, and for deep extensive learning in righteousness, so
> that the man of God may become perfect and complete
> for every good work."

The only thing circulating from what we currently call the New Testament during the ministry of Paul is the book of Matthew, and we see very clearly from the book of Acts, Corinthians, and Timothy that Paul had a copy of the manuscript of Matthew, because he quotes Matthew's account of the Gospel multiple times, but that is it from what is now given to us as the New Testament. However, other than that, when they are giving teachings and revelations, they are giving these understandings from what they would call "Scripture," which is Genesis through Malachi in an English Bible, or in a Hebrew Bible, the ordering of books is different, ending with 2 Chronicles, although still containing the same books in its entirety. Therefore, when studying the New Testament, the most important part we have to understand is context. We need to understand what passage in the Tanach is being referenced, because in their sermon they don't give the backdrop, but it is from some place in the Tanach, and mostly the Torah of Moses specifically, which is the foundational passage from which they are preaching or getting all of these revelations and principles. Without this understanding, we take things out of the context they meant for it to be understood, and this is how we get 41,000 denominations in Christianity, and so many contradictions with Scripture, yet all claim to be moving by the unifying Spirit of God.

The same goes for the concept of the anointing. Paul writes in 2 Timothy 2:19-21:

> "But the firm foundation of God stands, and it has this seal: 'the LORD knows those who are His,' and 'let everyone who invokes the name of our Master stand aloof from iniquity.' But in a great house there are not only vessels of gold and silver, but also of wood and pottery, and some of them for honor, and some for dishonor. If therefore, anyone purges himself of these things, he will be a pure vessel for honor, fit for the use of his Master and prepared for every good work."

Notice, the last verse starts out, saying, "if therefore," meaning, this last verse is dependent upon the first two verses, and even what precedes those. If the individual purges himself of "these things," which is the iniquity in the first verse. By purging oneself from iniquity, one will be used as a vessel of honor by Master Yeshua and prepared for every good work. Paul is speaking here about a certain vessel that can be used in the service of God, and the vessel can only be used if purged from iniquity, and continually being purged of iniquity, because it is a continual process of sanctification until the day of Messiah. The emphasis of this passage is on a vessel that can obtain an anointing, which will enable that vessel to be used by God in His service or Tabernacle.

The Biblical definition of an anointing is the authorization from heaven for one to be used in a very specific area of service for the Kingdom of God, as we will see. The question becomes, where is Paul's teaching to Timothy coming from, so we can deeper understand the anointing? Paul is making a reference to the Tabernacle in the book of Exodus. Paul is talking about vessels for honor and dishonor, and the vessels of honor can be used in God's service. He is talking about the vessels that were prepared in Exodus, in order to be used in the service of the Tabernacle for a very specific service or calling. Some had the calling and anointing for the altar of incense, some for the menorah, etc. We will see here shortly, that when these vessels were fashioned, and then anointed, the Scripture tells us that these vessels shall be anointed "and you shall sanctify them (Exodus 30:29)," or "and you shall sanctify it (Exodus 40:9)" in regard to these vessels. The Scripture says only once you anoint them, they are sanctified, which in Hebrew literally means to be "set apart for a specific service." The latter is dependent upon the former, meaning, by the anointing they will be sanctified (קדש) or set apart (קדש), as it is the same word in Hebrew, which is also the word for "holy." The anointing enables the vessels to be set apart for their service in the Tabernacle or in God's service, or as Paul says, fit for the Master's use and prepared for every good work. The anointing gives authority to now be used in a specific manner. Without the anointing, one can't be used as a vessel in the Tabernacle.

We must understand something about becoming holy or set apart. This word in Hebrew, (קדש) to be holy, sanctified, or set apart, by definition, has to do with what is removed from it, and not what is added. This means, one doesn't become holy because of what they add to their lives, just as these vessels didn't become holy because of what was added, but rather, what was removed or taken away. Think about the word holy as it is first defined in regard to the Sabbath in Genesis 2:1-3. The Sabbath isn't holy or set apart from the other six days of the week because of what is added to it, but rather due to what is taken away, such as typical work that is done on the other six days of the week. Taking away is what made it different or holy. This is the definition of the word "holy, sanctified, or set apart" in Hebrew. Reading your Bible, going to church, Bible studies, or even being baptized and adding these things is not what sets you apart and causes you to be holy or sanctified if you still are doing drugs, living in drunkenness, cheating on your wife etc.

Adding these things does not make one holy, it makes one a hypocrite. It is taking away the things of the world from your life that makes one holy or set apart and prepared for an anointing. So too, with these vessels, as Paul said, it is "purging oneself from iniquity" and removing worldly things that will enable one to be anointed and considered set apart for a specific purpose in the service of God. The anointing carries authority, as well as fear and trembling to those around them, just as the priests and Levites trembled at misusing any of the holy things. In fact, one of the six offerings in Leviticus 1-5 is based off of misusing God's holy things. When you carry an anointing, people tremble at your presence and word, because they know you don't come alone or on your own accord, but speak and act by the oracles of God, such as one who fears when a prophet walks in the room, as it is written in Deuteronomy 18:22:

> "When the prophet will speak in the Name of the LORD, and the word will not be, and will not come to pass, that is the word which the LORD did not speak. The prophet spoke in insolence, you shall not fear him."

Before one could receive the anointing, which will enable them to be used with power and authority, there was a process one had to go through, or that these vessels had to go through. Now we can talk about how we receive an anointing, and how we obtain it in an increasing manner. Paul says he who purges himself of sin is like a vessel that is being purified. What is this referencing specifically? The menorah in the Tabernacle. It is written in Exodus 25:31 "and you shall make the menorah of pure gold, it shall be made of beaten work," and again in Numbers 8:4 "this is the making of the menorah, beaten work of gold," as well as its vessels (Exodus 25:39). All of it was made of beaten work of gold (מִקְשָׁה זָהָב), pronounced "miksha zahav," which means, there is this big block of gold, nothing special. You have to take this massive block of shapeless gold, put it in great fire, and beat it intensely until you break off piece after piece, in order to shape it into the menorah that will give light, as well as its vessels. It is a painful process for the block of gold to be shaped in such a way, taking away things from it continually, in order to make it holy or set apart. That block of gold being greatly beaten, and beaten, is like one who is being purged from the inside out of iniquity and the things of the flesh, which include pride, ideologies, bad habits, comfortabilities, generational behaviors, thought processes, language, relationships, family ties, soul ties, etc.

You can drop gold on the ground, and it won't break, and the same goes for us, we can be told to do something, but a simple word or thought won't usually change us. To do this, there has to be extremely intense heat, and a "beaten work" for shaping. It is the only way to purge and shape, which then allows the menorah to later be anointed with oil, as it was in Exodus. The pruning process that brings the anointing, which will authorize you to be set apart for service is nothing short of a painful process. You may have a calling, just as God has a desire for a certain vessel to be transformed into something for the Tabernacle, but a calling is nothing more than a desire or plan from God upon your life. Jesus said many are called, but few are chosen (Matthew 22:14). Being chosen is because one has gone through the fire of that calling to now be a chosen vessel for the service, and to receive the anointing. Many have a calling, but a calling and anointing are totally different. The anointing gives you the authority to carry out the calling. I know many people that have been heavily called, but they couldn't take the fire and sacrifice, just as all of Israel was called out of Egypt, but only 20% were chosen to come out, and 80% actually died in the land of Egypt, yet, all were called, for many are called, but few are chosen.

All of us can be considered holy/set apart when we repent of our sin and have faith in Jesus, which now sets you apart from the world, but then there can be a new level of holiness and being set apart, even from the majority of the body of Messiah, and those are the ones who walk in power and are to be the Levites who were separated from the rest of Israel with a different authority in the LORD, but it comes with a price, and it will cost you everything. It is a new level of removing things. Now we aren't just removing sin, but even certain permissible things that may not feed the power of the Holy Spirit. It is important not to confuse the anointing I speak on here, which gives authority in the Holy Spirit in a given area or calling, to the anointing spoken of by John in 1 John 2:20, which says we all have an anointing from the Holy One. The context of that passage has to be read from verses 18-27, which is speaking about having an anointing to discern who is and is not the Messiah. That portion of Scripture has nothing to do with fulfilling a calling, but rather you having an anointing to know that Jesus is the Messiah, and not to follow a false messiah or anti-christ who claims to be Him. See, once again, context is key.

Receiving an anointing comes after one is made of beaten work (מִקְשָׁה), pronounced "mikshah" as I just showed, but it is important to note that this word comes from the three letter verbal root kashah (קָשָׁה), which means to be hard, difficult, severe, or harsh, and is the same word in Exodus 6:9 "and Moses spoke thus to the children of Israel, but they did not listen to Moses because of impatience and hard (קָשָׁה) labor." The word for "hard" in the phrase "hard labor" is the same word for where we get "beaten work" as it pertains to the vessels used in God's service. The connection shows us that being holy, and the pruning process it takes to get to the anointing can only come through the pains of Egypt and great hardship and suffering, which as it did then, will generally include some type of physical pain, whether it be in the body, or finances, etc., as they were oppressed physically. Something that will try and take your attention off of hearing the words of Moses/Messiah, because the physical burden is so tough and distracting (Exodus 6:9). The children of Israel were being sanctified in Egypt. It is the difficulties that we endure and see through until the end with faithfulness and meekness, and the pains we go through, where we will come out with the anointing and in the power of the Holy Spirit, as Jesus went through pains in the wilderness, fasting for forty days, and with faithfulness He endured, so then Luke 4:14 says He returned in the power of the Holy Spirit.

Egypt produces the anointing in the tough circumstances by humbling us, pruning us, and shaping us. The affliction that was taking place was a painful process of sanctification so that they could come out as pure gold and silver, and with clean garments (Exodus 3:22). All of the revelation of this entire book, and a few more that will be written came from the ridiculous pain I had to endure from the end of 2021 through 2023. Not only all of the revelation of this book, and a couple other books that will be written, but also many of my public teachings, and even the giftings and signs and wonders that have taken place in my life came through storms that broke me, and put me on my knees in tears, over and over again. But the Word of God and prayer has always been my plumb line, and the Holy Spirit continually nourished me, as it is written in Psalms 109:4 "in the place of my love they persecute me, but I pray."

That pain and pressing into God during that time of intense fire, is what brought the revelation and anointing that was produced by those circumstances. The pain enabled me to now teach with power, and through my experience, and I am now able to do a certain work in God's service or Tabernacle. I was pruned (and am still being pruned continually) in such a way that now I can be fit for the Master's use. What was once a calling, turned into an anointing due to the endurance (James 1:1-4). In fact, when God took Israel out of Egypt, it is written in Exodus 13:18 "and God turned the people the way of the wilderness of the Red Sea, and the children of Israel went up armed from the land of Egypt." The word for "armed (חֲמֻשִׁים)" is the same letters for the word "messiah's or anointed ones (משׁחים)." They came out armed with the anointing from Egypt, meaning, ONLY out of the pains of Egypt can one obtain the anointing, or the gold and silver, which is true wisdom and understanding, which is the reason for its juxtaposition in Scripture, as it is written in Proverbs 3:13-14 "blessed is the man who has found wisdom, and has obtained understanding, for its trade is better than the trade of silver, and its gain than fine gold," as well as in Proverbs 2:2-4:

> "To cause your ear to listen to wisdom, to incline your heart to understanding, for, if you will call out to understanding, and you will lift your voice to discernment, if you seek it like the silver, and you will search it like the hidden treasures."

Again, in Psalms 119:127 "therefore I have loved your commandments more than gold, and more than pure gold," as the Torah itself, which is filled with God's commandments, is the ultimate wisdom as we discussed in Chapter 6 on the Fear Of The LORD, which is said to be the true gold.

Our walk with Messiah is a process and walk of sanctification and pruning, however, there is also a threshold, where at a certain point, one obtains the anointing that will thrust them into the calling they've been called to since the beginning, as it is written in Ephesians 2:10 "for we are His creation who are created in Yeshua the Messiah for good works, which God has before prepared for us to walk in." This threshold for the anointing is also spoken of in Exodus 29:45-46:

> "I will dwell inside of the children of Israel, and I will be their God. They will know that I am the LORD their God, Who brought them out from the land of Egypt, in order to dwell inside of them. I am the LORD their God."

And again, in Leviticus 26:11-12 "And I will place My dwelling inside of you, and My soul will not abhor you, and I will continually walk inside of you, and I will be your God, and you will be My people."

Notice, in the Exodus and Leviticus verses, most English Bibles translate this as "dwell in your midst," rather than how I translated it "inside of you." The word "b'toch (בתוך)" literally means "inside" of someone, and in verses 11 and 12 above it is carrying a second person, masculine, plural pronominal suffix, meaning, God is not speaking to Israel as the nation, rather He is speaking to each individual, and that He will dwell in each of them individually. God is speaking about the indwelling of the Holy Spirit within us, and in context, Leviticus 26 says this will happen if we continually walk in His ways, obedient to Him and in purity, which is why it is written in Acts 5:32 "and we are witnesses of these words, and the Holy Spirit whom God gives to those who obey Him." It is also written in 1 John 3:24 "and whoever keeps His commandments is kept by Him, and He dwells in him. And by this we distinguish that He dwells in us, from His Spirit that He has given to us." John himself says this same exact revelation from Leviticus 26, that if we continually walk in His commandments, the Holy Spirit will dwell within us and walk within us. God says He will make His dwelling within us, and that He will "continually walk" inside of us, as Paul said in Galatians 2:20, we will be so possessed by the Holy Spirit and dead to ourselves that it will no longer be us who lives, but the Messiah within us.

God says in Leviticus 26:3-13, and mentions in Exodus 29:45, that if we walk in His ways, pruned by Him, we will have a vessel that He will dwell in, and as it is written above, "continually walk inside of." If we do not walk in His ways, we will grieve the Holy Spirit, and the anointing will not flow, as it is written in Ephesians 4:30 "and do not grieve the Holy Spirit of God, whereby you are sealed for the day of redemption," and again in Ephesians 5:18 "and do not be drunk with wine in which is rebellion, but be filled with the Spirit," and also in 1 Thessalonians 5:19 Paul writes "do not quench the Spirit." The Holy Spirit needs a holy vessel to operate in, or God will "abhor our vessels (Leviticus 26:11-12)."

The anointing is something that has to be entrusted to you. Can God trust one with authority, power, and responsibilities that can either glorify Him, or be abused, because Jesus said to whom much is given, much is required (Luke 12:48). This concept on the menorah is the meaning of Jesus' words in Matthew 5:14-16:

> "You are the light of the world. There is no city that is built upon a mountain that can be hidden. And there is no one who lights a menorah and places it under a bushel, but rather upon the stand of a menorah, and it gives light to all who are in the house. Thus, let your light

shine before men, so that they will see your good works
and they will praise your Father in the heavens."

Jesus says that we as the light have a menorah within us, but a bushel
could be covering it. He is making a reference to the menorah in the
Tabernacle, that before it becomes the menorah that shines light, it is one
big block, covered by excess and unnecessary gold, and must be pruned
to show that light, so too, our sin and flesh can be the bushel that is covering the menorah, the light of the Messiah within us from shining to all
who are around us. Genesis 2:7 says, "the LORD God formed man of
the dust from the earth, and He blew in his nostrils the breath of life, and
man became a living soul." The word for "breath" in the phrase "breath
of life" comes from the word n'shamah (נשמה), which is the same word
for "soul" in Proverbs 20:27 "the soul of a man is the lamp of the LORD,
searching all the inner rooms of the belly." Scripture calls our soul a lamp,
which the word for lamp (נר) is related to the word menorah in Hebrew,
meaning, this breath of God is like a menorah within us that can either
be covered up by sin and flesh, or revealed through purging and purification. There are seven lamps in the menorah. The point and connection
of Jesus' words above is that every man, having a soul, has a menorah
within them with a calling, but we are all like big blocks of gold, and it
is a matter of whether or not we go through the continual repentance,
beaten work and fiery trials of Egypt, so the menorah can be realized,
allowing us to be anointed. One will then go from being "called" to
"chosen (Matthew 22:14)" and fit for the Master's use and prepared for
every good work (2 Timothy 2:19-21).

Now that we have seen what it takes to obtain an anointing, what
about maintaining the anointing, or growing in the anointing? As I said,
one can absolutely lose the anointing. Many people use the verse Romans
11:29, that the gift and calling of God is irrevocable as a means to say

one will never lose their gifting, however, the context of Romans 11 has nothing to do with an anointing or gifts in the Spirit, but rather God's continual call to the Jewish people, which is irrevocable. Context must be taken seriously in order to properly divide the Word of Truth (2 Timothy 2:15).

The anointing is likened to oil in the Scripture, because when something was anointed in the Torah of Moses, it was using the anointing oil, and it is a representation of the anointing and authority in the Holy Spirit to be used in the Kingdom of God. The verse we have to focus on for understanding this concept that we can grow in the anointing or cause it to cease is Ecclesiastes 9:8 "let your garments be white at all times, and oil will not be lacking upon your head (בְּכָל־עֵת יִהְיוּ בְגָדֶיךָ לְבָנִים וְשֶׁמֶן עַל־רֹאשְׁךָ אַל־יֶחְסָר)." In Biblical Hebrew grammar, this verse speaks volumes. The phrase "let your garments be white," and "oil will not be lacking upon your head," is in the imperfect conjugation, which grammatically expresses habitual or customary action. Garments need to habitually be white and unspotted from sin continually. This verse is two phrases connected by what is called a "consequential Vav," meaning, the latter phrase, the oil not lacking upon one's head, is a consequence of the former phrase, keeping one's garments always white. ONLY IF your garments remain white at all times, the Scripture promises the anointing oil will not cease from upon your head. It will continue to flow. Keeping our garments white is a picture of what the menorah had to go through. It is a cleansing process of continual sanctification and beaten work.

This story of the vessels from the Torah, the anointing, and the anointing continuing or stopping is found within 2 Kings 4:1-6:

"One woman from among the wives of the prophets' disciples cried out to Elisha, saying, 'your servant, my husband, has died, and you know that your servant feared

God. But now the creditor has come to take my two sons to be his slaves.' Elisha said to her, 'what can I do for you? Tell me what you have in the house.' She said, 'your maidservant has nothing in the house except a jar of oil.' He said, 'go, borrow vessels for yourself from the outside, from all your neighbors, empty vessels. Do not be sparing. Then go in and shut the door behind you and behind your sons. Pour it in to all these vessels and carry away the full ones.' She went from him and shut the door behind her and behind her children. They brought vessels to her and poured. When all the containers were full, she said to her son, 'bring me another vessel.' He said to her, 'there is not another vessel,' and the oil stopped."

Notice she gathers a bunch of empty vessels, and for however much vessel there is, there is enough oil, but only once the vessels stopped, so too, did the oil stop. The vessels stopping is a revelation of the pruning/purging of the vessels stopping. When we stop in our beaten work of sanctification, the oil stops, but when we multiply in sanctification, so does the anointing. We have to be continually pruned so the menorah within us can continually give its light and be used alongside its vessels. The vessel is continually in repentance, and the vessel has to be continually repentant to receive new and fresh oil, as Jesus said in Matthew 9:16-17:

"No man places a new patch on a worn out garment or else its seam should tear away from that garment, and the hole will be greater. And they do not place new wine in worn out wineskins or else the wineskins should rip, and the wineskins are destroyed, and the wine should pour

206

out. Rather, they place new wine in new wineskins, and both of them are preserved."

In Jewish thought, the wine has to do with the anointing and secrets that the Messiah wants to reveal to us. It is well known in Jewish and rabbinic thought that the gematria (numerical value) of "wine (יין)" is 70, which is equivalent to "secret (סוד)." The Messiah wants to continually take those who are willing to walk into sanctification with a continually renewed vessel and wineskin, and bring us into the deep, secret places of revelation and anointing to walk in power, just as Jesus would take Peter, James, and John privately, even separating them from the rest of the 12 disciples, as it is also written in Psalms 25:14 "the secret of the LORD is to those who fear Him." The twelve disciples were set apart from the rest of Jesus' followers, but Peter, James, and John were even more set apart. It was as though all of Jesus' followers would be set apart from the world and enter into the outer court, but the twelve would enter into the Holy Place, and Peter, James, and John would enter into the Holy of Holies. Jesus says if new wine is poured into an old wineskin, the wineskin will break and be worse off, just like if new oil was poured onto an old vessel, because the vessel isn't mature enough to handle a new authority, it will bring a greater destruction for them, and others around them.

The anointing will keep growing the more we are taken into the process of beaten work, being pliable to the Holy Spirit in each tough Egyptian season. The anointing has to be deeply studied from Exodus and the order of pruning the vessel, then to be anointed in order to be used in the Tabernacle. This place of beaten work and sanctification births revelation and authority in the Spirit. Egypt is the place that separates the one who is called, and the one who becomes chosen. God will always be able to find someone He can use to do His work, as it is written in 2 Chronicles 16:9 "for the LORD's eyes run to and fro throughout the entire earth to grant strength with those whose heart is whole towards Him." We are vessels, meaning, if one vessel becomes corrupt, He will find another to fashion, as it is written in Esther 4:13-14:

> "And Mordechai ordered to reply to Esther, 'do not imagine to yourself that you will escape in the king's house from among all the Jews. For if you remain silent at this time, relief and rescue will arise for the Jews from somewhere else, and you and your father's household will perish, and who knows if for a time such as this you have attained the Kingdom."

So full circle, Paul talks to Timothy about the anointing, and being aloof from iniquity, being a vessel of honor or dishonor, and if you do "these things" by being sanctified through beaten work of hardship, obedience, humility, and meekness, you will be able to obtain an anointing, so that you may be a pure vessel for honor that is fit for the use of his Master and prepared for every good work (2 Timothy 2:19-21). This entire chapter I have explained is the context of that passage. Are you willing to count the cost and go through the fires? Through the pruning, the menorah shines bright, and you become a Tree Of Fire, ready to kindle everyone around you. Your circumstances are meant to be pruning. As we discussed, one cannot be armed with the anointing EXCEPT out of Egypt, but many don't make it through those fires, as I mentioned, it is well known in Jewish thought, only 20% of the Jews left Egypt. The other 80% died in the plague of darkness due to lack of faith and not being able to endure, but just as with our faith, so too with the anointing, and those who endure to the end shall be saved (Mark 13:13), so too, those who endure the pain will be anointed, and continually anointed. I am telling you firsthand, the anointing comes through the greatest pain imaginable. If one is wondering why we aren't walking in the miracles and anointing of the book of Acts, it is because we haven't paid the dues of desperation of the book of Acts, nor faced and endured its hardships.

People that run through the fires of marriage generally obtain the anointing to run marriage ministries or have had to go through tough freedom ministry and now have the anointing to take people through freedom ministry. The tough seasons bring anointing, but many today are trying to abide in the old anointing, and aren't learning the new things, and truth be told, their anointing stopped with the old revelation. One must humble themselves to receive the new wine. Your past qualification doesn't qualify you for this season. The Kingdom of God isn't impressed with the past doctoral degree or even the ancient testimony, but the continued pliability to the current river of the Holy Spirit. Telling old miracles is great, and should be continually remembered as a testimony, but if all you have are old ones, at some point, the oil and anointing stopped. As I abide in meekness to the Spirit, I realize I have miracles to proclaim that God is doing almost every week. Without a current and continual anointing, you can't be used in the Tabernacle service. Many who were once pillars in the Tabernacle, are now dust outside the camp, because they didn't stay with the process of anointing that only comes through the beaten work of humble garments before Him in the secret place at all times. The anointing separates, and God is no respecter of persons, so come and get what you were called for, and that is to be an anointed Tree Of Fire.

CHAPTER 10

Train My Hands For War

Around the time I moved to Iowa in May of 2022, there was a verse that the Holy Spirit had me praying over and over again. The Holy Spirit kept telling me to pray "train my hands for war (Psalm 18:35, 144:1)." To be completely honest, we say these words all the time, but most of us, including myself at the time, didn't understand what this really meant. I was in such an intense battle at the time spiritually. Every day I was having a hard time even getting out of bed, or not returning to bed by noon, and this verse became the theme of my prayers every single day, even without me understanding the meaning. I kept saying, "LORD, I don't know what this even means, but you keep telling me to pray it, so I will." Very, very quickly, I got its revelation in a way that changed my life and changed things for many around me. It brought a whole new understanding to spiritual warfare.

Going to war in the Holy Spirit isn't talked about enough, and even when it is, it is discussed in an abstract manner that doesn't enable others to really be raised up as a spiritual powerhouse, and to be equipped to warfare effectively. I say this even about people that are in ministry. If you were to just put them on the spot and ask them about this verse or ask them to explain in depth about spiritual warfare, pulling down strongholds, the true depths of the Jezebel spirit, witchcraft, etc., even the most experienced people I know couldn't elaborate if put on spot. I have spoken with pastor after pastor, teacher after teacher, none of which can elaborate on these concepts in great depth straight from the Scriptures. However, this has been something the LORD commissioned me on when I ended my sabbatical in November of 2022. A mighty passion of mine was now to really bring true depths of knowledge on the Holy Spirit, in order to equip His people, and raise up an army as Trees Of Fire.

The fact of the matter is, everyone considers everything a "Jezebel spirit," and there is no precision to the warfare in the body of the Messiah to call out things exactly as they are, rather than just this umbrella that everyone calls a "Jezebel spirit." It is immature or ignorant at best. We have become so familiar with certain verses, phrases, and the idea of spiritual warfare that it all has become watered down and powerless in our lives. The laziness in the knowledge of the spiritual things and the lack of hunger to deeply dissect them as students in the Word of God which overflows into powerhouse Trees Of Fire absolutely disgusted me. The body of Messiah has lost its edge. The Holy Spirit is about precision, and our prophecy needs precision, our warfare needs precision, and our revelation needs to be rightly divided (2 Timothy 2:15). Precision means a sharper sword in your armor (Ephesians 6:10-17). It is written in 2 Corinthians 10:3-5:

> "For, although we walk in the flesh, our warfare is not after the flesh. For the weapons of our warfare are not those of the flesh, but those of the power of God, by which we subdue rebellious castles, and we demolish imaginations, and every lofty thing that exalts itself against the knowledge of God and subjugate all reasoning to obedience to the Messiah."

And again, in Ephesians 6:12 "for our conflict is not with flesh and blood, but with principalities and with those in authority, and with the possessors of this dark world, and with the evil spirits that are under heaven." When we go to war, we are warring against spirits, which is something that isn't directly seen with the eyes, and so if our warfare is against something that isn't physical, how can we be precise with what specific evil spirit or scheme of the enemy we are warring against? As we will see in this chapter, we have to notice its pattern in how it manifests in the physical, and then we can find that pattern Scripturally, and learn how the man or woman of God combatted it. We see that when Jesus would disarm the power of these evil spirits, He wouldn't address the person, but rather the spirit that was operating, such as when He looked to Peter, and rebuked not Peter, but the spirit of Satan that was operating through him in that moment (Matthew 16:23). Another example of Jesus dealing with an individual, but focusing on the spirit(s) operating is in Mark 5:1-10:

> "And He came to the other side of the sea, to the region of the Gadarenes. And when He went out from the boat, a man who had an unclean spirit happened upon Him from the cemetery, and he was dwelling in the cemetery. And no man was able to bind him with chains, because whenever he was bound with fetters and chains, he would break the chains and would cut the fetters and no man was able to subdue him. During the night and during the day he was always in the cemetery and in the mountains and he would cry out and cut himself with rocks. And when he saw Yeshua from afar, he ran and worshipped Him. And he cried out with a loud voice and said, 'what have I to do with You, Yeshua the Son of the Most High

God? I adjure you by God that You not torment me.'
For He was saying to him, 'unclean spirit come out from
the man.' And He asked him, 'what is your name?' He
said to Him, 'Legion is our name, because we are many.'
And he entreated Him greatly not to send him out of the
country.'"

Notice, Jesus may seem like He is speaking to or addressing the man,
however, He is really dealing with the spirit(s) involved. We are to always
see with eyes the of the Spirit, so that we truly understand when warring,
although a person may be the avenue through which the spirit operates,
the patterns and methodology is something spiritual that we can find
directly out of Scripture, because nothing is new under the sun (Ecclesiastes 1:9-10). The patterns and schemes of the enemy don't change,
we just have to find which one it is that is operating, and only then
can we understand in which way we are to combat it, so that our hands
are trained for that specific war. By the end of this chapter, you will see
spiritual warfare, and a spiritual equipping in a way you have probably
never seen it, and if studied carefully, it will change your life. You will be
like a fiery vessel that causes spiritual manifestations everywhere you go
just by walking in somewhere as a powerful tree of fire, just as the spirit
manifested when Jesus came to the Gadarenes. I have personally had this
happen where a man started manifesting the moment I even walked into
the atmosphere, and the man began yelling at me specifically as we see
with Jesus. The Holy Spirit showed me what was taking place from this
very story with the Gadarenes. In fact, I have had demons and witchcraft
manifest in people while I was preaching on things regarding the Holy
Spirit. When one walks intimately with the Spirit and with the anointing, this is more frequent than one may realize.

For Passover in 2023, we had a room gathered with almost 80 people, and after I finished preaching, I called for a fire tunnel where nine of us laid hands on every person to have them receive whatever they needed from the Holy Spirit- freedom, devils cast out, baptized in the Holy Spirit and fire, impartation, etc. We had devils cast out, people laid out under the glory, even young kids getting baptized in the Holy Spirit, unbelievers getting hit with the Holy Spirit and becoming flames for God, and there was a woman who was going through and got hit by the power of God, and as she got hit, multiple demons within her manifested. My dad was at the end of the tunnel with two others, and the woman manifesting multiple demons leans over and began throwing up blood for probably over half an hour. It was a good learning experience for people there who had never encountered this before. A few days later, I sat my dad down to explain to him what was happening, showing him through the Scriptures that when Jesus would cast out devils in the gospels, you will see that the demon(s) causes a violent manifestation upon its exiting the individual. The night after this Pentecostal Passover experience, I had a dream that ravenous wolves surrounded my parents' home and were trying to kill us, and that I was to stay within the house and intercede. Within 48 hours of the dream, I was on my knees in my parents' home interceding because my mom was put in the hospital, very, very sick, and fighting for her life against sepsis.

The spirit realm and those walking in power are always targets, and I knew this attack was directly from every bit of witchcraft we broke off just a couple nights before at Passover, and the powerful movement of the Spirit of God that took place. We had doctors in the faith, pastors, teachers, elders, etc. all from different ministries that night getting hit with the power of God, being re-kindled in the Holy Spirit from the staleness they had been stuck in. Due to a revelation from the Holy Spirit, I knew the week prior to the Passover gathering that I was going to get attacked. I told certain leaders weeks before it happened because the LORD showed me through dreams. I was girding my loins from the get-go, making sure all of my doors were closed to the evil one and everything was covered in the blood of the Lamb. I was warring in the Holy Spirit for my mom as she fought for her life in the hospital. I was on my knees before God, tearing down the web of witchcraft string by string. None of this surprised me. In fact, during the time she stayed in the hospital, when I would visit her almost daily, I was meeting people there and ministering, including a pastor who needed to get touched by the Holy Spirit, and for his physical eyes to be opened. The LORD was frustrating what the Enemy meant for harm and was using it for good (Genesis 50:20). Do what you want to me, but wherever I go, I am about my Father's business. If Jesus commanded us to cast out devils, heal the sick, and cleanse the lepers (Matthew 10:8), we need to be equipped and knowledgeable in how to move in the Holy Spirit, but first as we discussed in Chapter 1, we must be baptized in the Holy Spirit and fire.

To unfold this entire revelation, I want to start out by sharing something the Father showed me one day. The Holy Spirit told me very clearly, "in every Garden of Eden, I have placed the serpent. There is a serpent in every Garden of Eden." Immediately He started to show me what this meant, and why He does this. What does He mean by every "Garden of Eden?" This means every group of righteousness, whether it be a righteous business, ministry, Bible study, etc. Literally, any group of righteousness that the LORD has planted, like the Garden of Eden, wherever Eden is, there the serpent is also, placed there by God Himself, because nothing is new under the sun (Genesis 3:1). The LORD started to show me the paradigms of this concept throughout Scripture, such as, with Moses, it was Korah literally in the courtyard of the Tabernacle. With King David, it was Ahitophel, his best counselor who joined and fueled the conspiracy of Absalom, David's son, against David. With Yeshua, it was Judas. With Paul, it was Demas (Colossians 4:14, 2 Timothy 4:10). In Colossians 4:14 Paul says that Demas is one of his closest partners in the ministry, then in 2 Timothy 4:10 Demas forsook Paul for the world.

God allows the serpent to be in our garden and in any righteous group for the LORD. If one isn't in righteousness, there won't be a serpent, because you aren't a threat, but rather, you might even be the serpent. However, when you walk in the power and intimacies of the Spirit of God, every group of righteousness will have the serpent, a Judas. Luke 22:3 says, "Satan entered Judas." So, we have to know how to expose the serpent/Judas, and how to go to war against these things, and not only that, but also to see the signs before it happens. There is a reason Satan could enter Judas, but not the others, because of certain doors, tendencies, and characteristics Judas had open, which gave access or legal right to Satan. As a leader, I am constantly scanning those around me daily, praying fervently with vigilance to not only see the full blown Judas, but who has the potential to get to that point due to certain signs that Judas had. There is a common theme with every serpent in the garden that we will see. They all want gain of some sort, and even more specifically, money and authority, just as Judas had a money problem (John 12:6), and Korah had a hunger for greater authority (Numbers 16:9-10). Greed and the love of money are the root of all evil (1 Timothy 6:10).

Judas was the one in charge of the money for the group. Jesus already knew who would betray Him, as it is written in John 6:64/70-71:

> "But there are some of you who do not believe, for Yeshua had known from the start who are those that did not believe, and who he was who would betray Him. Yeshua said to them, 'did I not choose you twelve, and is it one of you who is an adversary?' He was speaking now

concerning Judas Iscariot, the son of Simon, for he was
about to betray Him being one from the twelve."

This is why I say, we must be vigilant and know before it happens.
Notice, Jesus left Judas there the entire time and Scripture says, "Yeshua
had known from the start." As a matter of fact, Jesus kept Judas very
close to Him on purpose. Why? Well, for one, the Scriptures had to
be fulfilled, and the Scriptures that Jesus references about Judas, were
actually the same Scriptures David spoke of in regard to his closest and
wisest counselor, Ahitophel (John 13:18, Psalm 41:10, 55:13-15), because nothing is new under the sun. Now, we get to learn from these
things, in order to be equipped to go to war against them, and like I
said, we will see in this chapter that we can locate the exact spirit we are
facing and recognize its schemes and how that individual combatted it,
therefore, training us and our hands for that specific war.

All of these "spirits" are Satan and manifestations of the demonic,
but we can put names to them by seeing through which Biblical character and narrative they manifested, in order to now know what to do,
such as a spirit operating through the woman Jezebel we now refer to as
a "Jezebel spirit." The problem is, all of Christianity refers to everything
as a "Jezebel spirit," and it is a total lack of being truly equipped, and an
easy way out. One could be going against a spirit of Korah, or Ahab, or
Absalom, etc., and once you can locate its schemes and know which one
it is that is operating, go to that passage of Scripture and study exactly
how it was dealt with. This is what David meant when he said, "train my
hands for war."

The question first arises, why does God not only allow the serpent
there, but He places him there intentionally (Genesis 3:1), and this will
teach us why Jesus kept Judas so close. You see, if Jesus would have
kicked out Judas, another one would have come along, so rather than

kick him out, we need to know why the serpent, Korah, Ahitophel, Judas, or Demas is there in the first place. The book of Judges spells this out for us perfectly. As with the rest of Scripture, if we don't see this through the lens of the Holy Spirit, we will miss what's written right in front of us. When the children of Israel entered the Promise Land, God purposely left the remaining Canaanite nations in the land in order to teach Israel something, just as Jesus left Judas next to Him. Read this passage very, very carefully. Judges 2:21-3:5:

> I, too, shall no longer drive away any man from before them, from among the nations that Joshua left when he died, in order to test Israel through them, whether or not they would guard the way of the LORD to walk therein as their forefathers did. So, the LORD let those nations remain without driving them out quickly, and He did not deliver them into Joshua's hand. These are the nations that the LORD let remain, to test Israel through them, all those who did not know the Canaanite wars, only so that the generations of the children of Israel would know, in order to teach them warfare, but those who were before them did not know: the five governors of the Philistines, all the Canaanites, Sidonites, and the Hivites that dwelt on mount Lebanon, from the mountain of the plain of Hermon until the approach to Hamath. They were to test Israel through them, to know whether they would listen to the commandments of the LORD, which He commanded their forefathers through the hand of Moses. So, the children of Israel dwelt among the Canaanite, the Hittite, the Amorite, the Perizzite, the Hivite, and the Jebusite.

The Scripture says that God Himself kept the enemy camp within the land of Israel, which is the Garden of Eden, just as Jesus kept the enemy near Him, in order to teach Israel how to go to war in the Spirit! When Scripture is talking about people going to war, it is the word milchama (מלחמה), which is the same word in the New Testament for "warfare." God is allowing things with the serpent, with the spirit of Ahitophel, Judas, Ahab, Jezebel, Korah, Amalek, Demas, etc. in order to teach us how to go to war in the Spirit. This is part of the nature of our walk with God, being full partakers in the war against the kingdom of darkness and dismantling the works of the devil.

Jesus' bride is meant to fully partake in all of what He partook in while on the earth, because as the Father sent Him, so does He send us (John 20:21). All manifestations and schemes of the enemy remain in our lives, in order to teach us how to be girded and vigilant in the Spirit of God, as well as how to team up with Him on a daily basis. Our walks as believers are not meant to be passive, but with power (1 Corinthians 2:4, 4:20). Jesus also rebuked His disciples for not walking in power and being able to cast out a devil (Mark 9:18-19). This is an army. In fact, the moment you accepted Jesus as the Passover Lamb of God and came out of Egypt, you were enlisted as a soldier in a life-long contract, as it is written in Exodus 12:41 "and at the end of the 430 years, in that same day, all the armies of the LORD went out of Egypt."

In the Spirit, we are needing to learn how to warfare, for even Paul says in 2 Corinthians 2:11 that we are not to be ignorant of Satan's devices and tactics, yet, today, many are ignorant and, therefore, powerless. As a believer, you should be feared by the evil one. How many of us would have just read that Judges passage in the flesh, and saw it only as God allowing Canaanites to stay in the land in order to teach Israel how to go to war, without recognizing this is about spiritual warfare? We have a spiritual blue print right in front of us, yet many of us are only reading a spiritual Word according to the flesh, because as I said earlier in this book, they aren't letting the Interpreter interpret. This is why David says twice in the Psalms that God is "the One who trains my hands for war (Psalms 18:35, 144:1)." As I began learning to find the patterns of the enemy in the Scripture, my hands were being trained for each war I came against. I would read certain passages, and the exact passage would be the exact pattern of the enemy in my life. In those moments, I would devour those portions of Scripture, and learn how to counteract that scheme of the evil one.

During that time, I had pressed in so heavily to the Scriptures and prayer, the level of mightiness that I gained in the revelation and knowledge of the Scriptures was equally yoked with how mighty I became in the Spirit. Everyone around me and those following my teachings began commenting on this increase, as Paul told Timothy in 1 Timothy 4:15 "on these things meditate, give yourself wholly to them, that it may be obvious to all that you make advances." In fact, both John the Baptist and Jesus are described the EXACT same way in Aramaic in Luke 1:80 and Luke 2:40 "and the boy grew and became strong in the Spirit." What does this mean? When we see someone strong in the Spirit, it means they are strong and numerous in their revelation of the Word of God, because Romans 7:14 and 2 Timothy 3:16 says that the Scriptures are from the Spirit, and in order to become stronger in the Spirit, we must become mighty in the Scriptures and in them being revealed to us. In Aramaic, when it says John and Jesus became strong (מתחיל) in the Spirit, the verb is reflexive, meaning, they not only became strong, but THEY strengthened THEMSELVES in the Spirit, because they devoured Scripture (Jeremiah 15:16). It isn't by chance that one becomes mighty, nor is it by passivity, but by ones causing themselves to be such, for God is no respecter of persons (Deuteronomy 16:19, Romans 2:11, Galatians 2:6, Colossians 3:25, Ephesians 6:9, 1 Timothy 5:21, James 2:1-9).

As they became mighty in the revelation of Scripture, their spiritual stature grew and became known amongst the enemy camp. During this season from the end of 2021 through 2023 that I was multiplying in revelation on all things of the Spirit, witchcraft, warfare, etc., I had a mighty man of God come up to me in 2022 and say, "Nick, the enemy doesn't know everyone by name, but he now knows you by name because of the abundance of revelation that you have attained, and your walking in the power of the Holy Spirit." God began taking me to certain Scriptures in the New Testament and in the Torah on this very concept. It is written in Acts 19:13-16:

> "Moreover, certain Jews who went about exorcising demons, were disposed to exorcise in the name of our Master Yeshua over those who had unclean spirits, by saying, 'we command you in the name of that Yeshua whom Paul preaches.' And there were seven sons of a Jewish man whose name was Sceva, who was one of the chief priests who did this. And the evil demon answered and said to them, 'Yeshua I well know, and Paul I know, but as for you, who are you?' And the man in whom was the evil demon leaped upon them, and overpowered them, and threw them down, and they fled out of the house beaten and bruised."

I began seeking for this revelation straight out of the Torah of Moses, in order to know why demons know and fear certain people, but not others. God revealed it to me in Exodus 1:7-10:

> "The children of Israel were fruitful, and swarmed, and increased, and became very, very strong, and the land became filled with them. And a new king arose over

Egypt, who did not know Joseph. He said to his people, 'behold, the people of the children of Israel are more numerous and stronger than us. Come, let us deal wisely with them, lest they multiply, and war will come about, and they will be added to our enemies, and they will wage war against us and ascend from the land. So, they appointed task masters over them in order to afflict them with their burdens, and they built storage cities for Pharaoh, Pitom and Ramases. But the more they afflicted them, the more they multiplied, and they broke forth, and they abhorred the children of Israel."

The moment the children of Israel became a threat due to their multiplying in the numbers of their revelation, the evil one took notice of them and began afflicting them physically, in order to distract them from the things of the Spirit. In other words, their name (Israel) became known and feared amongst the enemy camp (Pharaoh and Egypt) due to their multiplying, that is, multiplying in the Spirit, in revelation, in disciples, and in mighty deeds. As I said, God was continually training my hands for the art of spiritual warfare through the abundance of revelations as I was picking up on different patterns of the enemy in Scripture, and He was teaching me how to fight accordingly. The more I was afflicted during that time, I only pressed in harder, and multiplied more and more in revelation. As I said in the foreword, the more the enemy trampled me like a wine press, the more new wine that began to flow. The evil one overdid himself. I became feared by the enemy camp, and I knew it with great reverence before God.

In fact, even leaders of other churches, ministries, synagogues, and institutions became intimidated by me, black-balling me because their pastors, teachers, and attendees were getting kindled by the Holy Spirit around me or through my teachings, and although I never went into other ministries with an Absalom spirit, people would come out to what God was doing through my life, because when people encounter the real power of God, their taste buds become bland to religion, or when they encounter the true bread from heaven and teachings of the Spirit, they no longer hunger for anything else. The Spirit of God will expose religious pharisees who are hypocrites and want to build their own kingdom, just as Jesus never went into ministries trying to "steal" people like Absalom, but people came out to Him, and the religious leaders were intimidated. As we have said, nothing is new under the sun (Ecclesiastes 1:9-10), and if this happened to Him, it will happen to us (John 15:18-20), as it has to me, and we are called to walk as He walked (1 John 2:6).

We will start with Ahitophel and Absalom. Ahitophel was David's main and wisest counselor. Scripture says that his counsel was so wise, it was even as the counsel of God (2 Samuel 16:23). David's son, Absalom, created a conspiracy against David, gathering people of his behind his back, in order to remove him so he can replace him on the throne. Then it is written in 2 Samuel 15:31 "and it was told to David, saying, 'Ahitophel is among the conspirators with Absalom.' And David said, 'LORD, I beg You, confuse the counsel of Ahitophel.'" During this time, I had been going against Ahitophel and Absalom. Even the people closest to me would betray me with a kiss as Judas betrayed Jesus (Luke 22:47-48). The LORD began showing me these things and said, "study David, and do as he did, and it will be well with you." Keep in mind, Ahitophel's name means "my brother slanders." This time was truly heartbreaking for me to encounter. It was involving my absolute closest relationships. As the LORD told me, the key is finding out what David did next... 2 Samuel 15:32-37:

"And it came to pass when David came to the top of the mount where he worshipped God, behold, Hushai the Archite came to meet him with his coat rent, and earth upon his head. David said unto him, 'If you pass on with me, then you will be burdensome to me. But if you return to the city and say unto Absalom: I will be your servant, O king, as I have been your father's servant until now, so now will I be your servant. Then you may defeat the counsel of Ahitophel for me. And don't you have there Zadok and Abiathar the priests? And it shall be that everything you hear from the king's house, you shall tell to Zadok and Abiathar the priests. And behold, they have their two sons with them, Ahimaaz to Zadok, and Jonathan to Abiathar, and through them you shall send to me everything you hear. And Hushai the Archite, the friend of David, came to the city, and Absalom was coming to the city."

David used Hushai as an informant to protect him, and to be able to defeat the enemy camp that he was now going against. At this time, the LORD started showing me that I needed an informant, and that He was going to be my Informant. The LORD was my Hushai. He began showing me everything I needed to know. He would come to me in dreams, over and over, and show me exactly what these people were saying and doing, just as the LORD did for Moses when Miriam and Aaron teamed up against Moses behind his back (Numbers 12:1-9). I teamed up with God, studying these passages and praying these Scriptures to Him, as I kept myself from evil and from returning evil for evil. Everything I needed to know, He revealed to me with revelation by day, and dream or angelic visitation by night. I cannot tell you how many nights this happened, and how supernatural this was. I could read people's mail before them, and they knew that I wasn't alone. One night, the LORD came to me in a dream, took me in the Spirit, and brought me into someone's home (Ezekiel 8:3-12). I hovered at their ceiling in the Spirit while listening to the conversation of this husband and wife, just as God took Ezekiel by the locks of his hair in the Spirit and brought him into the inner rooms of certain people to see and hear them. I literally hovered over them and heard their entire conversation, which this type of encounter was not my first with the LORD where He would hover me over something or someone in a dream.

I reached out to this married couple and said that we needed to have a conversation, and they had me come over to their home. I shared with them exactly what the LORD showed me, and they said, "Nick, how did you know this? This has literally been our conversation this entire week." I told them that I hovered over them during their conversation in the Spirit. God is my Informant, and He is the One who will protect His people, and deliver them from the mouth of the lion (Daniel 6, Psalms 33:17-21)), as Paul said in 2 Timothy 4:17 "but my Master stood with me and strengthened me, that by me the preaching might be fulfilled, and all the Gentiles might hear, and I was rescued from the mouth of the lion," and again, in Ecclesiastes 10:20 "even in your thought, do not curse a king, and in your bedroom do not curse a wealthy man, for the bird of the heavens will carry the voice, and the winged creature will tell the matter." The LORD is the bird of the heavens. By pressing into these passages of Scripture, and teaming up with God through expectancy, prayer, and integrity, I was going to battle in the Scriptural way, and my hands were trained for this war.

I remember back in September or October of 2018 I was invited to California to speak at a conference. My mom, a few of her friends, and some others went, and after the conference we went to an In N Out

Burger. While we were there at the table, I said to one of my mom's friends, "hey, the Holy Spirit showed me something about your family." Keep in mind, I have NEVER been in she and her husband's bedroom. However, the LORD showed me their bedroom through a dream, so I said, "you have a couch on the right side of your bed, and last week your husband was crying on the couch and was so upset because something your daughter's boyfriend did to your daughter." She began weeping at the table, while all my mom's friends look at me in complete shock of how I could have known this. I said, "this is the LORD." I was able to minister to her on the very subject matter as the LORD revealed it to me, and my mom's friends got to see the power of God (1 Corinthians 14:24). This is what happened in 2 Kings 6:8-12:

> "Then the king of Aram warred against Israel and took counsel with his servants, saying, 'in such and such a place shall be my camp.' And the man of God sent unto the king of Israel, saying, 'beware that you do not pass such a place, for there the Arameans have come down.' And the king of Israel sent to the place which the man of God told him and warned him of, and he was guarded there, not once or twice. And the king of Aram was greatly disturbed about this matter, and he summoned his servants and said to them, 'will you not tell us who from us told to the king of Israel?' And one of his servants said, 'no, my master, the king, but Elisha the prophet who is in Israel tells the king of Israel the words that you speak in your bedroom."

I don't say this to boast in my abilities, but I share my experiences to tell you, when you go against the spirit of Ahitophel and Absalom (Absalom is a conspiring spirit), or any other evil spirit for that matter, you can go to the Scriptures and team up with God, and you are prepared for the battle. As one who dreams almost every night, this is also how dreams are to be interpreted most of the time. Dreams from God will have a word, phrase, or scheme from the Word of God, and by knowing that passage, we can interpret what God is speaking to us. Many times, God speaks to me in such parables that if it were not for my deep study and being filled with the Holy Spirit, I would say, "there is no way that dream can mean anything." I have story after story with dreams, and I say this to say, do not write off even the most "random" dreams. Now that I have learned Hebrew, God will also speak to me frequently in the Hebrew or Aramaic. He has shared Hebrew from the Scriptures with me in dreams, as well as taking a Hebrew dictionary in my dreams and taught me from there. God speaks in one way or another, yet man does not perceive it (Job 33:14-18).

We have to be so well versed in Scripture, that we recognize every scheme of the enemy and message from God. Without being expertly dependent upon Scripture, you will fight the battle with the wrong weapon and tactics, and you will be powerless. You may bring a knife to a gun fight. You can also do the same thing with Demas as he was with Paul, or with Judas, whom Jesus kept very, very close to Him for over three years, and purposely placed the money within his authority, while knowing he was the one who would fall drastically, and ultimately betray Him. The LORD began showing me the reason that the theme of all of these individuals that do this are always amongst the ones closest to you, as God Himself placed the serpent in the Garden of Eden with Adam and Eve (Genesis 3:1). God uses those people closest to us to keep us vigilant and to make sure that we are abiding in integrity, so that you don't get lazy, and to make sure the places nobody else sees are always submitted to the LORD.

David had many counselors, many students, and many friends, but only Ahitophel, the wisest of his counselors would be next to him at all times, hearing all the secret conversations, and knowing all of the things David is doing behind the scenes. David could just seem righteous in the eyes of the public, but Ahitophel will know if David has open doors in the private places that nobody sees. Demas was one of the only ones with Paul. All of the churches from afar will know Paul is righteous, but Demas will know whether or not Paul has any open doors. Demas and Luke will know (Colossians 4:14). Judah's first two sons seem righteous, but God knows their sins in the bedroom that nobody sees (Genesis 38). So too, with Jesus. He seems righteous in front of the 5,000 men that He feeds and multiples bread and fish for, or even in front of the pharisees and chief priests, but the 12 will know in private if there is something to be used against Him, which is why Judas was chosen to find something they could try to use against Him. They see Him when He eats, sleeps, prays, His emotions, His reactions, whether he slanders or tale-bears, etc. Jesus did nothing wrong, but my point is, God keeps these people close to you, and always leaves a serpent in your Garden of Eden to keep you diligent in the Spirit, and this means there is only one way to overcome the serpent slithering in your Garden, and the answer is found in the book of Numbers, which is actually the same way that one can truly overcome one of the main forms of witchcraft-word curses.

As we have previously touched on from a completely different angle, in the book of Numbers 22-24, there is a man named Balak who wants to curse Israel, so he hires Balaam, the sorcerer, in order to come and curse them for him. Notice, the Scripture says that the way Balaam was going to curse Israel was through words, spoken word curses. Numbers 22:6 says that whomever Balaam blesses is blessed, and whomever he curses is cursed, but Balaam says that he can only curse those whom God allows him to curse (Numbers 22:18). So, the secret behind Balaam's cursing was that God would allow it, because someone had an open door, as it is written in Proverbs 26:2 "a curse without a cause can't come." Balaam speaks word curses and is called a sorcerer exercising witchcraft, so for those slanderers, they are no different than Balaam. Slander is a form of witchcraft, especially as it pertains to trying to control an outcome or situation. So, what I am going to explain is not only how you overcome the serpent in your garden, but how you overcome this specific form of witchcraft (there are many kinds of witchcraft), word curses, Judas etc., and how God will come to be your Informant as Hushai was to David. It is all found within this story in the Torah of Moses.

The key to overcoming all of this is realizing Balak's strategy. Balak and Balaam attempt to curse Israel three times, but the first two times reveal a significant approach, and are the keys to understanding the entire passage. In Numbers 22:41 and Numbers 23:13, Balak specifically says that he will not show Balaam the entire camp of Israel, but ONLY the outer edge of their camp. He could only see the edges of the camp, but this was going to be sufficient to curse the entire camp. What is the significance of the edges of the camp? We must understand, God's Tabernacle is in the center of the entire camp, which means all of the eyes of the people are toward the center of the camp, focusing on God's Tabernacle. Therefore, whatever is happening on the edges is the place that nobody sees, and it is the place of weakness, because all strength is on the inside of the camp. If the enemy or a wolf wanted to attack, it won't come to the center of the camp, but it will come to the place nobody sees on the outside, in order to attack a weak spot, which is why the enemy will come and tempt you in a time of weakness, as Amalek did with Israel (Deuteronomy 25:17-19), and as the enemy tempted Jesus with bread when He was hungry after fasting forty days. It is the place where no eyes are actually looking, just as nobody would have known or seen Jesus take the bread in the wilderness, because nobody else was there besides He, God, and Satan.

Although I won't get into it here, this passage in Numbers is the prophetic equivalence of Jesus' being tempted. Three times Balak tries to curse Israel in the wilderness at their weakness where nobody sees during their forty year journey, and three times Jesus is tempted by Satan in the wilderness during his forty day journey in the wilderness during His time of weakness that nobody else would have seen. Israel and Jesus both overcame the same way as well. This entire connection in detail will come out in another volume on overcoming witchcraft, God willing.

These edges are the places only Ahitophel, Demas, Judas, or the serpent will see. The stuff you watch on TV, the way you talk to your children or spouse, the way you talk about people, the places that only those closest to you will know about. It was this place, the outer edges of the camp of weakness and hiddenness that defined whether or not all of the camp of Israel was able to be cursed by Balak. Cursed, or blessed and protected by God. Notice in this story, Israel doesn't even know this is going on! Balak and Balaam are on a cliff, so God is being their Informant, and Israel is being guarded solely on integrity, just as Jesus was moving through His temptations completely on integrity. In Numbers 23:20-24, God says that He finds no iniquity or wrong in Jacob and Israel, and so as Proverbs 26:2 says, a curse without a cause cannot come, unless God allows it as He did with Job.

Every time Israel was being cursed behind their back, God transferred it into a blessing (Deuteronomy 23:5-6). The key to overcoming Judas next to you, and word curses, and having God be your Hushai is totally dependent upon your integrity in all areas. Your life has to be devoted to God on every line, so that even those closest to you say, "we can't find an open door with him/her," just as Judas, the pharisees, and the priests could not find a word against Jesus. When even those closest to you can't find anything, your life is probably consumed in holiness, and the other secret places will be for only God to see, as it is written in Deuteronomy 29:28 "the hidden things are to the LORD our God, and the revealed things are for us and our children forever, in order to do all the words of this Torah." But if the enemy can find even one open window, he has access to the entire house, and your entire life can crumble: money, marriage, kids, health, ministry etc. Just by cursing the edge of the camp, the entire camp is vulnerable. A little leaven leavens the whole lump (Galatians 5:9). Israel seemed righteous close to the Tabernacle, but what about where no eyes are? The secret places will determine whether or not God becomes your Informant.

For us, do we make mistakes? Of course. But mistakes are not what bring the curse. When we make mistakes, we are to have a perfect heart towards God that repents immediately when it is revealed, and turn away from these things, continually seeking how to draw nearer to the Father. I make mistakes all the time, but I fear God, and I surrender every area of my life to the Holy Spirit, and I am continually bringing all things before His light to be exposed, so I can walk before Him with a confident heart in intimacy. The fear of the LORD keeps us in a continual process of purification, as it is written in 1 John 1:9 "but if we confess our sins, He is faithful and righteous to forgive us our sins and to cleanse us from all our iniquity," and again, in Proverbs 28:13 "he who covers his sins will not prosper, but he who confesses and forsakes them will have compassion." When you walk in integrity and Psalms 37 meekness, God will confuse the counsel of Ahitophel, and slaughter that spirit from your life as He killed Ahitophel and Absalom, just as Judas, and ultimately even Balaam (Numbers 31:8). Demas, Ahitophel, and Judas left for money or authority and the things of this world. God always shows me patterns, and I continually ask Him "LORD, who is the next Judas in my life?" Sometimes I will find someone with Judas-like tendencies that hasn't fully blossomed into that yet (James 1:13-15), and I will begin inter-ceding for them that whatever tendency may be leading them into that direction be exposed to them and repented of.

I have watched people step into Judas-like tendencies and then end up as a full blown Judas, Demas, Ahitophel, or Balaam. But I have noticed it always has to do with money and higher seats of authority. Nobody is above this. With every one of my leaders, family, friends, etc., I keep eyes open and remain vigilant and abide in prayer for discernment. Your integrity will protect you from all witchcraft and plans of the enemy, and God keeps these enemies there as we saw earlier from Judges, in order to train your hands for war and keep you vigilant in the Scriptures, but also to make sure you are always abiding in the LORD, and not getting lax in the Spirit. The LORD will be your Informant and your Rear Guard.

During the summer of 2022, and again in 2023, I was going against the spirit of Balak and Balaam, and word curses were being spoken over me left and right, and as I said, even by those closest to me. I stud-ied that passage (Numbers 22-24) line by line, over and over again like you wouldn't believe. The LORD began coming to me in dreams with person after person that was word cursing me and what they were doing behind my back as Balak and Balaam did behind Israel's back. He con-tinually showed me this and protected me, not only so I could cancel the word curses, and confuse the counsel of Ahitophel, but also to give me a chance to bless those who curse me and pray and intercede for those who persecute me (Matthew 5:44), because as for me and my house, we serve the LORD (Joshua 24:15). I didn't retaliate, but rather I blessed. I walked with meekness. Only in person could I tell someone all of the dreams and stories that took place during this time. I will take them with me as a testimony forever. He was and truly still is my Rear Guard (Isaiah 52:12), and a firewall protection around me (Zechariah 2:9). My integrity has been tested again and again, and it is when I press into Him with integrity during these great trials that the revelation and anointing pour out mightily, and I leave with a greater power in the Spirit as it is written Jesus "returned from the wilderness in the power of the Spirit (Luke 4:14)" because of His integrity during Satan's testing Him while alone in the wilderness, the time that nobody else would have known except you, Satan, and God.

Psalms 34:8 says the angel of the LORD encamps around those who fear Him and delivers them. Scripture says again in Psalms 16:8 "I have kept the LORD continually before me, because He is at my right hand I shall not stagger." In all things, the LORD always has my focus and attention, and wherever I am, I always remain in the Presence of God. This is the only way to not only overcome Judas, but the only way to SEE Judas! The entire time Jesus was in ministry, God showed Him Judas. He walked fully aware of what, or who was sitting next to Him at the Passover seder before He went to the cross. John 2:24-25 says that Jesus had no need for anyone to testify of another person before Him, because He knew all men. I have walked next to Judas, while knowing it was Judas. I wasn't going to kick him out unless God told me too, because ultimately, I knew another one would come. I have to allow Judas, once I am aware of him/her, to do that work in my life, which is making sure I depend upon God even more, and remain even more diligent in the Holy Spirit. Ultimately, God always takes care of those individuals.

Being sent out as sheep among wolves (Matthew 10:16), our ability to overcome is not by physical strength, but by strategy in knowing the Scriptures inside and out, and through this, becoming strong in the Spirit to know how to war each individual situation. Hosea 4:6 says, "My people die for lack of knowledge," because God's people are not equipped in the things of the Holy Spirit. There was a woman in California who called me during the summer of 2022 when I moved to Iowa, and she is filled with the Holy Spirit. She was going against witchcraft that snuck in through someone in her real estate business, and she was asking for me to help her out. She said the LORD keeps showing her Judas and the things going on around her, and I said "the LORD is teaching you how to go to war against these things. You are a powerful woman of God, but He has to train your hands for war." I began explaining to her this entire concept of what David means when he said, "train my hands for war." I told her she has to know how to go to war and cast out devils, and you have to know what spirit you are dealing with, so that you can go to war accordingly. We must recognize the schemes, so that you can go, "oh, Korah and the sons of Reuben did this to Aaron and Moses. Now I can go study this passage and know what to do against gaslighting." You can learn how Elijah dealt with the gaslighting tactics of Ahab (1 Kings 18:17-18) or recognize the witchcraft of Jezebel and her manipulation of authority (1 Kings 21:1-16), or to be aware of the scheme of Amalek (Exodus 17, Deuteronomy 25:17-19).

This woman told me on the phone that she knew I was right, but she didn't want to do all of this, and was not wanting to go to war. I said, "woman, when you came out of Egypt to follow Jesus, you entered the army of the LORD (Exodus 12:41). There are no benchwarmers in the Kingdom of God. Benchwarmers get chewed up and spit out." King Jesus was not kidding when He said the enemy comes to kill, steal, and destroy (John 10:10). I have watched it before my eyes. He literally wants to kill you both spiritually and physically. He wants to steal your identity and your inheritance spiritually and physically and destroy all that God has for you. I must say, Satan is very good at his job, because many walk ignorant (Hosea 4:6, 2 Corinthians 2:11) and as doormats for their entire life. He will ruin your family, your marriage, your finances, your business, your ministry, your health, and everything else that deals with your existence all because of an open door or edge of your camp.

I told this woman that she is personally being called by the LORD by name (Exodus 31:2), and she needed to receive the invitation to the school of the Holy Spirit, and to allow Him to train her hands for war. Her business is righteous, it is a Garden of Eden, and she found the serpent right there in her real estate business. I commanded her to deal with it with power, boldness, conviction, and the authority of the Holy Spirit. Trees Of Fire don't sit passively. They either burn up the enemy camp around them and consume it with power, or they ignite the fire in those around them to become a Tree Of Fire, but regardless, Trees Of Fire walk with power on the front lines of battle (Numbers 32:20-22).

I want to share two more quick stories of our hands being trained for war that may not seem like much, but it is huge and practical in our daily lives. This concept is not for just things of witchcraft, but as you will see with these stories, it is for daily situations that take place in our lives. During the summer of 2022 when I came to Iowa, as I mentioned, this was the exact time the LORD showed me what it means to "train my hands for war." Unfortunately, through social media's, I tend to have women that will send me direct messages privately or however else, and will send me perverted messages, and even inappropriate pictures. I immediately block these individuals and step into prayer.

There came a time that summer that all of the sudden, now I was not only getting bombarded with them on social media, but now it reached a new level. I started getting text messages to my personal cell phone over and over again from random numbers of women hitting on me and sending me naked photos. I would continually block them. This was during the time where the word curses could not come in my life as Numbers 22-24 with Balak and Balaam. One morning as I was in prayer asking why this was happening, the Holy Spirit reminded me of the next chapter, Numbers 25, when Balaam sent women to entice the children of Israel, and what stopped these women, and the curse was Phineas taking his sword and piercing it through a woman's belly. Right then, the LORD said, "take the sword of Phineas." I rose up with authority and said, "right now in the name of Yeshua, I take the sword of Phineas and pierce it through the belly of that adulterous woman!" I also commanded every Midianite woman from Numbers 25 to be destroyed and pierced through with the sword of Phineas. My life was in direct sync with Numbers 22-25.

It was no coincidence this happened at this time. It was during this time that I was going against the word curses of Balak, which couldn't touch me because I was walking in integrity with God and had no open doors, as Balak's curses couldn't touch Israel for this very reason in Numbers 22-24. This was why Balaam sent in women, because he knew this would open a door, and now they could have a curse lay hold of them. During this time, I knew Balaam (the evil one) was trying to tempt me with women in order to open a door for curses to pummel me, but I was girded with the Word of God, and I unsheathed the sword of Phineas by the leading of the Holy Spirit. From that very moment, all of these messages ceased. Nothing is new under the sun. God trained my hands for that moment as I sought Him desperately in prayer.

A totally different story, nevertheless, a practical daily scenario with my pit-bull, Kaia. On the farm in Iowa in the summer of 2023, we were doing some work on the land, and Kaia got too close to the electric fence that we have for our goats and chickens, and she got shocked terribly. I have never heard her yell that loud. Well, as I kept working, once we finished, I called Kaia, and she didn't come to me. I called again and again, but I couldn't find her. I started walking all over the place, and after a while, I began to get worried. Right then, I stopped and prayed to the Father, and the Holy Spirit spoke to me about Hagar and Ishmael in the wilderness in Genesis 21. In Genesis 21:9-21, the two of them go into the wilderness of B'er Shava, and she runs out of water, fearing the young boy, Ishmael, would die. She asked that she would not see the death of the boy, for they had no water in the wilderness. God hears her, and it is written in Genesis 21:19 "and God opened her eyes, and she saw a well of water, and she went and filled the skin bottle of water, and she gave the lad to drink." There was a well of water right next to her that she was blinded too! In that moment, God reminded me of this and I prayed, "Father, open my eyes to find Kaia as you opened Hagar's eyes to see the well."

I cannot make this up. IMMEDIATELY the LORD opened my eyes, and I saw Kaia standing on the grass about 500 yards away. After Kaia got zapped by the electric fence, she was confused, thinking I zapped her because she also wears a shock collar that I control manually, and she thought I shocked her and she was in trouble, which caused her to run off that far. Even when I found her and went to her, she was cowering down, thinking it was me who did it. Keep in mind, the shock of that fence is extremely strong, as it is meant to ward off coyotes! The point is, many times, the LORD wants us to simply just be engaged with Him in all things, even in matters that may seem trivial to us. But once again, even with finding Kaia, my hands were trained from Scripture and hearing the Holy Spirit, and I was able to team up with God through His Word.

The better you know the Scriptures, the more trained you will be for every war, the more consuming your fire will be in the LORD (Hebrews 12:29), and the enemy will start to know you by name. Everywhere I go I break off witchcraft in people's lives, set them free from things by the Holy Spirit, help raise up their ministries, and trample the enemy camp, not I, but the grace of God in me (1 Corinthians 15:10). Luke 10:19 "Behold, I give authority to you to tread on snakes and scorpions and all the power of the enemy, and nothing will harm you."

CHAPTER 11

Working Your Garden Of Eden

Trees Of Fire is not just about being baptized in the Holy Spirit and igniting others in the flame of the Holy Spirit, the gifts, power, and revelation, etc., but really, all things need to flow from a place of overflow. What I mean, and what I want to emphasize in this chapter especially, Trees Of Fire is about partnership with the Holy Spirit and learning how to ride the river of the Spirit of God, in order to enter into the fullness of discipleship in Messiah Yeshua (Matthew 28:18-20). There is a Garden of Eden-like relationship with the Holy Spirit, which when we step into, brings about encounters, relationships, and fruit that is not only not forced in anyway in the flesh, but that will also enable us all to fulfill our ministry in the earth (2 Timothy 4:5).

In 2022 the Holy Spirit downloaded so much into me on the Garden of Eden, including partnering with the Holy Spirit. I actually had this revelation I will share in this chapter partially back in 2018, and its repetitive patterns were revealed to me in 2021, but in 2022 the revelation of all of this with the Holy Spirit was poured out upon me. I want to share what it means to abide in the Garden of Eden, or, as Adam was commanded, "to work it and to guard it (Genesis 2:15)." In other words, tilling our Garden of Eden with God. Each of us has a Garden of Eden with the LORD that He has placed each of us in, as it is written in Genesis 2:8 "and the LORD God planted a garden in Eden from the east, and He placed there the man whom He had formed." It is important that we truly understand this concept of abiding in the Garden of Eden with God and understand how to make it practical. The revelations in this chapter changed my life, and I know others as well that I have taught it too.

Many of us, if not all of us, are looking for something. We are seeking for things whether it be a spouse, clothing, money, job, calling, kids, the right relationships, business partners, etc. Many times, I have taught to others what I am about to teach in this chapter, because it is men or women looking for a spouse, and we will see that the Scriptural passages I bring up actually come from passages with a man and his bride, however, as we will see, it will apply to anything that we are seeking out or longing for. This revelation initially came to me in 2018 in the context of a spouse, but later, it expanded in a way that as I said, changed my life and my approach with how I really live my entire life, and the peace of God which surpasses all understanding began to flow like a mighty current in my life once I did this more and more in 2022 and 2023, because it was such a partnering or teaming up with the Holy Spirit (Philippians 4:7). I have noticed when I have slipped out of this concept, anxiety rushes upon me, but when I return to His Garden, peace overflows like the Jordan river overflowing its banks. In the Name of Jesus, I am telling you right now, many reading this chapter will be healed by the Holy Spirit from anxiety and depression through the revelation given in this chapter, as it washes over you by the Spirit of God.

The problem is, many times, we are seeking for these things beyond what is healthy or Scriptural. We are striving for things in the flesh, rather than being meek/submissive to our circumstances as we discussed earlier in this book. Rather than seeking in the flesh, we need to simply be available. If and when God brings it or takes away (Job 1:21), keep your hands open, but striving and stressing for things can be the wrong approach, and you will see what I mean as we dive deeper here. There is a formula given to us in the Torah of Moses, beginning in Genesis, the very same formula Jesus actually mentions in the New Testament, that when we grasp this concept of tilling our garden, as Adam was commanded, everything else flows properly. The grass is not greener on the other side, it is greener when you water your own garden, and fruit begins to over-flow. When we go and do things in the flesh, and all it brings are fruits contrary to the Holy Spirit: impatience, anger, stress, anxiety, etc., we don't leave room for the Holy Spirit. We have to go about things in a way that we always, and I mean always, leaves room for the Holy Spirit to bring increase, rather than ourselves (1 Corinthians 3:6-7).

When things develop in a way where you know it was God and not in your own flesh, it is not only so encouraging and empowering because we know it is from God and we love seeing the hand of God work in our lives, but it will also come on a sturdy foundation and incorruptible as I talked about in the foreword of this book. There are more than six passages in the Torah of Moses that reveal the same pattern to everything I am talking about, and as I said, most of those six that I will use have to do with a husband and wife, but we have to view things by the Holy Spirit, and not be so honed into the ten foot view, but see the 35,000 foot view and pattern in order to see the bigger picture as it relates to the Holy Spirit, however, this will also be a chapter that I think imparts things maritally for husband and wife. This same topic I am planning to put into another volume in great detail specifically in the context of marriage, but here, we will keep it 35,000 feet.

Starting with the Garden of Eden in Genesis 2:15, God tells Adam that He wants Adam to work and guard the Garden of Eden. To be in the Garden of Eden means to be in the Presence of God, to be in rela-tionship, to be vulnerable, to be naked before Him, as intimacy is based upon vulnerability and being bare and naked before His unapproachable light (1 Timothy 6:16), but most importantly for this context, to be about the Father's business (Luke 2:49). The Garden of Eden is the place of intimacy with God, doing what God has told YOU to do. We each have a garden to work that may be different than another's. We each have giftings, families, ministries, jobs, etc., and things that God has called us to steward and nurture, to work and to guard (Genesis 2:15). It is important to ask the Holy Spirit where your Garden of Eden is. The Garden of Eden is your business with the Father, and your calling in that specific season. Our gardens can change from time to time, or at least the work and fruit of it can, so we have to continually reflect on this topic with the Holy Spirit. Our Garden of Eden is the place that our focus needs to be. If your focus is on your garden with God, everything else will fall into place.

It is important that you make a list of what your Garden of Eden is, and whatever is not on the list, you need to remove it because it is a distraction from tilling your garden. It is also important to notice, the things you must remove may not be bad things, as we will see, but they are not God things, meaning, they could be Godly, but they aren't what God has designed for YOU in that season. I know people that want to go to every ministry event every night, and they want to help everyone, which are Godly things, however, it can distract your focus from what He has called you to do. Let those be someone else's garden, and you stay focused on yours with the LORD, while praying and interceding for the other people and their garden.

There was a time that I began getting so busy, helping many other people, visiting with so many people, and attending things and ministries with other Godly individuals that I began to slack on the very things God had for me and my ministry. The LORD gave me a very gentle rebuke, as the Holy Spirit told me Proverbs 27:8 "as a bird wanders from its nest, so too, is a man who wanders from his place." These things were all good, but they took my time and attention from my tasks and were taking me away from the garden He placed me in, as it is written in Genesis 2:8 "and the LORD God planted a garden in Eden from the east, and He placed Adam there whom He had formed." I wandered from God's garden in my life as a bird wanders from its nest. Although these were "good things" I was getting involved in, they brought stress to me as I tried to make things work in the flesh. I noticed that I wasn't performing in all things with excellence, and the LORD is all about excellence in our work with Him, as it is written in Colossians 3:23, "and whatever you do, do it with your whole soul, as doing it to our Master, and not to man."

Now, notice as Adam starts working on the Garden of Eden, God notices what Adam needs, and says in Genesis 2:18 "and the LORD God said, it is not good for man to be alone. I will make him a helper as his opposite." Notice, that without Adam even asking, God recognizes Adam's need, which is why Jesus said in Matthew 6:8 "therefore, do not be like them, for your Father knows what you seek before you ask Him." Jesus' sermon, and the entire context there in Matthew 6 on this topic is from the Garden of Eden. Before Adam even asked, God knew, and because Adam was about God's business, God was about Adam's business. As Adam focuses on the garden, God BRINGS the woman to Adam, and places her right before him, because although Adam may have wanted this in his heart, he didn't go out of his way searching for it, rather, he partnered with the Holy Spirit (God), and God brought what he needed, which is the meaning of Jesus' words in Matthew 6:33 "but first seek the Kingdom of God and His righteousness, and all of these will be added to you." As I said, sure, this speaks on a wife, but Scripture wants us to see much more than just getting a spouse. This is business relationships, finances, children, etc. Adam sought this in his heart, but rather than going out to use his time on finding this in the flesh, he simply focused on the garden he was called too and made himself available whenever God did bring this blessing. Adam partnered with the Holy Spirit.

As I said, Adam was about God's business, so too, God was about Adam's business. In December of 2019 I was in Punta Cana, and the LORD gave me a dream that night, however, the dream was only audible, and it was one word on repeat all night. The LORD said, "Haggai, Haggai, Haggai, Haggai, Haggai, Haggai," literally all night in the dream. For the next two months, I cannot tell you how many times I read Haggai, which is only two chapters. The Holy Spirit told me due to the book of Haggai "build My house, and I will build yours. The silver and the gold are Mine (Haggai 2:8)." This was in 2019, and I asked the LORD for almost four years what was the house He wanted me to build for Him. Earlier in 2019, the LORD showed me that I was going to build a worldwide school to raise people up in the Holy Spirit. I told a few people about it, however, I simply put it in my notes, and left it at that. When I first visited Iowa in 2019, the LORD gave me a dream that I was leading a school out on the property, teaching to great multitudes of children daily, alongside my brother, Todd Cleppe. I told Todd and Maria the dream, and they took me outside on the farm and showed me a massive foundation that was already laid in the ground for a building and Todd said:

> "The Father showed Maria and I years ago there would be a worldwide school for discipleship that had a headquarters built here, but the LORD said we will not be the ones who create the school, just as David had the desire to build God's temple, but God said David would not be the one to build it, rather, David's son, Solomon, would build it. The LORD showed us He would bring someone who would build the school."

That same trip to Iowa in 2019, as I was on the property praying, the LORD showed me an open eyed vision of a landing strip for planes, then He showed me the same thing in greater detail in a dream while there. I told Todd and Maria, and they took me to a certain part of the property and said, "a landing strip for planes to land and leave used to be right here. This is what the Father has shown to us again since this is a mission's base to receive people and send them out."

Ever since 2019 we knew the LORD had big plans, but the timing was not yet. In fact, while in Iowa in 2019, and continually after that, I had dream after dream after dream that I was packing up a trailer filled with all of my stuff, moving to Iowa. The move didn't take place in 2019 as we initially thought, and I left the school idea simply in my notes until I moved out to Iowa in 2022. That summer of 2022, during my four month sabbatical, the LORD began downloading so much revelation for the school, my hands couldn't type fast enough. The school was to be called "Trees Of Fire."

In the beginning of 2023, I took a break from the school for about six months, and Todd kept telling me again and again, "Nick, you need to focus on the school. Now is the time." For about six months I kept pushing it off, and finally, in July of 2023, the LORD got my attention, and I began working in great detail on every dimension of the school, and much more. The entire structure, curriculum, and all the books I would write for it was being given to me literally within a week from Genesis 41 with Joseph and Exodus 36 with Betzalel. I tore Genesis 41 apart daily. The downloads by the Holy Spirit were like a firehose. While working on it for just about a week, the Holy Spirit reminded me of my dream about Haggai from 2019, and said "do you remember I told you if you build My house, I will build yours? Trees Of Fire is the house."

I had a woman approach me one day after I preached, whose name was Miracle. I had never seen her before, nor have I seen her since. After

I preached, she walked up and told me, "God spoke to me about you as I walked in the building, and He is showing you all the details of the end-time apostolic structure and the prophetic anointing. It is your anointing." She then takes my hand, and places into it a cased silver dollar, and a cased gold Bitcoin and says, "The LORD says from Haggai, 'the silver and the gold are Mine.'" I absolutely lost it when she told me this. Nobody had spoken a word of Haggai to me since the dream in 2019, and she read my mail right before me. This is exactly what the LORD told me years prior. The same week I was studying Genesis 41 in Iowa as the downloads were coming, and a woman in Africa emails into the ministry out of nowhere and said, "Genesis 41:33 'and now let Pharaoh find a man of understanding and wisdom, and he will place him over the land of Egypt.' You are Joseph." I was so aligned with the Holy Spirit in that moment. Every day I was deeply rooted in the garden God placed me in, and because I was about His business, God was about mine. He began bringing me all the right people, from teachers, to lawyers, to builders, to computer programmers, etc.

I was then reminded at this time of a dream I had in at the beginning of 2019. The LORD Himself, massive and glorious, with hair white as wool, was standing before me in a glorious house that He had given to me. His face was not a face with eyes and a nose, but rather a countenance of great light that shone with joy or dimmed with sadness. He placed His hand upon a wall that had a map of the world on it, and He said, "Nick, what you will do will change the world." Then as He walked off, His presence was magnetic, the other end of the magnet was inside of me, and I followed after Him. He sat down, pulled out a massive book, and I sat down at his feet as He began reading to me from the book, which had the works He created for me to walk in. When I woke up, the LORD brought me to Daniel 7:9-10:

"I watched until thrones were put in place, and the Ancient Of Days was seated. His garment was white as snow, and the hair of His head like pure wool. His throne was a fiery flame, its wheels were a burning fire. A fiery stream issues and came forth from before Him. A thousand thousands ministered to Him. Ten thousand times ten thousand stood before Him. The court was seated, and the books were opened."

The house that was given to me in the dream by Him was the house He later told me in 2019 He would build for me as I built His, and His house is Trees Of Fire. Shortly before this in 2018, I had a woman in Houston reach out to me and say:

"Nick, I had two dreams about you that were the same, and I don't usually dream, especially not twice. In the dream, my mom and I were driving, and we saw this beautiful, massive house, and my mom said 'wow, look at that house.' I told my mom, 'that is Pastor Nick's house, and it is always filled with children He is teaching.' You were not older than thirty years old."

Just as these other dreams I had, the LORD would build my house as I built His, and just as I saw in Iowa in the dream that we were raising up people daily, so too, she saw in hers. The LORD also showed me why she had the same dream twice is from Genesis 41:32 "and the reason the dream is repeated twice to Pharaoh is because the matter is established before God, and God is hastening to do it." So too, was this matter established before God, and He was hastening it upon me. In the summer of 2023 in Iowa, God began connecting all of the dots from years prior, through everyone's words and dreams, and I had the deepest revelation of the garden He had called me too. As I said, in the garden, everything was being brought to me, as to Adam.

What we have seen with Adam is the first example where man partners up with God, and the Holy Spirit becomes the bridge to bring the increase in a given area, as the individual focuses on God's garden in their life. God knows what you need before you ask, and when you step into alignment with Him in the garden He has placed you in, all things will be brought to you by the Creator of the heavens and the earth, the one Who possesses all things. The next example we have of this is found in Genesis 24, which is when Abraham sends his greatest servant, Eliezer, and ten camels, to go and get a bride for his son, Isaac. Remember how with Adam, I brought up Matthew 6:8, where Jesus said that our Father knows what we need before we ask, just as God knew Adam needed a wife before he asked? The same thing happens here with Eliezer. When Eliezer gets to Aram, notice what God does before Eliezer even asks in Genesis 24:12-15:

> "And he said, 'LORD God of my master, Abraham, please cause to happen before me this day, and do kindness with my master, Abraham. Behold, I am standing by the fountain of water, and the daughters of the men of the city are going out to draw water. And it will be, the young woman whom I will say to her, please stretch out your pitcher and I will drink, and she will say, drink, and I will also water your camels, she will be the one You have approved for Your servant, Isaac, and by her I will know that you have done kindness with my master.' And before he finished speaking, behold, Rebekah was going out, who was born to B'tuel, the son of Milcah, the wife

of Nachor, the brother of Abraham, and her pitcher was upon her shoulder."

Just as with Adam, God knew what Abraham's servant needed before he asked (Matthew 6:8), and as Adam focused on the LORD and His righteousness, all things were brought to Him (Matthew 6:33), so too, "before he (Eliezer) even finished speaking" his request, as he was about Abraham's business, God was already orchestrating it. The peace that comes with not only understanding God's sovereignty, but also God's faithfulness to His Torah, that we need not stress or be anxious about a thing if we abide in His garden that He has called us too, as it is written in Matthew 6:27 "and who from you can add one cubit to his stature by his anxiety?"

Please notice in Genesis 24, the Torah never tells us that Isaac is going out and looking for a wife, but quite the contrary as we will see. Although he may have been longing for one, he was totally consumed in the Father's business. Notice, as Isaac is doing his father's will (and His heavenly Father), Isaac's father, Abraham, takes it upon himself to find a bride that will be brought for his son, as God did with Adam. Eliezer and the ten camels, which we will get to in a moment, go to Padan Aram in order to get Rebekah, and it is important to notice what Isaac is doing when she is finally brought to him. It is written in Genesis 24:63-64 "and Isaac went out to pray in the field before evening, and he lifted up his eyes, and he saw, and behold, camels were coming. And Rebekah lifted her eyes, and she saw Isaac, and she got off from the camel."

Just to be transparent linguistically, the phrase I translated as "to pray (לָשׂוּחַ)" can mean to meditate, to talk, to think, and some others, however, to pray is the best translation, because we know from Jewish thought that Isaac was known for one of the three prayer times in Judaism (Daniel 6:10), specifically the one in the afternoon that took place before

TREES OF FIRE

evening as Isaac was doing here. Isaac was out meditating in the field and praying with the Father in the garden when this bride was brought to him from Aram....from another country....God is not limited to our reach or grasp, for the earth and all of its fullness is His (Jeremiah 23:24, Psalms 24:1). Isaac is about the Father's business and while he is doing this, his father, Abraham is working on what he needs, a wife, or increase in any given area. Isaac was maybe longing for this, but he didn't leave his position to seek it out, rather, he made himself available for the Holy Spirit to bring whatever he needed while being obedient to where he was called. He partnered with the Holy Spirit while he was about the father's business, and as Jesus said in Matthew 6:8/33, our Father knows what we need before we ask, and if we seek Him and are about His business, all these things will be added to us.

You might ask, how do we connect this with the Holy Spirit? We have to notice some key insights to the Genesis 24 narrative. First off, there were ten camels that carried Rebekah from point A to point B. Secondly, notice what Eliezer places upon Rebekah in Genesis 24:22 is a nose ring of gold weighing half a shekel, as well as two bracelets upon her hands weighing ten shekels of gold. The nose ring of gold is a topic I won't discuss in this volume, as I have explained it in depth in my book *Joseph's Identity Crisis, Uncovering Messiah*. However, we must notice the ten camels, and the two bracelets weighing ten shekels of gold. This is a prophecy about the two tablets of stone given at Sinai with the Ten Words on them. It was the Torah that brought her, however, this is actually a reference to the Holy Spirit, because Romans 7:14 and 1 Corinthians 2:14-16 says the Scriptures and the Torah are of the Spirit. Not only that, but Ezekiel 36:26-27, Jeremiah 31:31-35, and Hebrews 10:16-17 says that the same Torah that was written on tablets of stone will now be written on the tablet of our heart by the Holy Spirit in the New Covenant under Messiah Yeshua.

250

The Torah, and the two tablets with the Ten Words is a revelation of the Spirit and are equivalent to the two bracelets weighing ten shekels of gold. Nothing is new under the sun (Ecclesiastes 1:9-10). We see that it was the Holy Spirit that bridged the gap and brought Rebekah to Isaac as he was about his father's business, just as the Holy Spirit (God) brought Eve to Adam as Adam was about his Father's business, by working and guarding the garden God placed him in. It was the Holy Spirit that brought increase. Rebekah is also called "the young woman (הנער)," but in Hebrew it is spelled irregularly, missing the final letter hey (ה), which actually is spelled in the masculine in its written form, also known as the "k'teev form," however, its vowels give us the feminine pronunciation, called the "k'ree form," due to the fact we are speaking about Rebekah. The Torah does this on purpose in order to connect other passages of Scripture that use the same spelling, as we will see. This is important to notice, because it will connect us to two more passages, as this word is used in those passages, and spelled the same way about other individuals.

The third example is found in Genesis 34 with Shechem, the son of Chamor, and Dinah, Jacob's only daughter, which was born to him by Leah. It is written in Genesis 34:3 "and his (Shechem) soul cleaved to Dinah, the daughter of Jacob, and he loved the young woman (הנער), and he spoke to the heart of the young woman (הנער)." Dinah is called by the same name (young woman) as Rebekah in Genesis 24 (verses 14, 16, 28, 55, and 57), which is once again, spelled irregularly. Shechem is also called by the same name with the same spelling as the "young man" in Genesis 34:19. The passages are connected, making this my third example of this pattern. Shechem's father, Chamor, was the one who was going out to get Dinah as the bride for his son. In Genesis 34, it is important to notice that Shechem had to get the consent of Dinah's ten brothers, as Benjamin was not yet born, and at this point, Joseph was too young to be involved, which is why even later in the Torah (Genesis 37)

Joseph was still too young to even go with the brothers on their journey then, so how much more so now before that even takes place when he is even younger. The ten brothers are a reference to the Ten Words on the tablets of stone, making it possible for Dinah to be with Shechem, just like the ten camels in Genesis 24 that carried Rebekah to Isaac, as well as the two bracelets weighing ten shekels of gold that was placed on Rebekah's hands. As we explained above, the ten's (Words on Tablets of Stone) and two's (number of Tablets of Stone) are a picture of the Holy Spirit (Ezekiel 36:26-27, Jeremiah 31:31-35). As Shechem didn't go out of his way, but trusted his father, Chamor, who got Dinah as his wife through the consent of the ten brothers, she was brought to Shechem.

The fourth story, which carries the same pattern is found in Genesis 43. Joseph is ruling in Egypt, and his ten brothers, not including Benjamin, come to him in order to buy grain, and Joseph says that they cannot come back to buy grain unless they bring him their brother, Benjamin. In Genesis 43:8, Benjamin is called "the young man (הַנַּעַר)," which is the same spelling in Hebrew for "the young woman" as Rebekah and Dinah are called, which is once again, done purposely by the Torah as God is wanting us to see the connection and patterns.

Joseph does not go out of his way to get Benjamin, but rather, he stays focused on where God has him in Egypt, in order to bring about salvation for the whole world. Joseph is tilling his garden God has him in. In Genesis 43:15, the ten brothers (although Simon was being held in Egypt) are responsible for bringing Benjamin to Joseph, which are once again, a representation of the Ten Words on the Tablets of Stone, which is a reference to the Holy Spirit as we saw earlier. The Holy Spirit is always the one bringing the increase as the LORD and His righteousness is being focused on (Matthew 6:33), and as one abides in his own garden. This story doesn't have to do with Joseph's wife, but it is with the prized possession that he is wanting, which he asks for, but doesn't go get in his flesh. He focuses on God and His work, and these things were all brought to him (Matthew 6:33).

The fifth story is found in Exodus 18:1-7, which brings us back to the bride and bridegroom. In Exodus 18 Moses is leading God's people in the wilderness. While Moses is leading them, Jethro brings Moses' wife, Tzipporah, and their two sons, to Moses. He doesn't go and get them himself, but he is concerned with the flock and work in the Garden of Eden that God has called him too, which is leading the entire house of Israel. Notice this time, it is Jethro who is responsible for bringing Tziporrah and the two sons. Jethro is a picture of the Holy Spirit, because Jethro's name (יתרו) has a gematria or numerical value of 616, which is equivalent to "the Torah (התתורה)," which as we saw, is a picture of the Holy Spirit according to Ezekiel 36:26-27 and Jeremiah 31:31-35, as the Torah was written on Tablets of Stone, the Holy Spirit would come write Torah upon the tablet of our heart. Moses and Tzipporah's two sons are also a representation of the two Tablets of Stone. As Moses focused on his garden, all these things were added to him (Matthew 6:8/33), and he teamed up with the Holy Spirit.

This story with Tzipporah, Jethro being a picture of the Torah and the Ten Words on two tablets of stone, as well as the two sons is directly connected to our third example in Genesis 24 with Rebekah, with the ten camels, and the two bracelets weighing ten shekels. Not only do we simply have the "tens" and "twos" at play, but also, Rebekah is from Padan Aram (פדן ארם), which has a gematria of 375, which is also equivalent to "Tzipporah (צִפֹּרָה)," the wife of Moses. God is continually connecting these passages to have us look deeper. The Holy Spirit continually shows me the patterns of Scripture, especially through numbers and mathematics, the quantitative dimension of the Torah.

The sixth story is within the same Torah portion as the fifth story with Jethro and is found in Exodus 20 as God gives the Torah, the two

Tablets of Stone with the Ten Words to His bride, Israel. Through the two tablets, and the Ten Words written on them, God is bringing Israel near to Him as His bride on Pentecost, as the Torah in Hebrew is called a "ketubah," which in Scripture comes from the word meaning "to write (כתב)." A ketubah is actually a marriage contract in Judaism. God uses the Torah, the Holy Spirit, to bring His bride near to Him, just as Messiah Yeshua sent the Holy Spirit to prepare His bride for Him.

The formula is clear, as we have seen at least six times in just the first two books of the Bible. If we focus on our gardens with God, the Holy Spirit will bring us everything we need, even before we ask. This is the same formula Jesus emphasizes to us in Matthew 6:8 when He said the Father knows what we need before we ask, or in Matthew 6:33, that we need to first seek the Kingdom of God and His righteousness, and all of these things will be added to us. In other words, Jesus is saying:

> "Till your garden, work it and guard it (Genesis 2:15), and the Holy Spirit will bring whatever you need, even if it comes from another country as Rebekah or Benjamin. The earth and all its fullness is God's (Jeremiah 23:24, Psalms 24:1)."

I assure you, if your focus is on God and where He has called you, you won't miss your train. He will preserve your spouse, your children, your ministry, your finances, your home, your calling, your business, etc. God can do all things (Mark 10:27, Luke 1:37, 18:27). He simply asks us to partner with the Holy Spirit by allowing the Holy Spirit to be the One who brings the increase (1 Corinthians 3:6-7). In each season, our job is to find out, where and what is our garden with the LORD? It can also be seen as establishing our priorities. The Holy Spirit is faithful to show you these things.

During the time I was getting all of this download on tilling our own gardens, as I mentioned, God had spoken to me Proverbs 27:8 and said "My son, just as a bird wanders from its nest, you have wandered from your place. Return to My garden, work it, and guard it (Genesis 2:15)." Other good and Godly things had gotten my attention, and my time and energy were being spent, and I was stressing a lot trying to get certain things I was wanting, which were great desires, but I went out of the garden to get them. Rather than requesting them and remaining in the garden for the Holy Spirit to bring them to me, while doing the work I was called too, I was trying to go out and seek them on my own. These things had to do with God, but those places, ministries, and people were not where God called me to be in that season. It was not my garden.

As I repented, I asked the LORD to show me my garden, and He gave me a list to write down of about 7-8 things. Just as an example, it was right before I wrote this book, just weeks before Passover 2023. Some of the things He told me were: this book, the big 2023 Passover seder, my blogs, my weekly broadcasts, the leaders I teach every week, my set routine of daily Scripture, as well as a couple other projects at that specific time. After Passover, that one left, and the LORD gave me new guidance that was now a part of my garden I was to work and guard. These, along with some others was my Garden of Eden with God at the time, that if I would focus on these things, He would bring everything else I needed even before I ask, or without me realizing I need it. Asking is a good thing (Proverbs 15:8, Matthew 7:7-8, Luke 11:9-13, James 4:1-4). I was continually asking for some of the very things that I was at first going out of my way to try and get, which brought great stress and anxiety to me.

For two or three months these things were bringing such stress to my life, although the things in and of themselves were great things, which can be the most deceptive part about it. It can even be something that is a part of your calling, but your efforts for them are at the wrong time, or in your own strength. As I also said, my attention was being brought away from doing the work in my garden with absolute excellence, which anything short of excellence is not Kingdom quality that God desires (Colossians 3:23).

I remember I went to the LORD and asked Him why I was so stressed, and that's when He showed me those things were not my Garden of Eden. When He listed out my garden responsibilities for me, I wrote them down and isolated myself to those things, removing any and all other things that were not within that garden. When I did this and prioritized my garden and life, I cannot emphasize to you how much the peace of God overflowed me like a mighty river (Philippians 4:6-7), and all the stress and anxiety was literally nowhere to be found. Even my desires started to change. The Holy Spirit removed the desires for those things, and even if some of them stayed, they weren't the anchor of my mind anymore, and held no power over me any longer, but rather, they were simply in my prayers and intercessions, while causing no stress or even a desire to leave the garden. When you eat of the fruits of the Garden of Eden intimacy, you refuse anything less, and have absolutely no desire for anything else.

The same goes for you, whether it be for a spouse, an assistant your needing, finances, understanding, resources of any kind, certain ministry or business doors to open, etc. The same thing happened in the book of Ruth with Boaz. Boaz didn't go around seeking a wife. God brought Ruth to Him as he walked as a man of God, focused on God and the garden God called him too. This could literally be used if we wanted to go deeper as a seventh example, as Ruth is taking place during the time of the wheat harvest (Ruth 2:23), which is when the Torah and the two Tablets of Stone with the Ten Words were given at Sinai during the time of Pentecost, once again, taking on the same pattern and variables as the first six examples I have given in this chapter.

I kid you not, I could go on and on with this concept, as there are still more examples of this even in the book of Genesis that we did not cover, nevertheless, the same goes for today, as nothing is new under the sun, and whatever has been, will be, and whatever has been done, will be done, because nothing is new under the sun (Ecclesiastes 1:9-10). The Holy Spirit will take care of everything as you focus on the garden you are called too. Leave the garden, and you are now a bird who has wandered from its nest (Proverbs 27:8), and outside the nest, is trouble, as it is known in Jewish thought that the "ken ha'tzipor (the bird's nest)" is the place of the Messiah. There is no need to stress when we walk with God in Eden, because He truly, and I mean truly, takes care of all things. He is such a good Father. Let the Holy Spirit shift the atmosphere into a holy peace even now as you read this.

Seek the Kingdom and His righteousness, meaning, focus on your Garden of Eden with God, and don't just prioritize Him, but ask Him to prioritize your life as I explained He had to do with me. Not just prioritizing Him in the sense of you are with Him in the morning, and then you go about your day, because I was doing the same thing. I am with the LORD every morning, and all day. Abiding in the Garden of Eden means you are not just with Him all day, every day, but you are working and guarding what you are called too, as Adam was called to work and guard it (Genesis 2:15). Trees Of Fire are planted by Him in a specific garden, bearing the fruits He has called you to bear, as it is written in Psalms 1:1-3:

> "Blessed is the man that did not follow the counsel of the
> wicked, neither did he stand in the way of sinners, nor sit
> in the company of scorners, but his desire is in the Torah

of the LORD, and in His Torah he meditates day and night. He shall be a tree planted besides rivers of water, which brings forth its fruit in its season, and its leaves do not wither, and all that he will do will prosper."

How can a tree of fire be on fire without the One who causes it to be aflame, which is the Holy Spirit and fire? As I said, being a tree of fire has to do with Holy Spirit intimacy, and that will take place as you find your garden with God. As you do this, the King of glory, the Unlimited Sovereign God, the Creator of the heavens and the earth, will know what you need before you even request it, and will bring it to you.

He is so faithful. The Holy Spirit jealously desires us to have this partnership with Him (Exodus 34:14, James 4:1-5). In the context of a wife, if you live in the United States, and God desires that your spouse be someone in Norway, I assure you, God can bring this individual as He brought Rebekah or Benjamin from another country. If He wants, He can rapture this individual to you as he raptured Phillip in Acts 8. If God has finances for you, He can multiply the very funds in your safe or bank account at this very moment. We have to stop limiting Him, and team up with the Holy Spirit, trusting that if we abide in the Garden of Eden with God, He will bring it all to us, as Jesus said "all these things will be added to you" in order for you to fulfill your calling with Him (2 Timothy 4:5).

My dearest friends, Pastor Todd and Maria in Iowa, I could have met them in the United States, but God brought all of us to Israel in December of 2017, and I met them in Jerusalem as we were all about the Father's business. Little did we know that trip for each of us would bring us across each other's paths, and the necessity of our relationship. When we abide in the Garden of Eden, you will notice not only the fruit of the Spirit as I mentioned earlier, such peace, joy, etc., but even the anointing begins to flow like a river with revelation, and His voice will become clear and evident. The Ark in the wilderness, where the Presence of God dwelt, went wherever the cloud and fire moved in the Torah. The cloud and fire is a picture of the Holy Spirit and fire, and when you move with the Holy Spirit, the Presence of God is tangible upon you. Many people aren't hearing the voice of God because they aren't in their garden. They are in someone else's and calling it God, although it is God's garden for someone else, but not for you. God speaks quietly to us in our garden, He doesn't want to yell. We must be close to Him, abiding where we are called, and in that place, we will hear the voice of God with such precision, because it is a still, small voice of intimacy, as it is written with Elijah in 1 Kings 19:11-13:

> "And He said, 'go out and stand in the mountain before the LORD,' and behold, the LORD passes, and a great and strong wind splitting mountains and shattering boulders before the LORD, but the LORD was not in the wind. And after the wind, an earthquake, the LORD was not in the earthquake. After the earthquake, fire. The LORD was not in the fire. And after the fire, a still, thin voice. And as Elijah heard, he covered his face with his cloak, and he went out and stood at the opening of the cave, and behold, to him was a voice, and He said, 'why are you here, Elijah?'"

The Garden of Eden is about stewardship, which is something Jesus discusses in His parables continually about the stewards that work the things He specifically gives to them while He is gone, and until He returns. Many wonder why they haven't been baptized in the Holy Spirit and fire, or received the anointing, or the provisions, the spouse, etc., and it is because they are in the wrong place, or not stewarding their garden properly, or if you are, be patient, for it is coming. Personally, even though the things I went off doing were good and Godly things, I had to repent, because it wasn't where I needed to be, and those things didn't need to have my focus.

In 2018, when I first began to have this revelation from the garden with Adam, but not the entire paradigm I now have shown in this chapter, there was something I was earnestly seeking, and not just desiring, but going out of my way to try and get on my own, and finally, after it was draining me for about three months, I decided, "I am done doing this. If I am to have it, He will bring it." I began to just focus on the LORD literally all day, every day. I became so exhausted for those few months, and I had to get to that place in order to see the flesh couldn't accomplish the desire in my heart. I kid you not, the very thing I had been seeking for three months prior literally just about knocked at my door one night as I was in bed. Technically, it came through a text message, but days later it was delivered right to my front door. I can't make this stuff up. God wanted me to have the desires of my heart, for He placed them there (Psalms 37:4). He just wanted to be the One to get it for me.

The revelation of this garden concept opened up for me in 2018, but the patterns that I gave on it and its understanding with the ten's and two's and the Holy Spirit did not come until 2022, and furthered in 2023, during times of deep pain and distress, yet, the more pain I had, the more I multiplied in the revelations and anointing of the Spirit (Exodus 1:7-12), as the children of Israel multiplied in Egypt the more the enemy afflicted them. Find your Garden of Eden, and work it well, and you will see the Holy Spirit do a mighty work. Numbers 11:23 "and the LORD said to Moses, 'is the hand of the LORD shortened? Now you will see whether My word will happen for you or not.'"

CHAPTER 12

Becoming Powerful In The Spirit

This whole book we have talked about being a Tree Of Fire, which means intimacy and partnership with the Holy Spirit, the baptism of the Holy Spirit, the gifts of the Holy Spirit, the anointing that flows from these things, and an overall overcoming life in the Holy Spirit that tramples serpents and scorpions, and overcoming the hardships that the evil one brings in our lives (Luke 10:19). A Tree Of Fire is such a mighty tree that the birds of the heavens come and nest in your branches as you become a person people get nourished by in the LORD (Matthew 13:32-33), and to be such a powerhouse that the evil one knows us by name and is threatened by us (Exodus 1:7-12, Acts 19:15). We have also talked about how to become powerful in the Holy Spirit anointing in order to carry this authority from Leviticus 26:3-13, and other places as well, however, now I want to reveal how we can continue practical steps to becoming this Tree Of Fire in a way that is fully practical, not that the rest of this book isn't, but what I include in this chapter will begin to summarize these things in a way that we can go out today and do this now. These are necessary steps that one will have to confront in their lives immediately, in order to begin walking in the fullness of God that He has for each of us individually, and corporately as the entire body and bride of Messiah. As I give revelation in this chapter on becoming powerful in the Spirit, I also want to note that everything I say here is also how to become powerful in prayer, so as you read this chapter, you can interchange these two concepts "Spirit/prayer," because not only is the formula the same for both, but also, there is nobody who is a powerhouse in the Spirit of God who is not a powerhouse in prayer.

When I talk about being powerful in the Holy Spirit (or in prayer), I don't mean this as some abstract concept. I am talking about genuine, tangible power in the Holy Spirit that shakes up atmospheres and ministries, overflowing with revelation, exposing the patterns and plans of the enemy, trampling the enemy, literally casting out devils as we see Jesus and His disciples do in the New Testament, getting baptized in the Holy Spirit and being used to lead others to this encounter, or how to know what form of witchcraft you are battling up against (all my teachings on overcoming witchcraft will be presented in another volume). In other words, all things moving in power in the Holy Spirit. There are two important concepts I will present that will enable everyone to walk in the power of the Holy Spirit as it is not only presented in the Scriptures, but also bringing insight to how these very things have even worked in my life or in the lives of those around me.

Up to the point of writing this book, I thank God for what He has done in my life in 5.5 years of being a believer, although I will not boast in my own abilities, because I have none apart from Him (Deuteronomy 8:11-20), as it is written in Romans 15:18 "for I presume not to speak of anything, which the Messiah has not done by me in word or in deed for the obedience of the Gentiles," and again in 1 Corinthians 15:9-10:

> "I am the least of the apostles, and am not worthy to be
> called an apostle, because I persecuted the assembly of
> God. But by the grace of God, I am what I am, and His
> grace that was in me was not in vain, but I labored more
> than all of them, not I, but His grace that was in me."

We see Paul say very confident remarks in regard to the work that Messiah has done through him, such as he mentions in 2 Corinthians 11:23 "if they are ministers of the Messiah, (in defect of understanding), I am superior to them: in toils more than they, in stripes more than they, in bonds more than they, in deaths more than they." Paul recognized the calling of God on his life and didn't shy away from it with a cloak of false humility, but he knew the power of God that he carried, and the authority given to him by God, as well as the abundance of revelations that he had, as it is written in 2 Corinthians 12:7 "and that I might not be uplifted by the excellence of the revelation, there was also given to me a thorn in my flesh, the messenger of Satan, to attack me that I might not be uplifted." I have learned, as Paul, to live in duality, and to recognize that I carry a deep anointing, walking in power, and receiving an abundance of revelations, while recognizing this power and wealth in the Spirit has been given to me by God, and not only is it from Him, but it is to be used for His glory and not my own, as it is written in Deuteronomy 8:11-18:

> "Beware that you do not forget the LORD your God, by not keeping His commandments, His ordinances, and His statutes, which I command you this day. Lest you eat and be satisfied, and build good houses and dwell in them, and your herds and your flocks multiply, and your silver and gold increase, and all that you have increases, and your heart grows haughty, and you forget the LORD your God, who has brought you out from the land of Egypt, out of the house of bondage, who led you through that great and awesome wilderness, serpent, poisonous snake, scorpion, and drought where there was no water, who brought water for you out of the flinty rock. Who

fed you with manna in the desert, which your forefathers did not know, in order to afflict you, and in order to test you, to benefit you in your end, and you will say to yourself, 'my strength and the might of my hand that has accumulated this wealth for me.' But you must remember the LORD your God, for it is He that gives you strength to make wealth, in order to establish His covenant, which He swore to your forefathers, as it is this day."

This duality is a recognition that you have it, while always recognizing Whom you received it from and Who it is for, that is God. It is from this posture that I will deliver not only this chapter, but the entire book. I won't walk in pride, saying, "look at me," as I said at the end of the foreword, but at the same time, I do recognize the revelations that the Holy Spirit has given me, the authority given to me, and the power that has been wrought by God through me, and I won't act in a false humility as if I am not aware, because it will not do anybody any good, nor respect the apostolic and prophetic office that God has placed upon my life. What I would prefer to do is discuss it very openly from the Scriptures, so that it may impart something to the people of God, so that you too, can become powerful and numerous in the Holy Spirit and in prayer.

As we have seen, it says in Acts 19:15, those who are mighty in the Holy Spirit, the evil one knows them by name and fears them, which was rooted in Exodus 1:7-10, as we saw earlier in this book. If, therefore, you take these two concepts that I will present in this chapter, which are both found in the gospel of Luke, you too, will become a powerhouse in the Holy Spirit, whom the enemy camp will know by name and tremble at even the very thought of you because of how possessed you are by the Holy Spirit. But I don't desire for you to be ignorant. Those whom the enemy knows by name will also be attacked and afflicted in every way possible by the enemy in a greater measure than you can imagine, just as when Pharaoh knew Israel by name because of their becoming powerful, and he afflicted them in every way physically (Exodus 1:7-12). The first concept is directly out of Luke 13:6-9:

> "And He (Yeshua) spoke this parable, 'a man had a fig tree that was planted in his vineyard, and he came to it, seeking fruit on it, and he did not find any. And he said to the vinedresser, behold, three years I have come seeking fruit on this fig tree, and I have not found it. Cut it down. Why should it ruin the ground? The vinedresser said to him, my master, let it be also this year, and I will tend it and I will fertilize it. Perhaps it will bear fruit, and if not, in the coming year you will cut it down.'"

We first have to notice that for the first three years, this tree has not given forth any fruit, which is a reference to the Leviticus 19:23-25 passage we went over earlier in this book, which states that when you plant a tree in the land of Israel, the fruit will not be ready for the first three years, but it says specifically in Hebrew in Leviticus 19 that the fruit is "orlah," which means it is uncircumcised. So, in this parable, there is something about this tree that is uncircumcised. Uncircumcised (ערלה) is the same letters as "for evil," or "to do evil (לרעה)," meaning, in this context, there is something causing this tree to not bear the right fruit. I know I said in Chapter 7 that this tree in Leviticus 19 was bearing good fruit, it was just simply not ripe yet, however, the great thing about Torah is what is known in Jewish thought as "shivim panim l'Torah (there are seventy faces to the Torah)." The Word of God has so many faces and revelations, which is why we must understand something in context.

As we said from Jesus' parable above, something is causing the tree to bear uncircumcised fruit, which is fruit that is not fit for the Kingdom of God. However, we must notice the antidote. The vinedresser says it will bear fruit after he tends it and fertilizes it. One thing I can tell you firsthand about working in a garden on the farm that you must do daily, by hand, you must continually pull out the weeds surrounding the plant. Weeds grow like crazy, and they will surround the plant and root, and begin to choke out that root so that it will die and cannot bear fruit. One must weed daily, which is similar to the third seed in Jesus' parable of the sower (Matthew 13, Mark 4, Luke 8), which is sown amongst thorns, and the thorns, which are the cares of the world and deceitfulness of riches, begin to choke out that seed so that it ultimately bears no fruit.

There is no difference when it comes to being strong in the Spirit. We too, have to continually weed out our lives, as Paul says in 1 Corinthians 15:33 "do not be deceived. Wicked conversation corrupts good attributes." Why does Paul start out by saying, "do not be deceived?" Because if you think you can surround yourself with these things and still bear fruit, you are literally deceived. Nobody is above this. We all need to be planted in a healthy garden, continually weeding our lives from people, relationships, music, shows, habits, social media, etc. We have to control our atmospheres as much as it depends upon us, otherwise, it can torment us and choke out the goodness of God from working within us, as it is written about righteous Lot in 2 Peter 2:6-8:

> "Burned up the cities of Sodom and Gomorrah and condemned them by an overthrow, making them a demonstration to the wicked who should come after them, and also delivered righteous Lot who was tormented with the filthy conduct of the Torahless, for that upright man dwelling among them, in seeing and hearing from day to day, was distressed in his righteous soul by their Torahless deeds."

Paul in 1 Corinthians 15:33 above isn't saying not to visit these things, such as Jesus who was sitting, eating, and drinking with sinners and tax collectors (Luke 5/15), but we must recognize that Jesus did not do that all day and night. Jesus controlled His surroundings, keeping a very tight group of twelve, and spent much time on His own in solitude with the Father. He would go into the synagogue and study, and then He would go amongst sinners and tax collectors. We must first protect our surroundings and cultivate a healthy atmosphere, in order to become strong in the Holy Spirit, as it is said, "birds of a feather flock together." Be surrounded by those whose cloth you want to be cut from. You will carry the same wineskin (Matthew 9:16-17).

Weeding and removing harmful things that choke out the fruit is not the only thing. This parable in Luke says the vinedresser needed to fertilize around the tree. After weeding and removing the wrong things, you now have to put the right things around you that will cultivate such results of growing in the power of the Holy Spirit, and to bear the fruit He is looking for. Ever since I came to the LORD in August/September of 2017, I have been surrounded by those who are baptized in the Holy Spirit and fire, and nothing less. From the get-go, this has been the case. It has always been the Holy Spirit, studying the Word of God daily, people speaking in tongues, interpreting tongues, prophesying, words of knowledge, supernatural healing, dreams, and visions, casting out devils, glory, fear of the LORD, repentance, etc. I have never known anything different since I have been in the LORD. Because I have always been surrounded by this, it has been a fruit-bearing contagion that has consumed my life with its expectancy of nothing less than such a walk with the LORD. It has always brought about a hunger and a thirst for those things in my life, but not only a hunger and thirst for them, but also as I mentioned, expectancy for them, and nothing less.

In my walk with God, I have been immersed at different times with Judaism, messianic Judaism, and different pockets of Christianity, and I have personally experienced the different highs and lows in the Holy Spirit in my life, depending on the fertilization of my atmosphere and whom I am around. The more I am surrounded by people who are filled with the Holy Spirit, the more I can't help but overflow, and the Holy Spirit becomes a reality in my life. For me, being a believer is not enough, you must be filled with the Holy Spirit and fire and help cultivate this atmosphere. If I go around people who are not overflowing in the Holy Spirit, or who once were, but at some point became dry, I can go there and be used by God to kindle that entire atmosphere like a forest fire, which I have seen happen time and time again, but if I dwell to long in a dead atmosphere with people who are not believing, or even worse, people who claim to be believers, but are a dry tree with no faith or hunger for the things of the Holy Spirit, but keep their mind on things below, such as politics, strife, gossip, money, etc., and not on the things above (Colossians 3:2), if I dwell there and make that my fertilizer, gradually, those weeds start to choke out the spiritual fervor in my life without me even realizing it.

It is like a frog in lukewarm water, but as it reaches boiling, it happens so gradually, the frog won't realize it and ends up dying in the water. The atmosphere begins to quench and grieve the Holy Spirit (1 Thessalonians 5:19, Ephesians 4:30). Rather than make that place my fertilizer or habitation, I have to do what Jesus did, and make the secret place of solitude, prayer, study, and worship my habitation, as well as being surrounded by like-minded fellowship, and then go visit those dry places, kindle them, leave, and repeat.

One has to feed the Holy Spirit in their life first and foremost. There are certain people I will be around, and atmospheres that I will go into, and prophecy, words of knowledge, the fire of God, and the glory of His

Presence etc., begin flowing through me like a river of living water. Their faith for those things pulls out of me the work of the Spirit of God, and He moves in a very tangible way. Then, I will go into other atmospheres that are so dry in the things of the Holy Spirit, nothing is pulled out of me. What is this a picture of? It is written in Luke 8:43-46:

> "And a certain woman whose blood was flowing for twelve years, who among the doctors had spent all of her money but was not able to be healed by man. She approached from behind and touched the wing of His garment, and immediately the flow of her blood stopped. And Yeshua said, 'who touched Me?' And while all were denying it, Simon Peter and those with Him said to Him, 'our Master, the crowds are pressing and thronging you, and you say, who touched Me?' And He said, 'someone touched Me, for I know that power went out of Me.'"

Her faith pulled power out of Jesus, just as atmospheres will pull power out of the Messiah within me as I am to walk as He walked (1 John 2:6), and it is no longer I who live, but the Messiah within me (Galatians 2:20). But then it is also written in Mark 6:1-6:

> "And He departed from there and came to His own city, and His disciples were following Him. And when it became the Shabbat, He began to teach in the assembly. And many who heard Him were amazed and were saying, 'where did this Man acquire these things?' And 'what is this wisdom that was given to Him that miracles such as these should be done by His hands? Is this not the carpenter, the Son of Mary and the brother of James, and Yosi, and Judah, and Simon, and behold, aren't His sisters

here with us?' And they were offended at Him. And Yeshua said to them, 'there is no prophet who is dishonored except in his own city, and his own kinsmen, and his own house.' And He was not able to do even one miracle there, except that upon a few sick He laid His hands and healed them. And He was amazed by their lack of faith, and would go around the villages while teaching?'"

This was a dead, faithless atmosphere of even religious believers in God, and they weren't pulling power out of Him. There was a time my mom was in the hospital, and my dad, the nurse, and two of her friends were in the room. I love my parents' friends dearly, but the conversation her two friends were bringing was so earthly and repulsive to me, I sent them out of the room as Jesus did in Mark 5:35-43 so that I could pray for my mom. Their conversation and carnal mind were greatly grieving the Holy Spirit within me. As I said, there are times when that power will be pulled out of us as it was pulled out of Jesus, or quenched within Him because of the atmosphere we are in. Around faith-filled atmospheres, there becomes an exchange with us and others in the Holy Spirit, as it is written, "iron sharpens iron (Proverbs 27:17)."

I make sure my core group of people that I engage with on a daily and weekly basis are those who are overflowing with the Holy Spirit, praying in tongues (although some don't, and that is okay. My point is, they operate in the Holy Spirit), seeking the Holy Spirit, and their mind is continually engaged with things above and not the things of the earth (Colossians 3:2). If there is sickness around, they immediately jump to the reality of the things of the Spirit, prayer, recognizing it could be a spirit of infirmity, or asking the LORD what doors may or may not have been opened, etc., and not wasting time focusing on the flesh, the science, the earthly realm. Knowing those things can be great, but they must come second to the perspective of the Spirit. We must abide in seeing life through the lens of the Holy Spirit. Notice when Jesus would cast out a devil, people would be healed at the same time, or even when people would repent and follow him, they would be healed at the same time. Sickness does not come for only one reason, there are many reasons, however, my point is, we have to seek the Father on all of these things, and not walk in ignorance to the realm of the Spirit as many believers do today. "My people die for lack of knowledge (Hosea 4:6)." Jesus rebuked Simon's mother-in-law's fever and she was healed (Luke 4:39).

At our 2023 Passover seder, two others (John and Jennifer Rowan) and myself are the ones who put this on, while I led the actual seder itself. Our seder in 2023 had nearly doubled in size from 2022, and we had about 80 people, and I remember as we were choosing who would sit at the leaders table, I was telling them the weeks leading into it as we were preparing for this event what I needed, and I hand-picked each person who sat at that leaders table (9-10 people). I had told them the reason I picked those whom I did was because they have all been baptized in the Holy Spirit and fire, and are full of faith, as Barnabas was explained to be "a good man, and he was filled with the Holy Spirit and with faith (Acts 11:24)." As the one leading the event, I needed the atmosphere around me from the leaders table, where I was going to be speaking and preaching from, holy and filled with expectancy, and feeding the same Spirit that I am governed by. When we go to war, we have to make sure that those we are fighting with are of the same mind and Spirit, as it is written when going to war in Deuteronomy 20:8:

> "And the officers shall continue to speak to the people and say, 'what man is there who is fearful and faintheart- ed? Let him go and return to his house, that he should not cause the heart of his brothers to melt as his heart.'"

This is why Jesus would clear the room with those having a lack of faith (Mark 5:35-43), as I cleared my mom's hospital room. The Torah is teaching us how to go to war in the Holy Spirit. The atmosphere is contagious. I needed an atmosphere saturated with the same faith I was walking with, or at the very least, weeding out anyone or anything that can choke it out.

I remember at the Passover seder that night in 2023, standing up and calling out everyone in the audience publicly at the beginning of the evening because the atmosphere seemed so sleepy. Many people looked like they were listening to Satan sing a sleepy, spiritual lullaby over them. Due to the Spirit within me and the surrounding I had at the leaders table, that whole place was kindled in the power of the Holy Spirit. In fact, due to the movement of the Holy Spirit, I didn't get home until almost 1am that night. I remember standing up in front of everyone at the beginning of the evening, this is around 6pm, and I told everyone that by the end of the night when we do the fire tunnel and lay hands on people, many were going to be baptized in the Holy Spirit and fire, and if you had already been baptized in the Holy Spirit, you will get re-kindled. This night we had people from all over and different ministries, including multiple pastors, prayer leaders, doctors of the faith, elders, etc., and I said:

> "Some of you have become stale in the Spirit. You once moved in the Holy Spirit years or decades ago, and you still believe in it, but the truth is, somewhere along the way you became stale, and there is no power in your walk anymore. Well, tonight is the night that changes, and demons will be cast out, the Spirit will pour out, and gifts of the Holy Spirit will be imparted."

At the end of the night I am giving a sermon on the power and baptism of the Holy Spirit as it pertained to the purpose of the blood of the Passover Lamb of God, as we discussed in Chapter 2, and I sent the leaders to the back of the room around 9pm, as we were about to do a fire tunnel, where half of the leaders stand one side, and the other half on this side, and it forms a tunnel that people walk through as we lay hands and pray and make room for the Holy Spirit. That night we had many people baptized in the fire of God, in fact, we were getting parents telling us their kids as young as 13 years old received the Spirit of God and explaining their experience. We had people laid out on the ground under the power, we had pastors and mighty men of God get hit and overflow with tears like children again before Him. We had people who are unbelievers get hit with the fire of God and they gave their life to the LORD on spot with drug addictions broken off. There was a pastor that went to their church the next day and told everyone what happened. By the time service started, my friends who attend that church had all leaders coming up to them, saying they heard how powerful the night was. This pastor doing this reminded me of the woman at the well in John 4, who went back to her village after experiencing the power of God through Jesus, and she told the whole village.

I am at the beginning of the fire tunnel, and I look at the other end, and I see a woman throwing up for about half an hour as multiple demons were being cast out of her and she is being set free. Although I wasn't on their end, seeing what happened, I knew what was happening, as this isn't a rare occurrence when devils get cast out. When planning this leaders table, I had placed my dad there on purpose who had never been in this scenario before, so that he would be in the fire tunnel laying hands, because I wanted him to encounter this, and for him to be surrounded by this kind of movement in the Holy Spirit firsthand, in order to raise his spiritual temperature, hunger, and expectancy for these things. This is how you raise up disciples in Word and in deed. I say all of this to say, that the dry trees that came in that night whom I called out at the beginning in front of everyone, they were surrounded by and stepped into an atmosphere of holy fire, and they left with a new wineskin. This night was a spiritual Pentecost. We chose the right leaders and brewed the right atmosphere for hours to then peak with all things Holy Spirit. The fire tunnel was a river of charisma, and this charismatic nature is what I have always made sure I surround myself with, and wherever I go, I will bring it, and if the people are hungry, He will move at any moment. I have seen it too many times in the airport, Walmart, gas stations, the gym, coffee shops, etc.

My dad, whom I chose to be at this leaders table in order to raise his spiritual temperature, he has been around me for years. At this point, he had been a diligent student of mine for almost five years, and he has seen me pray in tongues, prophesy, move in power, watch people get hit with the Holy Spirit, healings, witchcraft, etc. My concern was that outside of being with me and seeing these things, he has not seen it much anywhere else, with anyone else, so I had him in this tunnel to be immersed in that atmosphere that was not just me, but many other leaders and even having him fully involved, as Jesus would finally send His disciples to the towns in order to experience it on their own as well (Luke 10), and not just with Him. He was at the end where this woman was having devils cast out for half an hour. A few days later, after there was time to process the evening, I explained what happened and asked, "do you know what was happening when that woman was throwing up?" He said he assumed it was just a powerful encounter with the Holy Spirit. I told him:

> "Yes, the individual got hit with the Holy Spirit on my
> end of the tunnel, but by your end, devils within her
> started manifesting, which is why the couple next to you

recognized the manifestation and began casting things out. The reason this woman was throwing up is because when you cast out devils, there is generally a very violent exiting manifestation of the demons, which is why when you read the gospels, and Jesus would cast out devils, it would throw the individual violently to the ground, or start foaming at the mouth, or scream, or throw someone in the fire and then leave them, or something of that nature. So too, this person had a violent exiting of multiple demons for about half an hour."

I got to walk my dad through these events, and it cultivated something within him to be able to encounter things in a powerful way that raises his spiritual awareness and enables him to be raised up in the Holy Spirit. All of this doesn't happen by chance. As I said, the first concept of becoming powerful in the Holy Spirit when walking with Jesus is we have to manually weed out our life and then fertilize it with the right atmosphere daily. One of my disciples in Dallas at the time came down for this Passover event, and he was so marked by what God did that night. The next morning, I told him, if he needs to move to Houston to fertilize that atmosphere with he and the Holy Spirit, then do it. Obedience is better than sacrifice (1 Samuel 15:22), and nothing is more important than your obedience to getting into the best position to grow with God, even if it means losing relationships, moving towns, quitting jobs, etc. Be radical in your pursuit to be raised up in the Holy Spirit, so that you can bear the fruits of the Holy Spirit (Galatians 5:22-23) and be the fruitful fig tree that Jesus is looking for in the Luke 13 parable. Otherwise, you will be choked out by the root and not bear fruit, and any tree or branch that does not bear fruit and takes up space is cut down and thrown into the fire (Matthew 7:15, Luke 13:6-9, John 15:1-6).

Less than two months later for Pentecost, it was as if we had a spiritual overflow that built up for fifty days from Passover leading into the time of Pentecost. I had brought in just a few of those leaders from Passover to also be a part of Pentecost. It was truly a remarkable move of God. I had sent out an email about 10 days before, alerting people about a gathering God placed upon my heart, and hadn't really planned much for that Pentecost gathering. I remember that morning, the Rowan's and I were having coffee in their living room praying. We were also saying, "we may only have three people show up, but whoever shows up, they will encounter the Holy Spirit." This was a pure act of obedience and faith, just doing what the LORD had told me to do. As I looked at the footage from that night, I was amazed that literally every square inch of that place had been fully filled, with kids even having to sit under tables. People had to stand, sit on the ground, fit wherever they could as the chairs completely filled up. That night, I preached, and then the Holy Spirit came and cleaned house with a purging and igniting fire. The fire of heaven truly invaded that place that night. Many people reached out after the event, including one, who said, "wow, Nick. What an awesome teaching. The fire of heaven came down on that place. What an experience. I have never felt the presence of God that strong."

We had people come simply because they were being drawn by seeing others walk there. There was a glory that drew people in, similar to the stories of the Azusa street revival, where people said the glory above the building drew people in from blocks away. We had pastors from out of state, elders, evangelists, worship leaders, etc., all whom I had never met, all getting hit with the power of God. I remember towards the end of the night, a married couple came up to me for prayer to get touched by the fire of God, and I looked around and said, "there are bodies on the ground everywhere." There was almost no room to keep praying, as people were literally falling on each other as the power of God hit them.

We had children, youth/teens, young adults, middle aged, and older all of one accord under the influence of the Holy Spirit, for He makes no distinctions.

I had a child that was about five or six years old walk up to me and say, "I want to speak in tongues." As I prayed for him, the power of God hit him and took him to the ground, and I yelled at the man behind the child, "get him back up, I am not done with him!" As the child was picked back up, I prayed again, and the Holy Spirit hit the child again and marked him. The entire night, from the start of my preaching until the end of the evening was all about relentless pursuit for Jesus, repentance, full devotion to Him, and preparing ourselves as the bride that He is longing for. All of this came through cultivating the right atmosphere through preaching with the power of the Holy Spirit and having the right leaders there to raise the standard, spiritual temperature, and expectancy. A few leaders and myself were there earlier in my office in a meeting of prayer, and as we dove deep in prayer, one of the leaders told me later on, "Nick the fire fell in your office during the prayer meeting." We labored in cultivation for God to do something powerful. Have you noticed, as I continually explain in this chapter about the power of God, all of it is blended with us praying before, during, and after? As I said at the beginning of this chapter, nobody is powerful in the Holy Spirit without first being powerful in prayer, which both have to do with the first concept of this chapter-weeding and fertilizing.

As I mentioned in this chapter for becoming powerful in the Spirit or in prayer, I would mention two concepts. The first concept is weeding and fertilizing. One must manually develop that atmosphere and pray the right atmosphere in for God as the Vinedresser to bring the right people and reveal your instruction clearly on what you need to do. The second concept to be powerful in the Spirit/prayer is also from the book of Luke from the first two chapters, in regard to both John the Baptist and Jesus. In Luke 1:80 we are talking about John the Baptist as a child, and in Luke 2:40 we are talking about Jesus as a child. In the Aramaic Peshitta, as well as its Hebrew equivalent, those Scriptures give us the SAME exact words for each of them.

For John it is written in Luke 1:80 "and the child grew, and became strong in the Spirit," and the same for Jesus in Luke 2:40 "and the Child grew and became strong in the Spirit." The phrase "and became strong" in Aramaic (מתחיל) and Hebrew (התחזק) is "reflexive." For example, the sentence "David killed Goliath," David is active, the subject doing the verb (killing), and Goliath is the passive object, whom the verb is being done upon (being killed). Reflexive means both, which would be like saying, "David killed himself," where you are the doer and receiver of the verb. In Biblical Aramaic, reflexive verbs can carry either reflexive or passive nuances, so it shouldn't just be understood as John and Jesus became strong in the Spirit, but rather, they strengthened themselves in the Spirit. "Jesus/John strengthened Himself/himself in the Spirit." So, what does this mean that they became strong in the Spirit, or better yet, they strengthened themselves?

To understand this, it is important that we don't separate or distinguish between the Scriptures/Word of God, and the Spirit of God. They are harmoniously One and the same, as God is the Spirit and the Word, as it is written in 2 Corinthians 3:17 "The LORD is the Spirit, and wherever the LORD is, there is freedom," and again in John 1:1 "in the beginning was the Word, and the Word was with God, and God was the Word." Therefore, God is the Spirit and the Word, and God is One (Deuteronomy 6:4), therefore, the Word and the Spirit cannot be separated. If Jesus and John became strong, or strengthened themselves in the Spirit, it means they strengthened themselves in the Word of God.

It is written in 1 Corinthians 2:13-16 that the Scriptures have to be understood by the Holy Spirit, and in Romans 7:14 in Aramaic and

Hebrew it is written that the Torah is OF the Spirit, not as many of the English Bible's translate that 'the law is spiritual." It is OF the Spirit, meaning, apart from the Spirit, there is no Torah or Scriptures, as Peter also said in 2 Peter 1:21 "for at no time was it by the will of man that the prophecy came, but Set Apart men of God spoke as they were moved by the Holy Spirit." Ezekiel 36:26-27, Jeremiah 31:31-35, and Hebrews 10:16-17 tell us that in the New Covenant God would place His Spirit within us, and by the Holy Spirit He would write His Torah upon our hearts and minds. Apart from the Holy Spirit, we can't understand the Scriptures, the two are One, as He is One (Deuteronomy 6:4).

With this unified understanding of Torah, the rest of the Scriptures and the Spirit, when Luke says that John and Jesus strengthened themselves in the Spirit, or became strong in the Spirit, they caused themselves to be strong in the Holy Spirit by diving deep in Torah study and being strong in the Scriptures/Word of God! They were devout, revelatory, overflowing, well springs of living water in the Word of God. They were mighty in the Scriptures. This is what Luke 1:80/2:40 mean when saying that John and Jesus strengthened themselves in the Spirit. When Scripture talks about Stephen in Acts 6-7, or Barnabas in Acts 11 that they were full of the Holy Spirit, it means they were full of revelation in the Word of God, because the deeper revelations that you get in the Scriptures, it causes you to be more revelatory in the things of the Holy Spirit and vice versa.

This is why I said at the beginning of the chapter that although I will not boast in my own abilities, for he who boasts, let him boast in the LORD (1 Corinthians 1:31, Jeremiah 9:24), but I will share the things that God has done through me in my life, because I recognize the power and authority in the Holy Spirit that I walk in. One thing I am trying to emphasize is that all of that revelation in the Spirit and Spiritual authority that I have acquired is equally yoked with the depth of study and knowledge of the Scripture that I have given myself too. I have strengthened myself in the Spirit and in the Word of God.

I have taught an entire series just on witchcraft, which was just me touching the surface, which will be written in another volume, God willing. How do I have so much revelation on all the different forms of witchcraft and schemes of the evil one, as I touched on in the chapter "Train My Hands For War"? It is from the revelations I have received in the Scriptures. My diligence and studiousness in the Word of God has equipped me and trained my hands for war in all these different areas, equipping me to understand spiritual warfare from Judges 2-3, freedom ministry from Leviticus 4/Genesis 20, witchcraft, the baptism of the Holy Spirit and fire, etc. Where did I learn about freedom ministry and soul ties? I learned from the Scriptures, and more specifically, the Torah of Moses. How did I learn about why demons know certain people's names in the book of Acts and all of its details? The Torah of Moses. Where did I learn about casting out devils, or clearing out a room when praying for the sick as Jesus did? The Torah of Moses. The Holy Spirit has opened the eyes of my understanding to see the spiritual Scriptures through a spiritual lens, especially when I went those two years reading nothing but the Torah of Moses in Hebrew. My eyes were opened in a new way, as it is written in Ephesians 1:17-18:

> "That the God of our Master Yeshua the Messiah, the Father of glory, may give to you the spirit of wisdom and revelation in the knowledge of Him. And that the eyes of your hearts may be enlightened so that you may know what is the hope of His calling, and what are the riches of the glory of His inheritance in His holy ones."

The Holy Spirit renewed my mind during that time and is continually doing so as I study Torah each and every day (Romans 12:2, Ephesians 4:23).

My point should be clear. The deeper you know the Scriptures and walk in them, and not just knowing them like a pharisee by the letter, but by revelation of the Holy Spirit, the stronger you will be in the Holy Spirit, for they cannot be separated. I cannot emphasize enough that my revelations have come by God THROUGH the Word of God, not APART from the Word of God. I don't sit on the couch twiddling my thumbs and get downloads from the Holy Spirit. I toil in the Garden of God, and the more I sow into it, or better yet, the more it sows into me, the more I reap, as it is written in Genesis 26:12 "and Isaac sowed in that land, and in that year, he obtained one hundred fold, and the LORD blessed him." The phrase "one hundred fold (מֵאָה שְׁעָרִים)" is key, because the word for "fold (שְׁעָרִים)," which also means "to estimate," pronounced "sh'arim" is the same word as "lessons (שְׁעָרִים)," pronounced "shiurim," which in Hebrew are teachings/lessons of Torah. The more Isaac sowed into God's labor, he reaped one hundred fold of Torah revelation.

In fact, the LORD told Isaac ten verses prior in Genesis 26:2 to "dwell in the land (שְׁכָן בָּאָרֶץ)," which has a gematria of 663, which is equivalent to "all 613 (כל 613)," referring to all of the 613 commandments in the Torah. By God telling Isaac to dwell in the land, He is saying to walk in His ways and commandments, and by doing so, it is as Isaac is "sowing" in the land by studying and walking in His ways, which allowed him to reap one hundred fold as Jesus mentions in the parable of the sower (Matthew 13, Mark 4, Luke 8), when the seed of God's Word is sown, if it is applied into our lives, we can reap one hundred fold in revelation. As Isaac sowed in the land through walking in His ways and teaching, "the man became great, and went forth and grew until he became very great, and he had herds of sheep and herds of cattle, and many servants (Genesis 26:12-14)," which means, as he sowed, he acquired many disciples (sheep and cattle) and became great in the wisdom and understanding from Torah.

In this same chapter, Torah says in Genesis 26:7 that Rebekah is "beautiful," or literally "good of appearance (טוֹבַת מַרְאֶה)," which also has a gematria of 663, equating to "all 613 (613 כל)" just as Isaac "dwelling in the land." What this shows is that Rebekah's beauty was based upon her devotion to walking in God's ways as a Proverbs 31 bride, as it is written in Proverbs 31:26 "the Torah of kindness is upon her tongue." As Isaac and Rebekah walked equally yoked in the LORD as husband and wife, their house was in order, and Isaac reaped one hundred fold, as it is said in Jewish thought, "blessing only rests upon a home in the merit of the wife (Genesis 12:16)."

This phrase "one hundred fold (מֵאָה שְׁעָרִים)" in gematria is equivalent to 666, which is equivalent to "all of the Torah (כל התורה)." 666 is not a bad number, as many seem to think from the book of Revelation, however, I will not be unpacking the concepts of 666 in this volume, which will be explained in another volume, God willing. As Isaac and Rebekah sowed and labored in study, prayer, and walking in God's ways, God blessed Isaac's house by giving him all kinds of revelation in the Scriptures, to know all of the Torah, so too, as I have labored and sown in the fields of Torah study, prayer, and continually walk in His ways, God has allowed me to reap the revelations of Torah and the fruits of my labor as Isaac did.

I am immersed in the Scriptures. How else can we know all of the depths of the Jezebel spirit, the spirit of Ahab, the gaslighting spirit, the spirit of Korah, Amalek, Canaan, Ahitophel, Judas, Absalom, etc.? All of the teachings I have continually poured out come from the abundance of revelation and study in the Word of God, allowing me to strengthen myself in the Spirit, as it says for John the Baptist and Jesus in Luke 1:80/2:40. This is also where I have learned all about intercessory prayer, and warfare in the heavens in regard to our prayers being hindered or unanswered. Directly from Torah I can explain to anyone the book of Revelation, the four creatures, the twenty four elders, the man on a white horse with a bow and no arrows, the golden bowls of prayer, the 144,000, etc. It is all in the Torah of Moses, some of which can only be seen in Hebrew and through deeper levels of Jewish hermeneutics.

I didn't jump to the New Testament, as many do. I can explain all of it in great depth, beginning from the Torah of Moses, and going forward as Jesus, Peter, Stephen, John, and Paul did (Luke 24:27, Acts 28:23). We are to be desperate for the Word of God, because this will empower us to walk in the power Jesus has called us into, in order to be strong in the Spirit and in prayer, but we must know the Scriptures inside and out, and understand them within a community of on fire believers that will help sharpen our understanding, imparting things unto us and vice versa, and most importantly, we need to be in the secret place with Abba (Father) daily.

The Pharisees knew the Scriptures, but many of them did not know them through the lens of the Holy Spirit, and quite frankly, neither do many believers or Christian pastors and leaders today. Nothing is new under the sun (Ecclesiastes 1:9-10). Remember, as we spoke on earlier in the chapter with the "Interpreter," we need to read our Father's letter with the interpretation of the Holy Spirit. If we want to become powerhouses in the Spirit, if we want to change atmospheres, call down fire from heaven, cast out devils, trample sicknesses, break off witchcraft, and do the "greater things than these (John 14:12)" that Jesus said we would do, we need to weed and fertilize our atmosphere to be surrounded around living torches in the Spirit, and be devoutly studied in the Word of God seven days a week. It is daily bread, manna from heaven.

One also needs to be discipled under someone directly, in order to understand the depths and breadths of the Word of God and to be raised up in power. Church or synagogue is great, but that's not discipleship. Sitting personally before a teacher daily, now that is true discipleship. In the Scriptures, this was done daily (Acts 19:9). It should be such high priority, that you will move cities to get it. Many will move cities for a job for the unrighteous manna, how much more so should we move cities for the manna from heaven? Nothing comes before being saturated in the Spirit of God and growing strong in the Spirit. Peter did not concern himself with his future bills when he quit his job as a fisherman to follow Jesus. He recognized nothing supersedes the calling to "follow Me (Jesus)," and enter into his fullness in the Spirit of God. Matthew left his tax collecting. Desperation is a powerful force, and when channeled towards Him, it will turn the world upside down, beginning with yours (Acts 17:6). If He is your top priority in all of these areas, He will also make everything else work. Seek Him first and His righteousness, and I assure you, the Creator of the heavens and the earth can move whatever He needs to move in order get you what you need, as we discussed in Chapter 11 (Matthew 6:33).

John and Jennifer Rowan, my dear friends and family, it is they and I who run the Passover seder, as I mentioned. Ever since we met, Jenn has continually commented on something. Every time we talk about witchcraft, the baptism of the Holy Spirit, word curses, soul ties, warfare, casting out devils, the apostolic, the prophetic, fivefold ministry, dream interpretation etc., I always have Scriptures I bring up to reveal the depths of these topics, in order to show where these spiritual concepts are truly rooted in the Word of God, and I explain them beginning from the Torah of Moses, as Jesus and Paul would do (Luke 24:27, 44, Acts 28:23). She continually would say, "Nick I love how every time we talk about these things, you are so rooted in the Word of God, you have references to explain everything." When your revelation becomes deeply rooted in the Word of God, there is no guess work, because you have the road map.

When another dear friend and brother was talking about soul ties with me in 2022, he had revelation through the Spirit of God that they were real and knew some insight about it in regard to breaking them off, but could not explain in great depths about them, nor could he give me deep Scriptural insight on them, except for 1 Samuel 18:1, which doesn't really give us anything. That summer I asked the Holy Spirit to show me where soul ties are in Scripture, in order to equip me in ministry with soul ties, and sure enough, the Holy Spirit shows me the depths, causes, and consequences of soul ties, whether good or bad, and I can explain it very deeply in a way that has brought conviction through the Holy Spirit, and He has given me a revelatory authority in the Spirit to minister in these areas. However, like many other areas we have touched on in this book, soul ties won't be expounded on in this volume. There is so much to teach, impart, and learn, which is why we need to be discipled daily in these depths, as it is written in Acts 19:9 "and he (Paul) spoke daily with them in the school of a man named Tyrannus," which as we discussed earlier in this book on the school "Trees Of Fire," is the commissioning God has given me.

Everything I do and teach I can explain deeply from the Word of God with revelation of the Spirit, which enables me to walk in more power and authority, because I have a firm foundation in the Spirit through the rock of God's Word (Matthew 7:24-29). This chapter explains my vision of Trees Of Fire that I initially received through an open eyed vision in Iowa in April of 2022. One tree on fire in the Holy Spirit will kindle another, and another, and another, and soon, He will have His bride as a forest fire, burning for Him. The vision of Trees Of fire was literally birthed as I was in deep prayer in the War Room (the name of our prayer room in Chelsea, Iowa) during times of desperation. This is why I said at the end of the foreword that God found a desperate man, broke him, and baptized him in a season of prayer, so too, all Trees Of Fire must come and be birthed from that place of desperation, which leads you into a prayer life that you wouldn't have entered without it.

Revelation 22:17, 20:

> "And the Spirit and the bride say, 'come,' and let him who hears say, 'come.' And let him who thirsts come, and he that is inclined, let him come and take the living water freely. He who testifies these things says, 'Yes, I come quickly.' Amen. Come, Master Yeshua."

Made in the USA
Columbia, SC
10 June 2024

36980495R00163